Tallulah, Darling

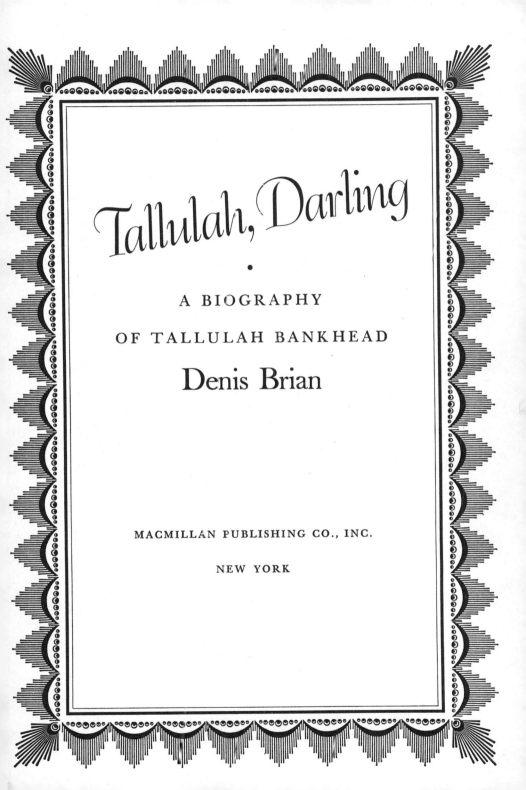

Tallulah, Darling

·

A BIOGRAPHY
OF TALLULAH BANKHEAD

Denis Brian

MACMILLAN PUBLISHING CO., INC.

NEW YORK

Macmillan Publishing Co., Inc.
866 Third Avenue, New York, N.Y. 10022
Collier Macmillan Canada, Ltd.

Library of Congress Cataloging in Publication Data
Brian, Denis.
Tallulah, darling.
Includes index.
1. Bankhead, Tallulah, 1902-1968.   2. Actors—
United States—Biography.   I. Title.
PN2287.B17B7   1980   791'.092'4 [B]   80-10930
ISBN 0-02-515200-9

First Printing 1980

Excerpts from "One Woman Show" reprinted by permission from TIME, The Weekly Newsmagazine; © Time Inc. 1948. Quotation from the *New York Times* on p. 145 © 1944 by The New York Times Company. Reprinted by permission.

Designed by Jack Meserole

Printed in the United States of America

To martine
with my love

CONTENTS

Curtain Up

"Codeine—bourbon!' were Tallulah Bankhead's last coherent words before she died in the winter of 1968. If you tried to epitomize her life in two words, those would be hard to top. Tallulah soaked up pain and pleasure in extravagant draughts and dished them out, too, generously and often.

Two summers before her death she was answering my questions in her thirteenth-floor Manhattan apartment, a portable oxygen tank at hand for gulps of relief between deep drags on her cigarette. She explained in a conspiratorial whisper, as she reached for another cigarette, that she was suffering from emphysema.

It was a night of confessions. "I probably need a psychiatrist more than anyone else," she admitted. "But what the hell, I've told EVERYTHING anyway."

But had she? Did frank, tell-it-like-it-is (and preferably in Anglo-Saxon) Tallulah take any secrets with her to the grave?

Tallulah Bankhead, like her grandmother, was named after a waterfall, Tallulah Falls. First mistake. It should have been after a hurricane, or better still a tornado, for Tallulah lovers and haters alike would agree that this tiny, tempestuous woman hurled herself at life, leaving behind devastated victims. Survivors recall her visits in the quiet aftermath with either stunned relief or incredulous excitement. An encounter with Tallulah was unforgettable.

She took off her clothes in public so often to reveal the

real Tallulah that it prompted her lifelong friend Estelle Winwood to ask: "Why do you do that, Tallulah? You have such pretty frocks."

Tallulah's reply, if there was one, is lost to posterity.* But at the same time this flouter of conventions was scandalized when she heard someone whispering in church.

Part of the secret of her fame was that she and the press were made for each other. Almost everything she did was reported on both sides of the Atlantic and throughout the then-flourishing British Empire, leaving the reader wondering—What Will Tallulah Do Next? She conquered the hearts of droves of men and women and a few children, took a lion for companion, and shocked the squares and even the tolerant with her taboo-breaking, bacchanal behavior.

She explained that the lesbian encounters of her youth were the result of her father warning her to beware of men but failing to mention women. Which sounds more like a Tallulah wisecrack than an attempt to tell the truth. But it just may be what happened. And although she was frequently surrounded by homosexuals and was broadminded about all sexuality except the sadistic, according to a friend "Tallulah hadn't a homosexual bone in her body."

The measure of her interest to the public was that even in a weak play that folded quickly, she rated a newspaper headline: "Tallulah Flops!"

At her best on stage, her performances have been called fabulous, but her more frequent bad performances were hammy, undisciplined, and a self-caricature. Those, she would explain, "darling, were in long, boring runs when I had to entertain myself to stop from going crazy." Ideally, she would have brought the audience home with her to give them a different show every night—words, music, direction by Tallulah; readings from Shakespeare, the Bible, and Ten-

---

* Tallulah's friends have intriguingly different explanations for why she had an irresistible urge to strip.

nessee Williams. A naked dip in the pool at midnight. A sentimental song at one, followed by highlights from past triumphs, and an account of how she couldn't stop laughing on stage one night after her leading man had fluffed and instead of saying of another character, "Her beauty took your breath away," said, "Her breath took her beauty away." And the audience broke down, too, and for what seemed hours laughed along with Tallulah. Refreshments would be on the house,—"and the first one to fall asleep is a shit. I can say shit, darling; I'm a lady."

But then there was the quiet, compassionate Tallulah who visited a hospital for lepers, invited one of them home to a party, and afterwards kissed him goodbye. And that never got in the papers. Nor did she ever boast of it.

She took advantage of a fleeting contact with J. Edgar Hoover to get blues singer Billie Holliday freed from prison, where she had been sentenced on a drug charge, helped people to escape from Nazi-occupied Europe, and waged a one-woman propaganda war against Hitler.

Tallulah attracted scandal as a small boy attracts dirt but idolized her father and was afraid her excesses might wreck his chance to be President of the United States, or even make him lose his job as Speaker of the House of Representatives. The fear of smearing the Bankhead name kept her from behaving so outrageously that she'd land in a drunk tank or worse. Her nature drove her to imitate a kamikaze pilot, but she throttled back when she realized the target might be her father.

When she couldn't help herself and her wild escapades did make headlines, she tried to cover her tracks by giving the affairs the most innocent if entirely implausible Tallulah explanations. Her cocaine sniffing became menthol snuff she took for a chronically sore throat. "Anyway, cocaine isn't habit-forming, darling, and I ought to know. I've been taking it all my life." And she probably explained her efforts to tempt evangelist Aimee Semple McPherson into admitting some indiscretion, as religious research, "in case I have to play a saint like you someday, darling."

Depending on your mood or temperament, her ploys to stay center stage and her monopoly of the conversation until it became monologue were entertaining or an ordeal. "I've just spent an hour talking to Tallulah for a few minutes," quipped her pal Fred Keating. And librettist Howard Dietz followed that with, "A day away from Tallulah is like a month in the country." Another friend timed Tallulah with a stopwatch and estimated that she spoke at least seventy thousand words a day, the length of an average novel. Words poured out of her (naming her after a waterfall wasn't so wrong, after all) in a stream-of-consciousness style, broken only by a quick gulp of whisky or a puff on her cigarette. She might pause for a fast question. But it had to be short or you wouldn't get to finish it.

Out came the highlights of her career, her phobias, childhood memories, funniest moments, political views, snippets from her latest reading, a new twist in the soap operas she watched religiously, appropriate quotes from the Bible, her latest plans, her latest malapropism—"I call people antisemantic when I mean anti-Semitic" and "Don't talk, darling, I've got laryngitis"—views on world problems. Tennessee Williams' torments, her father, her sister, her beautiful mother who died shortly after Tallulah was born, Lawrence of Arabia—"while I was posing for Augustus John to paint me, Lawrence used to drive off on his motorcycle to get me cigarettes." She'd point proudly to the portrait on the wall. "I've been offered a fortune for it, but I'd never sell." But the monologue is not over yet. If you tried to leave, Tallulah would demand that you return to hear how much she adored Winston Churchill, how fond she was of animals, how she hated Somerset Maugham, how she triumphed in England. . . .

Tallulah had the gift of endurance, the energy of two

women, and almost total recall. She could stick to a sentence longer than Proust and with more convolutions than Henry James, sometimes laughing at herself in a husky voice when she lost track: "Where was I? What was I saying, darling?" She would break into tears at some sad memory, into song to prove she couldn't sing, but couldn't resist trying. It was like listening to a bright child who has just discovered how to talk and has had all the wonders and woes of the world presented to her. She just had to talk about it. And nothing would stop her.

Her husband, for one, never tried. He was bedazzled, bemused, and then almost broken by the phenomenon he married. John Emery was a stagily handsome, John Barrymore look-alike, a genial, gentlemanly actor. He tolerated Tallulah for four years and then ran for his life—although they always remained friends. Before her one and only marriage, to Emery, Tallulah estimated her lovers at a round five thousand. But she was never good at figures.

The great love of her life got away. He was a titled Englishman with eighteen thousand acres and a casual charm. By several accounts he was also a tubercular bisexual, with something of a sadistic streak. She obviously wasn't making things easy for herself. Losing him was one of her big regrets. Later on, an overaged fighter pilot, he was killed in World War II. Had he survived—well, anything is possible. Remember, Tallulah watched soap operas as though she was getting special insight into real life.

To think of Tallulah as a wanton woman perpetually holding a drink in one hand and a warm body in the other is almost accurate. Sometimes she changed hands. But if that summed her up, her life wouldn't be worth exploring. In fact, she was a constant surprise with many hidden and unreported sides to her, both worse and better than she was painted.

What would you expect her to do when President Truman called her on the phone?

Tallulah asked him to call later—when she wasn't watching a soap opera. Nothing was ever allowed to interrupt that.

How would you think she'd respond when then-husband John Emery revealed that he'd just beaten up a man for insulting her?

She gave Emery a black eye—for not killing the brute.

Take a wild guess at what she did when producer Herbert Shumlin came to her home to offer her what was to be her greatest role, in Lillian Hellman's *The Little Foxes?* Whatever you say, you'll be wrong.

She led him to her bedroom and introduced him to husband John Emery, who was in bed. She pulled back the sheets and asked: "Just tell me, darling, if you've ever seen a prick that big." Shumlin must have said the right thing: Tallulah took the part. It's no wonder people claimed Tallulah would do anything for a laugh, or to shock the shockable.

She was a fiercely loyal friend, a vociferous enemy, loved children, animals, and Democrats, was scared of almost everything but rarely into silence, could pee in a washbasin while saying, "One thing I insist on is good manners," was funny, witty, outrageous, outspoken, curious as a cat, and would bet at the drop of a bottle top. She loved dogs passionately, but in a semicomatose state set at least one alight by dropping a lit cigarette on it. Naturally, she had enough liquid at hand to put out the flames.

How witty was she?

Her first recorded wisecrack was a happy fluke. Theatergoing with critic Alexander Woollcott, she said of a Maeterlinck play they were watching: "There's less in this than meets the eye." Woollcott grabbed at it for his column. Tallulah later confided she thought that was the correct expression.

But she learned.

On hearing of a promiscuous young woman who had broken her leg in England, Tallulah's friend Dorothy Parker whispered: "Probably sliding down a barrister." Nobody outclassed Parker at that sort of remark. Tallulah might easily have been the lady in question, though she would deny that she was ever promiscuous—there always had to be a spark. Years later Tallulah played a role in *Midgie Purvis* in which she had to slide down a bannister.

Never able to top Parker, Tallulah had some great near-misses. In a public toilet devoid of tissue, Tallulah called to the woman in the next stall: "I beg your pardon, darling, do you have any toilet tissue?" "No," replied the woman. "Well, then, darling," Tallulah said, "do you have two fives for a ten?"

Trying to make an omelette, Tallulah dropped an egg on the floor. "Oh, my God!" she cried out, "I've killed it!"

Failing to outwit Dorothy Parker at one party, Tallulah turned cartwheels and indulged in other wild gyrations as her contribution to the gaiety. "Oh, has Whistler's mother gone?" murmured Parker after Tallulah made a shaky exit, with George Cukor as navigator. Next morning, told of Parker's parting shot, Tallulah moaned: "The less I behave like Whistler's mother, the more I look like her the next morning."

Nobody would expect to see the risqué Tallulah quoted in the *Christian Science Monitor*, but it was almost as surprising to find her in *The New York Times*.

The quote appeared in only one edition. Then a puritanical pressman pulled it—no doubt with the approval of a higher power. But several hundred thousand readers had a chance to see it. The edition's probably a collector's item by now.

Tallulah was quoted as saying she didn't feel comfortable in a conventional lovemaking position, but of the alternatives one gave her claustrophobia and the other lockjaw.

Comedians and gossip columnists were constantly quoting and misquoting her. And today it would be impossible to separate fact from fiction—especially as she was inclined to accept the better fiction as her own.

When Stan Laurel of Laurel and Hardy fame died, he left behind an envelope full of gags. One was:

[BANKHEAD *in ladies room at Ciro's.*]

FRENCH WOMAN [*enters*]: Oh, Miss Bankhead, didn't we meet in Cannes?

BANKHEAD: Which one, this one, or the one at the Mocambo?

Could she act or was she simply putting on an act?

Lynn Fontanne said Tallulah was the greatest natural talent of her time. Of her performance in *Dear Charles,* the New York *Mirror*'s Robert Coleman wrote: "It reminds one of a Heifetz or a Horowitz bestowing his genius on a pop trifle."

"She and Bert Lahr are the two best muggers in the business," said John Chapman of the *New York Daily News.*

John Mason Brown described her in *Private Lives* as "the only volcano ever dressed by Mainbocher."

She gave 408 performances on Broadway as Regina Giddens in *The Little Foxes* before going on tour with it. Brooks Atkinson of *The New York Times* wrote: "As the malevolent lady . . . she plays with superb command of the entire character, sparing of the showy side, constantly aware of the poisonous spirit within. . . . It is a superb example of mature acting that is fully under control . . . not only the finest thing she has done in this country but brilliant acting according to any standards."

She played in Noel Coward's *Private Lives* everywhere, she claimed, but under water.

The New Yorker's Brendan Gill saw her in it as "a fabulously interesting trouper with a worldly style based on a fine Southern upbringing and a cavernous voice that shivers the galleries. . . . Dressed as expensively as possible, she gives an exciting and hilarious performance. 'Ferocious' might be the word."

Critics had a fine time searching for the words to describe her voice. They threw away the thesaurus and J. C. Trewin came up with "voice like hot honey and milk, a face like an angry flower." Not bad. John Crosby claimed "her voice has more timbre than Yellowstone Park." Hah! Walter Kerr called her "a blithe spirit with a rusty voice."

Told she looked much taller on stage, she replied: "I'm only five foot three, but I play tall parts." If she was five foot three, it was in very, very high heels.

Should anyone doubt her acting talent, she could always quote the man who turned her down for the role of Scarlett in *Gone With the Wind,* choosing instead her friend Vivien Leigh. A note David O. Selznick sent Tallulah on May 15, 1945, read: "I did want you to know that, more and more, I am convinced you are the great actress of our time."

Empathy was one of Tallulah's strongest and most endearing points. She used to listen to a late-night radio show in New York City called "Happiness Exchange" in which the losers phoned in for help and advice. Tallulah often called up and joined the conversations with the heartbroken, offering sympathy, encouragement, and cash. She sent one desperately needy woman one of her best fur coats.

Her affection and admiration for John Barrymore were enduring. And when he was a dying and forgotten man, his brain almost drowned in alcohol, his behavior unpredictable and sometimes dangerous, she got in touch with him and invited him to a party. It was a comparatively staid affair, but Barrymore changed that—shocking all the guests into stunned silence with a string of obscenities. Tallulah quickly came to his side, took his arm fondly, and said: "John, darling, we've all heard those words before. Kit Cornell used them on the radio last week."

That was the kind, warm, thoughtful Tallulah. But she could be just as shocking as Barrymore.

What seemed the endless run of *Private Lives* got to her when she reached Marblehead, Massachusetts. Until then she had tried mild tactics to keep herself sane, like slowly lowering her long glued eyelashes out of sight of the audience as she stared at the performer opposite her, until they both broke up and had a fit of the giggles. But now she exceeded herself. She rented a mansion from a Mrs. Blaisdell, insisted on calling her Mrs. Bloodshot, and kept all the lights blazing from dusk to dawn so that her pet parakeet Gaylord would feel at home. The cops stayed away until Tallulah threw a noisy party and aroused the neighbors. Tallulah faced the police naked—of course—and in a fighting mood. A cop advanced on her and Tallulah hit him. She spent some time in the local jail and left town under cover of darkness.

Tallulah never stayed in the dark for long. The Marblehead romp escaped press scrutiny, but Tallulah was falling prey to her own excesses—and though she might hide behind smoked glasses and other disguises, her voice was a dead giveaway.

As she reached her forties and fifties, she burned and broke and cut her body in freak accidents, accounts of which reached the news desk of any city where she was holding court. But, by some alchemy, plus her reputation, reports that might have been sordid or pitiful gained new hilarious life in the telling and often seemed straight out of *Hellzapoppin*. Tallulah was a happening before anyone coined the word. Jaded deskmen rallied when tales of Tallulah's troubles fell on their littered desks. Now they could think up zany headlines to fit the unlikely facts.

New York Daily News reporter Theo Wilson chronicled one of Tallulah's follies in 1958 when she cut her arm on a vase doing God knows what and a howling ambulance raced to her home.

The headline for the story was: WELLDAHLINGITWASLIKE-THIS,THISLAMPWASBYMY . . .

And the story, in part, runs: "Tallulah had just been through one blankety-blank of an evening, complete with cops, doctors, five stitches in her arm, and a house guest with hepatitis and no sleep—but she came roaring on the phone yesterday with a full head of steam and went right into a magnificent denunciation of those 'fantastic' reports that she had tripped and fallen on a 'blankety-blank' vase. . . ." (Tallulah said she simply cut her arm on a vase which she knocked over reaching for the telephone.)

" 'Well, after the maid called an ambulance,' said Tallulah, 'these three enchanting policemen came, and then there was this perfectly charming doctor who put five stitches in my arm. I didn't have a thing while it was done. I was noble.'

"Tallulah insisted she was not ill. 'If I were no one would dare to call me at this blankety-blank time of the day.'

" 'Why, there were reports that I was murrrrrderrrrred,' she roared, 'when I became ill with acute nephritis last year and had to be carried from the house.' There was some more roaring, and Tallulah hung up after telling the reporter, 'God bless you darling.' "

That report got Tallulah's picture on the front page.

Another anonymous deskman gave a new word to the language with his double-barreled headline:

TALLULAH IS HOSPITALIZED,

HOSPITAL TALLULAHIZED

And here's a taste of the story: "Tallulah Bankhead has entered Flower-Fifth Avenue Hospital for 'a general checkup' and some of the other patients there are positive that the doctors aren't going to find anything wrong with the lady's lungs.

"One patient called the *News* yesterday to say that he knew Tallulah was on the floor, on account of 'I could hear her bellowing that she wanted an air-conditioner pronto.'

" 'Did she get one?'

" 'I guess so,' said the patient. 'From the hammering and noise going on in that room, she's getting everything she's hollering for.' "

To be fair to the young and innocent—actors, playwrights, doctors. nurses among them—Tallulah should have worn a label: This Lady May Be Hazardous to Your Health. Because sustained encounters with Tallulah could drive them bonkers.

She was mean and generous, cruel and incredibly kind, cold and warmhearted and unpredictable as a flash fire. Those who came to love-and-hate her protest when the legends of her outrageous behavior and penchant for strong drink and language swamp the truth about the woman.

She was much, much more than the caricature the public knows, they say. She could, it's true, be as cruel as Caligula, but she was also funny, entertaining, sensitive, caring, and devastatingly honest. And even the walking-wounded playwrights who watched her switch in midsentence from tiger to pussy cat and back again, slashing their plays in rehearsal into a chaotic travesty came out of their traumas to write new plays—about her.

Inevitably publishers panted after her, hoping she would tell all between hard covers, expecting to get the frankest confessions since Saint Augustine's. The prestigious house of Harper & Brothers finally trapped her—and their new author-in-the-making began to set the record straight, after a fashion. She scorned quill, ball-point, or typewriter, preferring, being Tallulah, to talk into a tape recorder and let her press agent eliminate the grocery lists and unscramble any incoherencies.

She was spurred by her passion for telling the truth, curbed by her fear of the consequences.

And friends and foes wondered and worried—which would win out?

II

Darling Tallulah

Of all the people that ever came out of Alabama,
I think Zelda Sayre Fitzgerald and Tallulah Bank-
head the most fascinating.
—PLAYWRIGHT LAWTON CAMPBELL

For a woman with the gift of gab who called herself "as pure as driven slush," there were many questions Tallulah Bankhead left unanswered, even when she wrote her own frank life story. She had the guts to tell almost all the truth about her "legend in her own time" life—but not the whole truth. That she didn't dare. When cornered, she'd avoid revealing herself by a maneuver worthy of a poker player. She routed sex researcher Alfred Kinsey when he asked Tallulah to tell him the facts of her sex life by replying: "Of course, darling, if you'll tell me yours." While playing Cleopatra—on her working honeymoon with John Emery—she cut short a woman reporter's probing questions by shock tactics, a family trait:

"Miss Bankhead, what is your definition of love?"

"Do you mean fucking?"

And those were the don't-tell-it-like-it-is days, when such language was the preserve of D. H. Lawrence, James Joyce, and front-line fighting men.

High-voiced columnist Earl Wilson asked husky-voiced Tallulah if she'd ever been mistaken for a man on the phone. "No, darling," she answered. "Have you?"

Many actresses, stars especially, are largely made of press agents' puffs, trick lighting, and plastic surgery. Tallulah eventually used all three, but even without them she was as arresting as an angry volcano, and so strikingly beautiful in her youth that fifty years later people would recall her looks with what sounded like the same shock of delight.

Who called her a legend in her own time? Her press agent, Richard Maney. But before he made that claim, British newspaper tycoon Lord Beaverbrook had confirmed it. "The only three names that are instantly recognized throughout the entire British Empire," said Beaverbrook, "are Bernard Shaw, the Prince of Wales, and Tallulah."

Winston Churchill hadn't much time for women, literally, but he was so attracted by Tallulah that he saw her five times in Coward's *Fallen Angels*. Even today, just mention Tallulah's name and a smile will come to most lips. Who else can arouse that reaction?

Why did she call everyone "dahling"? "Because, dahling, I meet so many people and simply can't remember all their names."

Eight astonishingly successful years in England (1923–1931) were her happiest times ever, even though she was hounded from theatre to theatre by a man who threatened to murder her, even though she appeared in only two plays worth recalling (*They Knew What They Wanted* by Sidney Howard and *Fallen Angels* by Noel Coward). She danced and drank and delighted in those golden years in which she, Noel Coward, and the Scott Fitzgeralds came to epitomize the spirit of the times.

There she is in London with her first car. But with so little sense of direction that she hires a taxi to drive ahead of her to show her the way. There she is, the toast of the town, introducing the Scott Fitzgeralds to her pal, the Marchioness of Milford Haven. And when a Rumanian prince dares her to turn cartwheels in a London street in the early hours she dares, ending up with her toe at a policeman's throat. He must have been the toast of his division.

But there was rarely triumph without torment: the young man said to have committed suicide because she scorned him; the strange, evasive behavior of the man she loved—and his eventual escape.

Back in America Tallulah shook gloomy Garbo out of her doldrums at a party with antics like a wound-up Charlie Chaplin. She compensated for white, anemic lips by hiding them under generous slashes of gleaming lipstick. The white face and the vivid red lips somehow added credence to the growing legend of her wickedness. She smoked almost nonstop. She drank when she wasn't talking. She took cocaine. She took lovers.

Tallulah was afraid of many things but she masked most fears with a wisecrack.

She hated a liar, strangely, even more than a murderer—which is some indication of her love for the truth. Plain-speaking President Truman was so impressed by her 1952 autobiography *Tallulah* that he called it "the best book I've read since I've been in the White House," and at that time he'd been in seven years. Yet, frank and truthful as it was, it left a lot untold, good and bad.

Tallulah didn't tell how she lay weeping on a movie studio floor, harassed beyond endurance by Ernst Lubitsch. She never mentioned how she helped save Jews from Hitler's Europe, nor the ghost she saw in Hollywood—in bright light. She hid the truth about her drug taking. Rarely the woman to resort to a euphemism, Tallulah was evasive about her love life. She didn't say a word about Tennessee Williams. Yet by that time she had known him for ten years and he had brought her—at least in the world of the theatre—the promise of immortality. Nervous, shy, tormented Tennessee found his inspiration in an actress who appeared to be a smoky-voiced extrovert cavorting through life. He knew her, in fact, to be a complicated woman, like a piece of cut glass that reflects the colors of its environment, yet with a secret core, apparently transparent, but as elusive as light itself.

Her friend Greta Garbo became famous by hiding from the world; Tallulah, by burning the candle, as Cecil Beaton says, "at every end," and by diverting lords, ladies, and cab drivers with her offstage antics.

She gave one of her most memorable performances in New York General Sessions court, during the closing days of 1951. Her former secretary, a one-time striptease artist, was on trial for forging Tallulah's checks. Tallulah was a witness for the prosecution, but in a switch that would have been more appropriate on a TV soap opera, the accuser became the accused. Miss Bankhead, thundered the defense attorney, had written the checks to pay for marijuana, cocaine, booze, and sex. Tallulah thought her career was over, that this accusation alone would wreck it. But eventually Tallulah triumphed, and the judge commended her for her spirit. She almost took a curtain call.

Sleepless nights, nicotine, liquid breakfasts, and mixed drugs took their toll. She was often dangerously ill.

In a 1957 interview with Mike Wallace she said of the United States: "I think it's a bloody sick country . . . everybody's scared of the atom bomb . . . everybody's going to psychiatrists . . . the only sane thing I've encountered lately is Senator McClellan and that divine Bobby Kennedy."

She said her rule was never to practice two vices at once and explained her love life this way: "I'm bored to the point of suicide when I'm not in love. But I'm not promiscuous. Promiscuity implies that attraction is not necessary. I may lay my eyes on a man and have an affair with him the next hour. But the attraction is serious." Then in the same breath she added: "I'm really very shy."

Tallulah appeared on Broadway in Mary Chase's *Midgie Purvis* in 1961. It was Mary Chase who first gave me a key to Tallulah Bankhead. "Tallulah," she said, "is seven different women, at least." And each one, she might have added, complex.

That is why Alfred Hitchcock would call her a woman without inhibitions," and her friend Eugenia Rawls describe her as "secretive." Vincent Price says: "She was magnificent. There ain't nobody like her. In her heyday nobody had a bigger ball." Virginia Graham believes "she had the honesty of the very rich. She just couldn't give a damn. She said it and she meant it. She was a warm, sensitive, loving, emotional woman who put a slip cover on herself because she didn't want the world to know." Lee Strasberg found her "fascinating." Billy Rose: "I've staged shows that called for the management of a herd of buffalo, and I've shot actors out of cannons for fifty feet into the arms of an adagio dancer, but both of them were easier than saying 'good morning' to Miss Bankhead." "A wonderful human being," says Estelle Winwood. "She frightened the bejesus out of me," said Joan Crawford. "I think she was slightly insane," says Tamara Geva.

I began to find out how complex, shocking, secretive Tallulah was when I interviewed her for four hours in her New York apartment on East Fifty-seventh Street one evening in 1966, and later, in 1968, after her death a month short of her sixty-seventh birthday, by speaking with over one hundred people who had known her in every aspect of her life. Few who knew Tallulah, even those who could be called enemies, refused to talk. The loves beat the hates by about twenty to one.

My aim has been to penetrate the legends, the press agentry, and Tallulah's own fancies, to get as close to the facts as possible, a fascinating task because the facts were often hidden. Even her friend Tennessee Williams, inspired, startled, hurt, amused, enraged, touched by Tallulah Bankhead, failed to solve the mystery of this tiny, feverish phenomenon, although he wrote four plays with her voice, her presence almost in the room with him.

She was daring because she was always herself. She saw

people and things clearly, as a child does, and if her words insulted they were never hypocritical. At times, like a child, she was cruel.

There was this surprising, sometimes startling innocence in Tallulah, who seemed the epitome of sophistication, partly because she had a child's inclination to do and say the forbidden. And, too, she restored the magic of childhood for some adults. "If you could meet anyone in the world, who would it be?" she asked some friends.

James Kirkwood believed it was only a game of make-believe, but to his amazement, Tallulah granted his wish—an afternoon with Mrs. Eleanor Roosevelt. For Ted Hook there was an evening with Dorothy Parker and Truman Capote.

There's a scene in Christopher Morley's novel *Thunder on the Left* in which the child-personality in the body of a man walks across the room, arms stretched before him, to meet the hostess just before dinner. And the hostess, who is in love with the man she sees, believes he is about to take her in his arms and kiss her. But all he says is: "You didn't look at my hands . . . are they clean enough?"

Tallulah had something of this child-spirit in her.

Women who hated her (few men did) were still smarting from the loss of stolen lovers, or couldn't tolerate Tallulah's comic efforts to keep stage center against all comers, or were Republicans. Or were shocked beyond endurance.

"Everything they say about me is true," she sometimes said. At other times she'd say: "If everything they said about me was true, I'd be dead by now." I tracked down and demolished one apocryphal tale. She did not say to Norman Mailer after he published *The Naked and the Dead*, which, in those more evasive days, was full of "fug" and "fuggin": "Are you the young man who can't spell fuck?" When they met, says Mailer, they merely smiled and said hello.

After her last film, *Die, Die, My Darling*, which she made in England in the summer of 1964, Tallulah left gifts of St. Christopher medals for her coworkers and she gave the director, Silvio Narizzano, a medal inscribed with a devil and the words: "It takes one to know one. Love Tallulah."

When she died suddenly of pneumonia complicated by emphysema on December 12, 1968, she left behind an estate valued at two million dollars and memories to top that.

"No one will ever know what she really was," said her best friend, actress Estelle Winwood. This book is an attempt to find out.

...hey
...most
...at her

...ned how
...ry opportu-
...ergarten, she
...was throwing
...governor of Ala-
...local doctor. All
...petition judged by
...instruments played,
...r a change of pace—
...e Wright brothers knew
...e and gave her first prize.

...us in Birmingham provided
...t the contortionist. Tallulah
...a week of strain and pain she
...pick up a handkerchief from be-
...uld stand on her head and turn
...ple didn't gasp, but at least they

...cinated Tallulah she wanted to make
...When she was five, her father took her
...ow in Birmingham. The hit was a risqué
...mitated the singer all the way home and her

...ts later he came home in high spirits. As he

III

Shock Tactics

When charm and reason failed, [...] they wanted by shock tactics. Duri[ng...] to persuade the reluctant Senate [...] E. Lee, grandfather John Ban[khead] dressed in his old army unifo[rm...] Senate as a rebel capt[a]in, s[...] night curtain call. Tall[ul]ah [...] genia, sixteen, watched f[...] and crying with the oth[...]

Tallulah's Aunt M[...] hospital crippled w[...] lacerated tongue. [...] first, she scrawle[d...] but a Bankhead wi[...] Alabama." He got the m[...]

Tallulah herself was the [...] Eugenia Sledge, whose name wa[s...] in the South. Engaged to a Virgini[an...] Huntsville, Alabama, to buy her wed[ding...] months later she married—another ma[n]. Du[ring...] ping trip, Eugenia met William Bankhe[a]d. Then[...] also Eugenia, was born the following year, and Tallula[h...] born on the second anniversary of their surprise wedding— January 31, 1902.*

* The many reports giving Tallulah's birthdate as 190[2] or 1904 are inaccurate.

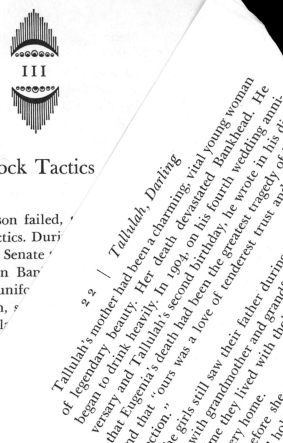

22 | *Tallulah, Darling*

Tallulah's mother had been a charming, vital young woman of legendary beauty. Her death devastated Bankhead. He began to drink heavily. In 1904, on his fourth birthday, he wrote in his diary that Eugenia's death had been the greatest tragedy of his life, and that "ours was a love of tenderest trust and consuming affection."

The girls still saw their father during vacations when [...] stayed with grandmother and grandfather in Jasper. But [...] of the time they lived with their father's sister, Marie [...] Montgomery home.

Almost before she could talk, Tallulah had lea[rned...] to attract and hold attention. And she sought eve[ry...] nity to demonstrate. Hurrying home from kind[...] joined a celebrity-studded party her aunt Mari[e...] for aviators Orville and Wilbur Wright, the [...] bama, judges, lawyers, congressmen, and th[...] the guests had to take part in a talent co[...] the Wright brothers. Songs were sung[...] poems recited or brayed. Tallulah—f[...] imitated her kindergarten teacher. Th[...] Tallulah was on her way.

What next? A visit to the cir[cus...] a force of nature when they saw on[...] answer. Everyone gasped. [...] wanted to be gasped at. Afte[r...] still couldn't bend back and [...] tween her feet, but she c[...] flawless cartwheels. Peo[ple...] stopped and stared. [...] Everything that fas[...] hers—by imitation sh[...] to a vaudeville si[nger...] singer. Tallulah [...] father loved it. [...] A few nig[ht...]

rector, Silvio Narizzano, a medal inscribed with a devil and the words: "It takes one to know one. Love Tallulah."

When she died suddenly of pneumonia complicated by emphysema on December 12, 1968, she left behind an estate valued at two million dollars and memories to top that.

"No one will ever know what she really was," said her best friend, actress Estelle Winwood. This book is an attempt to find out.

III

Shock Tactics

When charm and reason failed, the Bankheads got what they wanted by shock tactics. During World War I, in 1917, to persuade the reluctant Senate to pay for a statue of Robert E. Lee, grandfather John Bankhead, senator for Alabama, dressed in his old army uniform. And when he stood in the Senate as a rebel captain, sword and all, it was like a first-night curtain call. Tallulah, then fifteen, and her sister Eugenia, sixteen, watched from the gallery applauding, cheering, and crying with the others. Bankhead got what he wanted.

Tallulah's Aunt Marie was hit by a truck and taken to the hospital crippled with a broken kneecap and silenced with a lacerated tongue. When the doctor started to examine her leg first, she scrawled a hurried note: "To hell with the kneecap, but a Bankhead without a tongue is no good to the state of Alabama." He got the message, and her mouth got priority.

Tallulah herself was the result of shock tactics by Adelaide Eugenia Sledge, whose name was synonymous with beauty in the South. Engaged to a Virginia planter, she went to Huntsville, Alabama, to buy her wedding dress. Three months later she married—another man. During the shopping trip, Eugenia met William Bankhead. Their daughter, also Eugenia, was born the following year, and Tallulah was born on the second anniversary of their surprise wedding—January 31, 1902.*

* The many reports giving Tallulah's birthdate as 1903 or 1904 are inaccurate.

Three weeks after Tallulah was born her mother died of complications resulting from childbirth.

Tallulah's father, William Bankhead, an amiable, tall, broad-shouldered man with a resonant voice and a sense of humor, appeared completely untheatrical, but as a lawyer and politician he knew the value of understatement and timing and used them effectively. From before the Civil War the Bankheads had been prosperous Alabama planters. After the war they were, without exception, anti–Ku Klux Klan. William, a fullback for the University of Alabama's football team and a Phi Beta Kappa, received his B.A. in 1893 and his M.A. two years later. In the meantime he'd earned an LL.B. from Georgetown University. He won a medal in college for oratory and was tempted to become an actor until his mother sent him an emotional letter warning him of the "disaster and disgrace" that would follow. He stuck to law.

Law took him to politics. He was city attorney of Huntsville (1900–1914), and campaigned first for fellow Democrats and then for himself. He was elected to Congress in 1917 as Democratic member of the sixty-fifth Congress from the seventh Alabama district.

While he was campaigning for Al Smith, Ku Kluxers pelted Bankhead with eggs. Brushing himself off, he said quietly to the chairman: "Sir, I have been treated discourteously . . ." then continued with his speech. He showed the same calm when his house caught fire in the early-morning hours. He dressed carefully, and when firemen arrived he climbed down the ladder as if it was the way he normally went to work.

Bankhead, eventually to be Speaker of the House, was called "the best-loved man in Congress."

To daughter Tallulah he was and always would be the best-loved man in her world. All other men in her life had to measure up to her father—and few could. Although there were years when they rarely saw one another, his influence was as constant as the North Star, and much warmer.

Tallulah's mother had been a charming, vital young woman of legendary beauty. Her death devastated Bankhead. He began to drink heavily. In 1904, on his fourth wedding anniversary and Tallulah's second birthday, he wrote in his diary that Eugenia's death had been the greatest tragedy of his life, and that "ours was a love of tenderest trust and consuming affection."

The girls still saw their father during vacations when they stayed with grandmother and grandfather in Jasper. But most of the time they lived with their father's sister, Marie, at her Montgomery home.

Almost before she could talk, Tallulah had learned how to attract and hold attention. And she sought every opportunity to demonstrate. Hurrying home from kindergarten, she joined a celebrity-studded party her aunt Marie was throwing for aviators Orville and Wilbur Wright, the governor of Alabama, judges, lawyers, congressmen, and the local doctor. All the guests had to take part in a talent competition judged by the Wright brothers. Songs were sung, instruments played, poems recited or brayed. Tallulah—for a change of pace— imitated her kindergarten teacher. The Wright brothers knew a force of nature when they saw one and gave her first prize. Tallulah was on her way.

What next? A visit to the circus in Birmingham provided the answer. Everyone gasped at the contortionist. Tallulah wanted to be gasped at. After a week of strain and pain she still couldn't bend back and pick up a handkerchief from between her feet, but she could stand on her head and turn flawless cartwheels. People didn't gasp, but at least they stopped and stared.

Everything that fascinated Tallulah she wanted to make hers—by imitation. When she was five, her father took her to a vaudeville show in Birmingham. The hit was a risqué singer. Tallulah imitated the singer all the way home and her father loved it.

A few nights later he came home in high spirits. As he

opened Tallulah's door to see if she was sleeping, she woke. Before he could tiptoe out, she was into her imitation of the risqué singer, and he was a captivated audience.

Bankhead the father tried to control his fiery daughters by bribing them with candy. Grandmother used direct methods. When Tallulah, in a rage, screamed herself from pink to purple, grandmother put her back in the pink with a bucket of water.

Bankhead the frustrated actor seized every opportunity to share his passion for Shakespeare with his daughters. And he dramatized stories from the Bible, with additional dialogue by Bankhead. Inevitably they were sad, and Tallulah and sister Eugenia would drown his last words in sobs. He'd quickly console them by promising a happy sequel, then had the devil's own job finding an upbeat ending in either testament for next Sunday's Bible story.

He was often carried away by his enthusiasm—to Tallulah's delight. Campaigning for his brother John who was aiming to represent Alabama in the Senate, William Bankhead drove over the state line into Tennessee by mistake. A group of men there invited him to speak and Tallulah watched him hold their interest for an hour—although of course he knew they couldn't vote in Alabama.

One terror-filled day Tallulah was bitten by a rattlesnake. Her father sucked the poison from the wound and saved her. But the poison got into his system and he was sick for several days.

When her father wasn't around to listen to her plans and dreams, to save her life, to tell funny stories which made her roar, to make "To Be Or Not To Be?" a real life-or-death question, she filled her time doing things that would make him proud when he heard about them—and she made sure he heard.

Aunt Marie and her husband Dr. Thomas M. Owen were in charge of the Department of Archives and History in the Capitol building at Montgomery. Whenever Tallulah visited there she'd turn the streets into an open-air theatre. Another girl about her age, Zelda Sayre (later to marry Scott Fitzgerald), was also attracting attention by her offbeat antics.

"I had a ringside seat for Zelda and Tallu's performances on Goat Hill," wrote Sara Mayfield in *Exiles from Paradise* (about Zelda and Scott Fitzgerald). "Even in those days, both of them had dash, a style and daring that left me wide-eyed and open-mouthed with admiration, for Zelda and Dutch, as we called Tallulah, were personalities and performers long before they became famous. Tallulah specialized in cartwheels, back bends, mimicry and song-and-dance routines."

As Tallulah grew, so did her temper, and Bankhead looked around for a school that might contain it. Although he was a Methodist and his wife had been Episcopalian, he decided that the best bet would be the well-disciplined nuns. He took Tallulah and her sister to the Academy of the Sacred Heart in New York City. Apart from the mistaken trip to Tennessee, it was the first time Tallulah had been out of Alabama.

Walking from the school, Bankhead heard ten-year-old Tallulah screaming, "Daddy don't leave me! Don't leave me Daddy!" But he kept moving, convinced he was doing the right thing. Tallulah had to be tamed, and the nuns were the ladies to do the job. He faced his mistake a year later, in 1913, when he and his sister Louise attended the end-of-term exercises.

They stared at a long procession of girls walking through the chapel as an organ played ethereal music. The girls all wore white veils and clutched lilies, a testimony to their virtue. Among them, like a smudge, was one girl in a black veil, without a lily. It was Tallulah. She had bitten someone in a temper and thrown an inkwell against a wall. Now she was being purged. "I felt like an untouchable," she said later. And when she glanced up and saw her father and Aunt Louise, she broke down and bawled.

From New York the sisters went to Mary Baldwin Academy

in Staunton, Virginia, spending their weekends riding Shetland ponies on Cordell Hull's estate. At least her father was within calling distance if Tallulah bit someone again. But no school could hold Tallulah for long, and she finally ended up at Fairmont Seminary in Washington.

While the Washington world was being diverted by Alice, the provocative, outspoken daughter of President Theodore Roosevelt, Alice was watching Tallulah. She recalls: "Tallulah and her sister Eugenia were charming, pretty little creatures in their early teens. They used to go swimming with the children of their father's senatorial friends, in the canal along the Potomac. Tallulah's accent was a rather exaggerated Southern accent and she loved to shock people by saying words over and over again that wouldn't be considered shocking now." "Goddam" was a favorite.

She never used such language if her father was around. He was one of the rare people for whom she tried to present a picture of perfection. Invariably aiming to please him, she couldn't always make it. She shocked him once while they were dining at a hotel by punctuating with her laughter the funny story he was telling—and even in those days her laugh was slightly Rabelaisian. "Don't laugh so loud, Baby," he whispered. "Never make yourself conspicuous. It's bad form. Bad manners."

That was advice she could only have followed after a major operation.

Tallulah was completely in agreement with his other advice. "If you know your Bible and your Shakespeare and can shoot craps, you have a liberal education."

And she resolved to heed his warning to be careful of "men and drink," two things to keep in mind not to keep in mind.

Tallulah bounded out of school for good in 1917, when she was fifteen. What had she learned? A smattering of French, a few fancy sewing stitches, and how to read movie magazines in class without being caught. In *Pictureplay* she saw her chance to become a movie star. The magazine offered screen contracts in New York to the ten girls and boys judged most attractive from their photographs.

The next mail carried Tallulah's photograph to *Pictureplay,* but she'd been in such a hurry she forgot to identify herself. She explained her mistake in a follow-up letter, describing the photo in detail.

Waiting to see if she was one of the winners was such a strain that after the first few months of grabbing the monthly issue from the drugstore and finding that the pages were filled with photos of runners-up, she made an effort not to stake her entire life on the outcome. She tried to fill the time between issues with other excitements. It was almost a surprise one day when she turned to the back page of *Pictureplay* and saw her own photograph there.

They'd obviously lost her letter explaining who she was, because above her photo was the questioning headline: "WHO IS THIS?"

Who Is This? ran back to the family apartment on Connecticut Avenue and broke the news to her father and grandfather. Her thwarted-actor father immediately wrote to the magazine identifying the mystery girl as his daughter. More proof was needed, replied the editor, explaining that fifty other moms and dads claimed the photo was their daughter. A duplicate photo was needed as proof. It was found and sent and the editor accepted it as proof. No one would ever doubt Tallulah's identity again. Within a few weeks the fifteen-year-old contest winner set out for New York with conquest in mind.

g
Al-

, very
the icy
and tried
script. She
she heard
n. Her gloves
the tremble in
eling she'd made
ried.
el Crothers. By in-
the lines that called

Hot Springs to represent
speaking engagement on
imitation of Constance Bin-
lf an hour before he realized
up there on the stage. Tallulah
when Broadway actors went on
was that her father hadn't had a
n.
ankhead hurried up to New York to
coma. She'd fainted in her room at the
been carried down the freight elevator
rushed to St. Elizabeth's Hospital. Doctors
pendix had burst. They told Bankhead: "She
ngrenous appendiix, complicated by perito-
e the order to operate.
lulah tottered out of the hospital six weeks later

IV

Tallulah Conquers
the Round Table

1917–1923

The film contract proved to be a dud. And there was Tallulah stuck in New York with Aunt Louise as a chaperone and every face a stranger's. Even the way they spoke seemed foreign. But there was such a sense of excitement in the air that summer of 1917, she felt she could touch it, as if destiny lingered around the corner. Not this one: the next.

The United States had just joined in the war against Germany, actors were leaving plays to join the army, and playwrights were turning out entertainment for a new mood.

Tallulah decided she'd shock, startle, and enchant the city into surrender yet. But it wasn't going to be easy. She shared a bedroom with Aunt Louise, who kept her awake by snoring. And in the afternoons and evenings when Tallulah wanted to haunt theatres, theatrical parties, and producers' offices, her aunt had other plans. Aunt Louise was mourning her eighteen-year-old son not long dead, and her goal was to attend spiritualistic services, hoping to hear from him. Tallulah was torn: groggy from lack of sleep, sorry for her aunt, she gave in and went to the services. Months passed and Tallu-

lah became more familiar with the strange voices of me[n]
in trances than the alchemy of actors and actresses b[ringing]
imaginary characters to life.

Then Aunt Louise made a decision that was to [have an im]-
mense effect on Tallulah's career. She moved the[m into a not]
too-large apartment on West Forty-fifth Stree[t, near the Algon]-
quin Hotel. Why she chose that hotel is a m[ystery, but],
accidentally it seems, she put Tallulah at th[e center of the world]
she aimed to conquer. Through that m[ove Tallulah came to]
meet and delight some of the most pow[erful writers and]
critics in the nation—known to frien[ds as the Round Table]
and to nonfriends as The Vicious C[ircle—who made the]
Algonquin their informal club v[here they praised and]
insulted each other for publicat[ion.]

Even Aunt Louise became d[...]
a while shared Tallulah's en[...]
to Alabama. Then Frank [...]
to keep a fatherly eye o[...]
husky-voiced sixteen-ye[...]

She lived on four [...]
an allowance of fift[...]
that went for th[...]
French maid. P[...]
scrimp on food and c[...]
table hopping, but there [...]
early, hungry and afraid, hop[...]
for both.

If Tallulah had been asked then wh[...]
most like to meet she'd have said: "Ethe[l...]
when she found herself alone with the actress [...]
quin elevator, she almost fainted from the excitem[ent...]
more remarkably, was unable to say a word.

One evening in the dining room she was introduced to [...]
Estelle Winwood, an English actress with such huge eyes she'd
been called "cow eyes" at school. Estelle looked down at Tallulah and said: "I don't want to sit at the same table as this

---

prouder when Samuel Goldwyn shortly afterward cast her in
one of his silent films called *Thirty a Week*. The movie and
World War I were both in the can by November, 1918.
And then came her chance to TALK on stage before an
audience. They wanted a summer replacement for Constance
Binney in *39 East*. "You'll be one of sixteen girls auditioning
for the part," warned actress Jobyna Howland, another Algonquin friend. "Act your age and don't dress like a tart."
Tallulah, not yet eighteen, turned up: very pale,
direct, with flopping ash blonde hair. She stood on the
theatre stage, which was lit as if for a horror movie.
couldn't, she began to turn the flimsy pages of the [...]
to pull off her gloves. Then it was her turn [...]
someone being bawled out. She was so anxiou[s...]
half off, she was shaking so much. Ahead of h[er...]
her voice matched the tremble in her legs. F[...]
a hopeless mess of it, she broke down and [...]
"The part's yours," said author Rac[hel...]
credible luck, Tallulah wept just befo[re...]
for her to be emotional. [...]
Her grandfather came up from [...]
the Bankheads at Tallulah's first [...]
Broadway. She gave such a good [...]
ney that he watched her for h[...]
that it was his granddaughter [...]
had played six performance[s...]
strike. Her biggest regret [...]
chance to see her in acti[ng...]
Three weeks later B[...]
find his daughter in a [...]
Algonquin and had [...]
on a mattress and [...]
discovered her ap[...]
has an acute g[...]
nitis." He ga[ve...]
When Ta[...]

IV

Tallulah Conquers
the Round Table

1917–1923 The film contract proved to be a dud. And there was Tallulah stuck in New York with Aunt Louise as a chaperone and every face a stranger's. Even the way they spoke seemed foreign. But there was such a sense of excitement in the air that summer of 1917, she felt she could touch it, as if destiny lingered around the corner. Not this one: the next.

The United States had just joined in the war against Germany, actors were leaving plays to join the army, and playwrights were turning out entertainment for a new mood.

Tallulah decided she'd shock, startle, and enchant the city into surrender yet. But it wasn't going to be easy. She shared a bedroom with Aunt Louise, who kept her awake by snoring. And in the afternoons and evenings when Tallulah wanted to haunt theatres, theatrical parties, and producers' offices, her aunt had other plans. Aunt Louise was mourning her eighteen-year-old son not long dead, and her goal was to attend spiritualistic services, hoping to hear from him. Tallulah was torn: groggy from lack of sleep, sorry for her aunt, she gave in and went to the services. Months passed and Tallulah became more familiar with the strange voices of mediums in trances than the alchemy of actors and actresses bringing imaginary characters to life.

Then Aunt Louise made a decision that was to have an immense effect on Tallulah's career. She moved them from their too-large apartment on West Forty-fifth Street to the Algonquin Hotel. Why she chose that hotel is a mystery, but, quite accidentally it seems, she put Tallulah at the hub of the world she aimed to conquer. Through that move Tallulah was to meet and delight some of the most powerful playwrights and critics in the nation—known to friends as The Round Table and to nonfriends as The Vicious Circle. The group made the Algonquin their informal club where they ate, drank, and insulted each other for publication.

Even Aunt Louise became dazzled by the company, and for a while shared Tallulah's enthusiasm, until she had to return to Alabama. Then Frank Case, who ran the hotel, promised to keep a fatherly eye on Tallulah. And the eager, anxious, husky-voiced sixteen-year-old was on her own.

She lived on four dollars a week. Her grandfather gave her an allowance of fifty dollars a week, but twenty-one dollars of that went for the hotel room and twenty-five dollars for a French maid. Putting up a front meant Tallulah had to scrimp on food and clothes. She survived by making an art of table hopping, but there were times when she went to bed early, hungry and afraid, hoping sleep would be an antidote for both.

If Tallulah had been asked then which actress she would most like to meet she'd have said: "Ethel Barrymore." But when she found herself alone with the actress in the Algonquin elevator, she almost fainted from the excitement and, more remarkably, was unable to say a word.

One evening in the dining room she was introduced to Estelle Winwood, an English actress with such huge eyes she'd been called "cow eyes" at school. Estelle looked down at Tallulah and said: "I don't want to sit at the same table as this beautiful girl. She makes me look plain." But she stayed.

Tallulah soon learned that Estelle had been on the stage for thirty years, toiling through four years of repertory in Liverpool, England, where she appeared in a different play every week. And now, recently arrived from England, she was starring in Broadway's most talked-about play, *Why Marry?* It had been awarded the first Pulitzer Prize. Tallulah wondered why Estelle wasn't more excited.

"I can't wait to play my first part," she said.

"Acting's a hell of a life," Estelle warned. "Stay off the stage if you possibly can."

At thirty-five Estelle had made few friends in the theatre. A cool, controlled, balanced woman, she regarded the excesses of her fellow actors with a mixture of scorn and amusement. But listening to the outpourings of this teenager, Estelle, almost twenty years older, felt the protective instincts of a mother. Tallulah was so amusing, so vital, so proud of her father and grandfather, and so broke.

They were friends almost on sight. After a few meetings Estelle realized that Tallulah couldn't both pay her hotel bills and eat, and invited Tallulah to share her apartment for a while so that she could save some of her allowance and return to the Algonquin solvent.

Tallulah faced her first Broadway audience in 1918, but only as a nonspeaking walk-on in *The Squab Farm,* which *The New York Times* called "a garish travesty of life in the movies, all in bad taste." Tallulah worked in that, as a mute, for four weeks. She infuriated other girls in the cast by whistling in the dressing room. "It's bad luck!" they shrieked and almost blamed her for the play's short life.

A week after *Squab Farm* closed, movie director Ivan Abramson told Tallulah he'd seen her in it and "Because you have poise and beauty I want you for a part in *When Men Betray.* I'm filming it on Long Island next week." Acting in that silent film was less fun than listening to insults at the Algonquin. But she was proud to say she'd made it and even prouder when Samuel Goldwyn shortly afterward cast her in one of his silent films called *Thirty a Week*. The movie and World War I were both in the can by November, 1918.

And then came her chance to TALK on stage before an audience. They wanted a summer replacement for Constance Binney in *39 East*. "You'll be one of sixteen girls auditioning for the part," warned actress Jobyna Howland, another Algonquin friend. "Act your age and don't dress like a tart."

Tallulah, not yet eighteen, turned up: very pale, very direct, with flopping ash blonde hair. She stood on the icy theatre stage, which was lit as if for a horror movie, and tried to pull off her gloves to turn the flimsy pages of the script. She couldn't, she was shaking so much. Ahead of her she heard someone being bawled out. Then it was her turn. Her gloves half off, she began to read. She was so anxious the tremble in her voice matched the tremble in her legs. Feeling she'd made a hopeless mess of it, she broke down and cried.

"The part's yours," said author Rachel Crothers. By incredible luck, Tallulah wept just before the lines that called for her to be emotional.

Her grandfather came up from Hot Springs to represent the Bankheads at Tallulah's first speaking engagement on Broadway. She gave such a good imitation of Constance Binney that he watched her for half an hour before he realized that it was his granddaughter up there on the stage. Tallulah had played six performances when Broadway actors went on strike. Her biggest regret was that her father hadn't had a chance to see her in action.

Three weeks later Bankhead hurried up to New York to find his daughter in a coma. She'd fainted in her room at the Algonquin and had been carried down the freight elevator on a mattress and rushed to St. Elizabeth's Hospital. Doctors discovered her appendix had burst. They told Bankhead: "She has an acute gangrenous appendiix, complicated by peritonitis." He gave the order to operate.

When Tallulah tottered out of the hospital six weeks later

the actors' strike was over. Her father took her back to Washington with him to regain her fighting spirit. It didn't take long. She was soon back at the Algonquin, and soon faint again, this time with excitement. She phoned her father the news: "I've been cast in a leading role in *The Hottentot*. It's a farce about horse racing." "I'll be there," he said.

Two days later she got the news from manager Sam Harris that she'd been fired because "her voice wasn't strong enough." Voice wasn't strong enough? Why, her whisper was strong enough! Maybe Estelle was right and the stage was a hell of a life. Especially being off the stage. If the family heard of this humiliation it might encourage them to discourage her from any more tries. That night she made her plans.

Next morning she walked into the manager's office, ignoring his spluttering receptionist, and said:"If Daddy learns I've been discharged he'll take me back to Washington and I'll have to suffer through those goddam dinner parties all season. If you don't write me a letter saying you didn't think the part was good enough for me, you'll be responsible for ruining a great career."

Harris had his pen in the ink before Tallulah finished talking. He even added his own thought to the letter: "I admire you very much as an actress."

Tallulah enclosed this letter with her own to her father who replied: "Every little bit of experience counts." If Sam Harris had heard her sigh of relief he'd have recast her in *The Hottentot*.

The summer heat settled over the city like a wet and warm enemy gas attack. Estelle had six weeks' vacation owing, during which her understudy would take over. "Let's go to Atlantic City," Tallulah suggested. "It's on the sea. You'll love it."

The train was so crowded they had to stand in the corridor, until Estelle recognized the man struggling toward them. She introduced her friend John Barrymore to Tallulah and he invited them to join him in his drawing room on the train.

Nobody could top Parker for wit but Tallulah was learning, watching, and even listening and the time would come when they were well matched.

Out of work, out of money, Tallulah shared an apartment on West Fifty-seventh Street with actress Bijou Martin. Almost everyone would arrive at the place, five flights up, panting for breath. It was a perfect setting for a farce because all the rooms—two bedrooms, living room, bathroom—opened onto the public corridor. When Bijou brought home a bottle of port, Tallulah looked shocked. When Bijou said, "How about a drink?" Tallulah looked horrified. "I promised Daddy I'd never drink if he let me go on the stage."

"But this isn't drink," Bijou said. "In Europe even little kids drink it."

"But I promised Daddy . . ."

"And you always say you want to try everything once."

"But I . . ."

"You can get his permission to drink wine next time you see him."

"But . . ."

"Here, just a sip."

"Cheers!"

That was Tallulah's first drink. They finished the bottle. Bijou took a shower with all her clothes on. Tallulah crawled away on all fours looking for a spot to die. When they woke next morning, they found a note from Bijou's father under the door. "I called last night to take you out to dinner, but you were both out."

Tallulah went back to cocaine.

Ruth Hammond remembers Tallulah in those days as "full of personality and charm and kindness and generosity. I just loved her. She was an egomaniac, but in a nice way. We were in a play together called *Danger* by Cosmo Hamilton. Leslie Howard and H. B. Warner were the leading men. It was a ridiculous play: didn't run long. While we were playing in it I had done a caricature of Tallulah which she adored. And beautiful girl. She makes me look plain." But she stayed.

Tallulah soon learned that Estelle had been on the stage for thirty years, toiling through four years of repertory in Liverpool, England, where she appeared in a different play every week. And now, recently arrived from England, she was starring in Broadway's most talked-about play, *Why Marry?* It had been awarded the first Pulitzer Prize. Tallulah wondered why Estelle wasn't more excited.

"I can't wait to play my first part," she said.

"Acting's a hell of a life," Estelle warned. "Stay off the stage if you possibly can."

At thirty-five Estelle had made few friends in the theatre. A cool, controlled, balanced woman, she regarded the excesses of her fellow actors with a mixture of scorn and amusement. But listening to the outpourings of this teenager, Estelle, almost twenty years older, felt the protective instincts of a mother. Tallulah was so amusing, so vital, so proud of her father and grandfather, and so broke.

They were friends almost on sight. After a few meetings Estelle realized that Tallulah couldn't both pay her hotel bills and eat, and invited Tallulah to share her apartment for a while so that she could save some of her allowance and return to the Algonquin solvent.

Tallulah faced her first Broadway audience in 1918, but only as a nonspeaking walk-on in *The Squab Farm,* which *The New York Times* called "a garish travesty of life in the movies, all in bad taste." Tallulah worked in that, as a mute, for four weeks. She infuriated other girls in the cast by whistling in the dressing room. "It's bad luck!" they shrieked and almost blamed her for the play's short life.

A week after *Squab Farm* closed, movie director Ivan Abramson told Tallulah he'd seen her in it and "Because you have poise and beauty I want you for a part in *When Men Betray.* I'm filming it on Long Island next week." Acting in that silent film was less fun than listening to insults at the Algonquin. But she was proud to say she'd made it and even prouder when Samuel Goldwyn shortly afterward cast her in one of his silent films called *Thirty a Week*. The movie and World War I were both in the can by November, 1918.

And then came her chance to TALK on stage before an audience. They wanted a summer replacement for Constance Binney in *39 East*. "You'll be one of sixteen girls auditioning for the part," warned actress Jobyna Howland, another Algonquin friend. "Act your age and don't dress like a tart."

Tallulah, not yet eighteen, turned up: very pale, very direct, with flopping ash blonde hair. She stood on the icy theatre stage, which was lit as if for a horror movie, and tried to pull off her gloves to turn the flimsy pages of the script. She couldn't, she was shaking so much. Ahead of her she heard someone being bawled out. Then it was her turn. Her gloves half off, she began to read. She was so anxious the tremble in her voice matched the tremble in her legs. Feeling she'd made a hopeless mess of it, she broke down and cried.

"The part's yours," said author Rachel Crothers. By incredible luck, Tallulah wept just before the lines that called for her to be emotional.

Her grandfather came up from Hot Springs to represent the Bankheads at Tallulah's first speaking engagement on Broadway. She gave such a good imitation of Constance Binney that he watched her for half an hour before he realized that it was his granddaughter up there on the stage. Tallulah had played six performances when Broadway actors went on strike. Her biggest regret was that her father hadn't had a chance to see her in action.

Three weeks later Bankhead hurried up to New York to find his daughter in a coma. She'd fainted in her room at the Algonquin and had been carried down the freight elevator on a mattress and rushed to St. Elizabeth's Hospital. Doctors discovered her appendix had burst. They told Bankhead: "She has an acute gangrenous appendiix, complicated by peritonitis." He gave the order to operate.

When Tallulah tottered out of the hospital six weeks later

the actors' strike was over. Her father took her back to Washington with him to regain her fighting spirit. It didn't take long. She was soon back at the Algonquin, and soon faint again, this time with excitement. She phoned her father the news: "I've been cast in a leading role in *The Hottentot*. It's a farce about horse racing." "I'll be there," he said.

Two days later she got the news from manager Sam Harris that she'd been fired because "her voice wasn't strong enough." Voice wasn't strong enough? Why, her whisper was strong enough! Maybe Estelle was right and the stage was a hell of a life. Especially being off the stage. If the family heard of this humiliation it might encourage them to discourage her from any more tries. That night she made her plans.

Next morning she walked into the manager's office, ignoring his spluttering receptionist, and said:"If Daddy learns I've been discharged he'll take me back to Washington and I'll have to suffer through those goddam dinner parties all season. If you don't write me a letter saying you didn't think the part was good enough for me, you'll be responsible for ruining a great career."

Harris had his pen in the ink before Tallulah finished talking. He even added his own thought to the letter: "I admire you very much as an actress."

Tallulah enclosed this letter with her own to her father who replied: "Every little bit of experience counts." If Sam Harris had heard her sigh of relief he'd have recast her in *The Hottentot*.

The summer heat settled over the city like a wet and warm enemy gas attack. Estelle had six weeks' vacation owing, during which her understudy would take over. "Let's go to Atlantic City," Tallulah suggested. "It's on the sea. You'll love it."

The train was so crowded they had to stand in the corridor, until Estelle recognized the man struggling toward them. She introduced her friend John Barrymore to Tallulah and he invited them to join him in his drawing room on the train.

Barrymore led the way, turning to whisper to Estelle: "Lord, that girl's pretty, isn't she?"

But Barrymore was otherwise occupied. He had a woman waiting for him at the other end and intended to spend the weekend with her.

Tallulah didn't sleep that night. Soon after daylight she dressed and walked out of the Ritz Hotel to the boardwalk. Maybe he'd be walking there to get an appetite or just for exercise. She looked for him for almost two hours. Then Tallulah crept quietly into Estelle's room and sat waiting for her to open her eyes. As soon as she did, Tallulah said: "I've been up since seven, sitting on the boardwalk hoping to see Jack. I want you to tell my fortune."

Tallulah had the cards all ready. At least six times that day she persuaded Estelle to go through them, just to see if there was a chance she'd meet John Barrymore again. Each time the message was negative. "But maybe you will when we get back to town," said an exhausted Estelle. "He often visits his sister Ethel at the Algonquin."

Estelle enjoyed the break from work and the heat of the city, but Tallulah couldn't wait to get back.

When she did she sat at tables in the Algonquin ignoring the conversations, on the lookout for Barrymore. Every time the elevator stopped she looked to see if he was aboard. She mistook several men for him from the back. Once she followed footsteps in a corridor and caught up with a fat little ten-year-old, Douglas Fairbanks, Jr. He had an air rifle with him. He smiled innocently, then, when he thought she'd gone, sneaked into Vinton Freedley's suite and fired his rifle at the electric lights of the Hippodrome sign across the street.

Barrymore remembered her when they did meet again, and she greeted him with the enthusiasm of old friends reunited.

Fairbanks recalls: "My parents joked about young Tallulah Bankhead who was so terribly in love with John Barrymore. They saw her waiting for him to come in and out of the hotel and then cling to him like a stagestruck teenager—

exactly what she was. My parents used to tease Barrymore about his attempts to shake loose from this fan who was a daughter of the Speaker of the House."

But however nonchalantly Barrymore behaved with Tallulah in public, he invited her to his dressing room after a matinee of *The Jest* with passionate intent.

John Barrymore's explanation of his effect on women and his reputation as a magnificent lover is remarkable. He told his friend Gene Fowler: "I was working so assiduously that a succession of heart flip-flops began to annoy me. Whenever I became excited, one of these harmless yet startling cardiac beats would make me jump or call out like a moose. One evening, when enjoying the company of a lady, and with romance at its meridian, the heart went 'Zoom.' I reacted with a sudden bound and cries. The lady mistook this for sheer ardor. She confided in some other lovely creature, and so help me God I had a similar experience with that one. The results of word-of-mouth advertising were incredible. Likewise the series of heart flutters. It got so that I was being exploited all over town like a patent medicine. Never could shake the reputation, even after the heart returned to its former monastic serenity."

Barrymore was going through this moose phase when he opened the door of his dressing room and invited Tallulah in. He told her that he intended to star in a movie version of *Dr. Jekyll and Mr. Hyde.* "Would you like to be my leading lady?" he asked, leading her to the couch with one hand and locking the door with the other.

Animal instinct told Tallulah to resist the moose call, which she did. "I would have cheapened myself in my own eyes if I'd given in," she said afterward. Her virtue cost her the part in the film—if it had been seriously offered. But she continued to be fascinated by Barrymore, going to see him thirteen times in *The Jest* (in which he played a poetic, effeminate man who overcomes a brute played by brother Lionel)—only stopping there because thirteen was her lucky number.

She told Estelle of her encounter with John Barrymore.

Estelle was only half listening. She'd found little bags of cocaine in Tallulah's room and had flushed them down the toilet.

"You're a damn fool to take it," Estelle said. "It only makes you rude and say things you regret afterward."

"Don't make such a fuss," Tallulah said. "All the girls take it."

When Tallulah found Estelle had dumped her cocaine *and* her marijuana cigarettes, she flew into a tantrum. Between outbursts, Estelle said: "You're just a little Miss Nobody. . . . This is stupid. . . . You're only punishing yourself. . . . Nobody else cares a damn."

Estelle's technique was as effective as Tallulah's grandmother with her bucket of water.

To the casual observer, if Tallulah could be observed casually, she was a strikingly beautiful young woman, with the manners of a Southern belle, the language of an army drill sergeant, the daring of a trapeze artist, and the zest and energy of the whole bloody circus. But to those who were close to her, she was a sensitive, emotional child, frantic to be a spectacular success, to honor the family name; with a dread of making a fool of herself; tortured when she couldn't act and scared silly when she got the chance.

She resisted Barrymore and yet, soon afterward, was found kissing a young woman at a party. She borrowed the handkerchief of one of the Round Table titans, and then, to his chagrin, used it to wipe off the other girl's lipstick.

To her friend Estelle Winwood she explained: "I want to try everything once."

It was a year since Sam Harris had fired her from *The Hottentot*. But he really meant it when he said he admired her as an actress. It was just that that first time around she was too young and inexperienced for the role. Now, in the spring of 1921, he offered her a part in *Nice People*, as beautiful Hallie Livingston who "sips her Scotch whisky with a slow and self-centered enjoyment indicative of her general psychology." The Round Table prize critic Alexander Woollcott described Tallulah in the part as "comely and competent and luxuriating in a feline role." She played it for twenty weeks: her longest run so far.

Although the aftereffects of mumps had left Woollcott unable to consummate a romance, he was otherwise the most romantic of critics who fell in love with actresses more often than he panned plays. Tallulah intrigued him and he invited her to his first night of Maeterlinck's *The Burgomaster of Stilemonde*. She was bored silly by the end of the first act and it was then she said her oft-repeated: "There's less in this than meets the eye."

While Woollcott was shocking outsiders with the carefully cultivated putdown delivered with a smile—which may have earned The Round Tablers their other nickname, The Vicious Circle—Tallulah was using her own conversation shock tactics

An example of Woollcott in action, greeting Frank Sullivan: "Hello Frank, you greasy mass of Gentile self-pity." (Sullivan looked wounded and puzzled: "Why 'Gentile'?" he replied.)

An example of Tallulah's: "I was raped in a driveway when I was eleven It was a terrible experience because we had all that gravel."

To the lighthearted Round Table wits, the ideal game was one where you could sit down, sip a drink, and let fly— with words. Tallulah joined their word games with feverish gusto. There was "I-Can-Give-You-A-Sentence." The sentence might be: "I can give you a sentence with the word 'burlesque.' I had two soft-burlesque for breakfast." Then the listener was given a chance to top it. Dorothy Parker triumphed over all with her: "I can give you a sentence with the word 'horticulture.' You can lead a whore to culture but you can't make her think."

Nobody could top Parker for wit but Tallulah was learning, watching, and even listening and the time would come when they were well matched.

Out of work, out of money, Tallulah shared an apartment on West Fifty-seventh Street with actress Bijou Martin. Almost everyone would arrive at the place, five flights up, panting for breath. It was a perfect setting for a farce because all the rooms—two bedrooms, living room, bathroom—opened onto the public corridor. When Bijou brought home a bottle of port, Tallulah looked shocked. When Bijou said, "How about a drink?" Tallulah looked horrified. "I promised Daddy I'd never drink if he let me go on the stage."

"But this isn't drink," Bijou said. "In Europe even little kids drink it."

"But I promised Daddy . . ."

"And you always say you want to try everything once."

"But I . . ."

"You can get his permission to drink wine next time you see him."

"But . . ."

"Here, just a sip."

"Cheers!"

That was Tallulah's first drink. They finished the bottle. Bijou took a shower with all her clothes on. Tallulah crawled away on all fours looking for a spot to die. When they woke next morning, they found a note from Bijou's father under the door. "I called last night to take you out to dinner, but you were both out."

Tallulah went back to cocaine.

Ruth Hammond remembers Tallulah in those days as "full of personality and charm and kindness and generosity. I just loved her. She was an egomaniac, but in a nice way. We were in a play together called *Danger* by Cosmo Hamilton. Leslie Howard and H. B. Warner were the leading men. It was a ridiculous play: didn't run long. While we were playing in it I had done a caricature of Tallulah which she adored. And she was going to have supper with Alexander Woollcott that night and wanted to show him the caricature. But she said: 'I don't want to take the original, darling. I'm afraid I'll lose it.' So she traced it off on toilet paper to show him. And for ever after she went around telling people: 'Ruth does the most divine cartoons on toilet paper.' She loved to shock people and would if they were stuffed shirts, but if you introduced her to your mother or grandmother, they'd think she was the nicest girl they'd ever met, because she wouldn't try to shock them. She wouldn't do it where it would destroy her image where it counted. She was a glamorous, exciting girl. I really was terribly fond of her. And she was in love with everyone around."

But there were in fact, apart from her father, only two men Tallulah would truly love. And she was just about to meet one of them, Lord Napier Alington, a man who would enchant and torment her. "I always fall for cads," she explained.

It happened at a party in Bijou Martin's apartment. Jeffery Holmesdale, theatre critic for *The Morning World,* was trying to think who could remedy the man shortage. "I've got it. Napier," he said, and phoned him. "I've told him about you Tallulah, and he's dying to meet you." Napier was in bed when he got the call but the party sounded promising.

"Don't bother to dress. Come as you are," Holmesdale said. Napier took him literally: arrived in pajamas and with a bottle of gin.

Tallulah first noticed Napier's thick, almost repulsive lips, then his English accent. "Mrs. Cornelius Vanderbilt invited me over to America to study banking," he said, "but it was a bore having to take her to the opera all dressed up and looking like a peppermint candystick and being made to endure all those formal dinners. Now I'm staying with Teddy Gerrard in the Village. Much more fun."

Tallulah knew Teddy Gerrard as an English musical comedy actress reputed to be half-mad and wholly delightful.

Napier was astonished to hear that at nineteen Tallulah

was still a virgin, and his eyes reflected a crusader's enthusiasm as he told her he would be thrilled to make her a woman of the world—that night. After all, he was dressed for the part. Tallulah said no with a rising inflection. He was fascinating, almost compelling, but at the same time his air of nonchalance and sometimes of cruelty was less than endearing.

They met again for brunch on Sunday at the Brevoort in the Village. Another time they joined a lean and hungry friend—Noel Coward, living on herbs and hope—at Reisenweber's in Columbus Circle, where they danced until nearly dawn. Before they rode a cab home Napier took off his shoes and socks and walked barefoot through the snow. "It's very healthy!" he called out, vainly trying to persuade them to follow him.

And then he was gone. With just a hint that he wouldn't be staying much longer, Napier suddenly returned to England. All his faults now seemed attractive to Tallulah. So he was reckless, and cynical. So he had lots of women. So he gambled. But in him it was charming . . . and why the hell doesn't he write? Weeks, months went by without a word. She tried to appear casual when she asked visitors from England: "How's Napier?" But nobody knew. He seemed to have disappeared.

Tallulah had been out of work for six weeks. Her last play, hopefully titled *The Exciters,* had folded after a five-week run. Cutting the Bible and searching for guidance didn't seem to help. There was no prospect of another play. But more painful than that was that there seemed no hope of ever seeing Napier. She had last seen him a year ago and had not heard one word from him since.

So she went to Evangeline Adams, a fortuneteller sometimes consulted by banker Pierpont Morgan. Miss Adams seemed to be trespassing on the banking business—she charged Tallulah $50, and told her: "Your future lies across water. Go, if you have to swim."

To Tallulah across the water meant England and Napier.

But having spent her last dollars on the fortuneteller she had nothing left for a transatlantic ticket. And no means of surviving if she got there.

A few days later she received the first cablegram in her life. It was from London, dated December 10, 1922, and read: POSSIBILITY ENGAGEMENT WITH GERALD DU MAURIER IN ABOUT EIGHT WEEKS. WRITING FULLY. CABLE IF FREE. CHARLES B. COCHRAN.

Free? She was frantic. She cabled her acceptance and told everyone from the Algonquin to Washington, D.C., and Alabama that all her dreams were coming true. She would soon be acting with Sir Gerald du Maurier, as famous in England as John Barrymore in America, and she would be seeing Napier.

Then came a second cable: TERRIBLY SORRY. DU MAURIER'S CHANGED PLANS. CHARLES B. COCHRAN.

She hurried for consolation and advice and to share her humiliation with her friend Estelle Winwood. Estelle knew of her love for Napier Alington and was a friend of producer Cochran. "Don't let it upset you," she told Tallulah. "Go to England anyway. When they see your beautiful hair someone will offer you a part."

Tallulah cabled Cochran: I'M COMING ANYWAY.

Cochran cabled back: DON'T COME. THERE'S A DEPRESSION HERE. THERE'S NOTHING GOING ON.

She showed the cable to Estelle.

"Pretend you never got it," said Estelle.

Tallulah, now twenty-one, borrowed a thousand dollars from a family friend and set off to conquer England—and to find Napier.

V

Tallulah Conquers
England

1923–1931   The day after she arrived
in London, Tallulah went
from her room at the Ritz
to see Sir Gerald du Maurier. He was playing in a matinee
performance of *Bulldog Drummond* at Wyndham's Theatre.
Du Maurier was a world-weary actor who thought kissing a
woman on the stage should be performed with the same
casualness as lighting a cigarette or tying a shoelace. Other
actors took their cue from him and helped transform the
theatre of bombast into the gentle art of underplaying.

Offstage he found an adolescent pleasure in taking many
of his leading ladies to secret rendezvous in darkened cinemas,
where he gave them expensive-looking rings bought in Wool-
worths. Then he'd go home to giggle over these affairs—and
describe them round by round to his doting wife and
daughters.

Tallulah watched him play *Bulldog Drummond* without
hearing much of it. As soon as the curtain came down on the
final act she hurried to his dressing room.

"Well, here I am," she said.

Du Maurier showed more astonishment than he ever did

onstage. "But we cabled you not to come. Another girl has been engaged for the part, and we open in a fortnight."

Tallulah feigned surprise. "I'm happy to be in England anyway," she said. "And perhaps she'll break a leg."

Cochran, waiting in the background, admired her nerve and invited her to dinner. Over the meal he suggested a last-minute strategy that might change du Maurier's mind. "He's never seen your lovely hair," he told Tallulah. "Try to see him again and this time, take your hat off. Give him a chance to see how unusually beautiful you are."

Tallulah gave du Maurier the chance. Du Maurier gave Tallulah the part. And that's how she came to star in *The Dancers* while the actress she replaced was paid full salary to stay at home for the run of the play.

With barely a week to learn her lines, moves, and dance numbers (she played an orphan who graduated from dancing in a British Columbia dance hall to ballet dancing in Paris), Tallulah still found plenty of moments to wonder if she would impress the staid, undemonstrative British audience.

Why, if they were anything like Sir Gerald du Maurier they'd show ecstasy by raising their eyebrows and disapproval by clearing their throats.

On opening night during the first act, Tallulah made her first exit and heard a roar from the audience, like a huge gas jet suddenly catching fire. She could hear it clearly as she ran for her dressing room—a menacing mixture of screams and shouts. She fell onto a chair, trembling, weeping with disappointment, sure that her acting had baited the British into an extraordinary demonstration of disapproval.

And suddenly her room was full of other members of the cast. One was shaking her. "Why are you crying?" she asked. Tallulah tried to explain. . . . "But they loved you," the actress broke in. In a jumble they explained to Tallulah that the audience had been shouting with delight, not disgust. And for almost eight years, that roar of approval was to follow

Tallulah wherever she went, whatever she did. Admirers would line up thirty hours in advance of a performance to be sure of a seat. The frenzy Tallulah caused became known as "Tallulahbaloo."

"With her golden hair flying in the wind, husky voice, a soft Southern accent, and utter scorn of convention, she had become, almost overnight, the idol of all the up-and-coming working girls, who saw in her the embodiment of their dreams of a free life," said producer Basil Dean.

Working girls were not the only ones who were wild about Tallulah. Alfred Hitchcock, a versatile young filmmaker, saw her in *The Dancers* and thought she was marvelous.

So did Somerset Maugham, who tried to stammer his approval to playwright Marc Connelly at the party after the first night. Tallulah sat between them, almost gasping for breath in a sea of approval. Then everyone was clapping and calling on Tallulah to say something special. "Speech! Speech!" She was that strange combination, part shy, part extrovert. And now the shy side took over. She stood up but couldn't think of a thing to say, so she just stood, looking absolutely gorgeous, responding with "Hi! . . . Hi! . . . Hi!" to the smiles and cheers of her newfound friends. She blinked a lot, a sure sign she was nervous. "I can't make a speech," she said. But she wanted to show how pleased she was—so she did a handstand.

Tallulah had conquered London on her first night. The rest of the British Isles fell soon afterward.

Tallulah woke from the second night of her greatest triumph, to hear a voice on the phone, saying: "Lord Napier Alington is waiting to see you."

Her resolve to be cool, calm, and detached lasted long enough for her to put down the phone. In minutes she was hurrying across the deep carpet of the lobby and was in his arms. "Napier, darling!"

Napier, indifferent to fame and fortune, once fought with Michael Arlen on the steps of White's, an exclusive London club, after accusing Arlen of wearing a made-up bow tie. Their antagonism may have been fanned by Arlen's novel *The Green Hat* in which a Napier Harpenden is pursued by a young woman, Iris March, with a slightly husky voice, who loved only him. Says Iris: "I have never said I loved him to any man but Napier, for it hasn't been true. I have given myself, in disdain, in desire, with disgust, with delight, but I have kept to that silly, childish boast." If Arlen hadn't modeled his characters on Alington and Tallulah, it was another case of fact following fiction and proving more unlikely.

Like John Barrymore, Napier had many traits in common with Tallulah—he was restless, outspoken, unpredictable, reckless, living on the crest of the wave—and it was as if the almost-mirror of herself would always attract, yet always elude her.

Tallulah appeared in only the first and the last act of *The Dancers,* so she had a forty-minute wait in her dressing room. But she was seldom there. Napier would hurry her off to dinner almost every night and then race her back to the theatre. Then he'd wait and take her out after the show.

"When he was in London I was with him constantly," she wrote in her autobiography, *Tallulah,* "fascinated by his rakishness, his pranks . . . then he'd disappear for months and I'd not hear a word from him. When he bobbed up without warning, again I'd be hypnotized, though inwardly ravaged by my inability to break off a relationship that was part ecstasy, part torture. His cruel insistence on doing only such things as pleased or interested him, his contempt for the desires of others both fascinated and repelled me." (And must have reminded Tallulah of herself.) "Invariably I got furiously angry only to melt in submission when he turned on his charm and bravado. Torn by tuberculosis, Napier went to Switzerland to take the Sparlinger Cure. Ordered to follow a Spartan diet, he violated every rule, stayed up all night drinking and gambling. He would flee the sanatorium, disappear for weeks, then blithely return as if he'd been to post a letter."

Tallulah's sister Eugenia recalls those times of triumph and torment: "We were both very young and anything in England was intriguing if it had a title. But Naps was exceptionally intriguing. He had great charm of manner. I wouldn't say he was the most handsome man in the world. He was never a well man: he had a very weak chest and was always having to go to Switzerland or somewhere. I'm sure he was her greatest love. There's no question about that."

A few weeks after she'd found him again, Napier disappeared.

Tallulah's life now took on the aspects of a French farce. While she was spending her free time chasing around trying to find Napier (Lord Alington), another titled Englishman, Sir Francis Laking, was chasing her. It was further made farcical because Laking was, according to Tallulah, "a witty young man of cloudy gender." In those early days she found his obsessive, frantic interest in her some compensation for Napier's disappearing tricks.

When Laking, Viola Tree (coauthor with du Maurier of *The Dancers*), and Olga Lynn (who taught Tallulah to sing for the play) revealed they were going to Venice for a vacation, Tallulah browbeat du Maurier into letting her go with them—although the play had been running only eight weeks. They all shared a palazzo in Venice. On their first day there Tallulah went sailing with Francis and insisted on staying out so long that she was savagely sunburnt and had to spend the rest of the vacation recuperating in the shade.

The Dancers took Tallulah into 1924 when she starred in "a stinker" (Tallulah's words) called *Conchita,* by Edward Knoblock, and set in Cuba. Again she played a dancer. But this time she carried a monkey with her in the second act. On opening night the monkey jumped onto Tallulah's shoulders, grabbed her black wig, and, to her horror, ran with

it to the footlights. There she stood, a Latin from the eyebrows down, a tawny blonde on top. The audience went from
giggles to hysteria in seconds and Tallulah climaxed the
situation by turning a cartwheel not in the script. At the end
of the play Tallulah was afraid to take a curtain call, expecting to have to endure her first British booing. But she was
persuaded to go out and face the crowd and when she did they
howled their approval—of her—not the play.

After the short-lived *Conchita*, Tallulah tried to steal
Herbert Marshall from Cathleen Nesbitt in *This Marriage*.
The play was another bomb, but Tallulah now had so many
thousands of loyal fans that if she had played the part standing
on her head while gargling champagne, they'd have remarked
on the clarity of her diction and the beauty of her movement.
They adored her: so she could do no wrong.

Offstage she was mourning the disappearance of Napier by
indulging in wild love affairs, strangely following the script
outlined for her in Michael Arlen's prophetic novel *The
Green Hat*. And trying to avoid jealous outbursts from Sir
Francis Laking who resented her having affairs with other
men, although incapable of replacing them.

Early in 1925 Tallulah was playing in a mediocre melodrama, *The Creaking Chair*, when producer Basil Dean told
her there might be a chance for her to star as a whore, Sadie
Thompson, in Somerset Maugham's *Rain*. In America Jeanne
Eagels had already made a sensation as Sadie. After eighteen
months in England it was Tallulah's first sight of a part with
guts. And she mapped out a strategy to persuade Maugham
to give it to her.

What she planned to do was this. Go to America, watch
Jeanne Eagels playing Sadie, then confront Maugham and
convince him that she was the actress for the London version.

The Creaking Chair creaked its last in February, and before
the month was out Tallulah was on the *Berengeria* bound for
Pittsburgh, U.S.A., where she eagerly watched every move
and intonation of Jeanne Eagels as Sadie.

She found out that Maugham was in Washington and she went there to see him.

Maugham listened to her pitch, then told Basil Dean that it was all right to start rehearsals with Tallulah in the part, but that he would have to give his definite approval before it was hers.

Tallulah had booked to travel back to England on the same boat as Maugham until Dean warned her. "Don't, whatever you do. Keep away from him as much as you can."

Mystified, Tallulah canceled her booking and traveled back on a cattle boat.

The rehearsals began. "Maugham sat in the dark auditorium throughout the first rehearsal," wrote Tallulah in her autobiography. "Sure of every line of the role thanks to weeks of study, I gave what I'm sure was a brilliant imitation of Jeanne Eagels. If Maugham was electrified, he didn't show it. He avoided me after the rehearsal. This frightened me. At the second rehearsal Maugham remained mute and inscrutable. Alarm started to gnaw at me. Audaciously I glided up to Dean: 'Basil, who the hell's going to play the part?' His answer chilled me: 'An angel from Heaven. God only knows!' "

What Tallulah was never to know is that Maugham hated to be pressured by anybody and he resented her having traced him to Washington to ask him for the part.

Two days after Tallulah started rehearsals for *Rain* she read that Olga Lindo was to play the role.

Basil Dean called Tallulah into his office and tried to soften the blow. She left in tears—to kill herself. That rejection had hurt and the scar always stayed with Tallulah. It was a lifelong mystery to her why she had been fired and who was behind the firing.

Sobbing like a child, she hurried home—refusing to be consoled by an actress friend en route—swallowed a handful of aspirins and waited for the end.

The telephone woke her—feeling great—next morning.

Noel Coward was on the line sounding desperate. An actress in his play *Fallen Angels* had suffered a nervous breakdown four days before opening night. Could Tallulah learn one hundred pages of dialogue in that time?

"Four days? I could learn them in four hours."

"How much d'you want?" Coward asked.

"One hundred pounds a week," Tallulah answered.

"But you were only going to get forty for *Rain*."

"That's true," Tallulah admitted. "But I wanted to play Sadie Thompson. I don't give a good goddam if I play in this or not."

Coward agreed to her price.

"Tallulah Bankhead came flying into the theatre," wrote Noel Coward in his autobiography *Present Indicative*. "Her vitality had always been remarkable, but on that occasion it was little short of fantastic. She took that exceedingly long part at a run. She tore off her hat, flipped her furs into a corner, kissed Edna, Stanley, me, and anyone else who happened to be within reach and, talking incessantly about *Rain,* which Maugham had just refused to allow her to play, she embarked on the first act. In two days she knew the whole part perfectly, and on the first night gave a brilliant and completely assured performance. It was a tour de force of vitality, magnetism, and spontaneous combustion. The press notices for *Fallen Angels* were vituperative to the point of incoherence. It was described as vulgar, disgusting, shocking, nauseating, vile, obscene, degenerate, etc., etc. The idea of two gently nurtured young women playing a drunken scene together was apparently too degrading a spectacle for even the most hardened and worldly critics. *The Daily Express* even went so far as to allude to these wayward creatures as 'suburban sluts.' All this was capital for the box office and the play ran for several months."

Tallulah made the most of her line in *Fallen Angels:* "Oh, dear, rain!" which she rendered: "My god, RAIN!" and got an understanding roar from the audience.

She surprised novelist-critic Arnold Bennett, who explained why in his diary on April 23, 1925: "I had been saying for weeks that Tallulah Bankhead couldn't act, and she gave a superb comedy performance. (She would not have been much good in Maugham's *Rain*.)"

When she wasn't working or sleeping, Tallulah continued to have love affairs with the most unlikely people, and there were even wilder stories of her antics. One angry wife complained that her life had been ruined because the man she married turned out to be a homosexual. Then she complained more bitterly still, because Tallulah had stolen him from her. Cecil Beaton recalls seeing Tallulah at supper clubs and parties. "She drank quite a lot and she would get crying jags like a lot of people who drink a lot do. Her nervous system was very much put to it. She was very sympathetic. There was never anything unattractive about her drunkenness, but she did whoop it up and she was someone who just burned her candle at every end."

Estelle Winwood was upset because she knew that Tallulah, now the darling of the English bluebloods, had got in with the "cream of the worst."

Scotland Yard men were watching Tallulah. Her dresser had handed a threatening letter to them. The writer said he was going to kill Tallulah because her father, William Bankhead, had "done him a dirty deed" in Birmingham. Tallulah's father had never been to Birmingham. Obviously he'd got his men mixed. Tallulah wasn't told of the danger until it was over. Then she thought: "If he had killed me I wouldn't have minded, but being an actress, if he had injured me it would have been hard to make a living."

And then she began to get threatening phone calls. When she went on tour the calls followed her—as far as Scotland. Again Scotland Yard men were called in to protect her. They caught the man one evening as he was trying to go through the stage door and he was put away. He turned out to be a doctor in an insane asylum for women. Afterward Tallulah thought: "Although Scotland Yard men were sent to protect me, how could they really protect me while I was acting on the stage? If the man had been in the audience and had decided to shoot me, what could the police have done to stop him?"

It was a humbling and frightening thought that among those cheering fans were people with murder on their minds.

Because of Tallulah's penchant for the peerage, and the fact that the Duke of Kent had watched her put life into *The Creaking Chair* every week of its thirty-week run, one of the many stories told about Tallulah went like this: "Tallulah Bankhead invited a taxi driver to stay for the weekend. As he left on Monday morning, exhausted, she called down from her bedroom: 'Dahling, you're as good as the King of England!'"

Another story was how a titled young man wanted her to leave a party with him and make love. Tallulah was enjoying the party but her friend was persistent. She finally turned to him and said: "Dahling, you go on ahead—and if I'm not there in half an hour, start without me."

Her own stories of life with the aristocracy have a more macabre twist. "I once went to stay at the Duke of Manchester's house. They told me about a ghost there. Next to my huge room was a tiny one in which Catharine of Aragon died: she was put there for twenty years by Henry VIII. You know queens always like tiny little rooms because they're so tired of those great big walls and palaces and halls. There was supposed to be a ghost there, with chains, but I wasn't hearing it because I made everyone stay in my room till dawn. They sat around the fire with me and I wouldn't let anyone leave. Apparently a young prince had been thrown out of the window years ago: somebody wanted to get him out of the way. One stone in the wall of the building had blood underneath it. The Duke of Manchester had married three American wives in succession and apparently the third American wife, the Duchess, was uncomfortable having that stone there, and she had it removed. It was a huge rock embedded way down into the earth, and the next day the blood came up. The Duke's daughter, Mary, told me to take pumice stone and peroxide, to try to get rid of the blood. And I scraped and scraped on the spot until it faded to pale pink, which was the color of the rest of the stone. But next day the blood came back again."

Tallulah went from the Ritz Hotel to live in a service flat in Curzon Street and then shared a house in Catherine Street with Gladys Cooper, Olga Lynn, and Lady Idina Gordon. Finally she took a house of her own on Farm Street.

When Tallulah was in a play there was often as much theatre offstage as on—sometimes more. Feverish groups of young women in the gallery chanted her name with religious fervor. Playwright Charles Morgan watched groups outside staring at the audience going to see Tallulah, and "uttering little breathless squeaking ejaculations, for all the world like mice in a bag."

Memoirs of the twenties seem incomplete if they omit at least one scene of Tallulah in a Thames-side restaurant, waving a cigarette, surrounded by broken glasses, and whooping it up before a pageful of Debretts Peerage.

In those days Tallulah often teetered on the brink of wedlock. Lord Mandeville, son of the Duke of Westminster, proposed six times. Obviously she gave him some hope. She almost became the wife of Tony Wilson, son of Sir Matthew Wilson and grandson of the Earl of Ribblesdale. There was a commoner in the running too—Michael Wardell, editor of the *Evening Standard*. Tallulah loved him almost as much as she did Napier. And she came so close to marrying Count Tony de Bosardi that photographs of the two of them were distributed with the caption JUST MARRIED on them. They weren't, because Tallulah suspected he was exploiting her for business reasons, and she returned his engagement present— a Rolls-Royce—with regret.

She had great affection for Winston Churchill and it was

apparently mutual. He saw her five times in *Fallen Angels*—
so she returned the compliment and went to see him at work.
Lord Beaverbrook took her to Churchill's home, surrounded
by hop fields and apple orchards in Westerham, Kent, and
they watched the master politician proudly prove he was a
master bricklayer too, as he cemented bricks together for a
garden wall.

Tallulah and Churchill shared a passion for politics and
Ethel Barrymore. Churchill had fallen in love with Ethel
Barrymore when he was a member of parliament in his
twenties and she was a teenage actress on the London stage.
Churchill arranged for Ethel to meet Neville Chamberlain,
Lloyd George, and Lord Roseberry at a dinner party, as a
test, to see if she would enjoy living in a political atmosphere
and listening to political conversation. The trial-run was a
mistake. Ethel was bored, and turned down his marriage
proposal. But they remained life-long friends.

Tallulah played in Michael Arlen's *The Green Hat* in
1925, in which, as Iris March, frustrated and desperately in
love with Napier Harpenden, who had jilted her, she followed him to the fashionable European resorts, trying to
quench her passion for him in other arms too numerous to
detail. It's interesting that she failed to remark how it echoed
her own hunt for Napier Alington. Instead she said that the
play reminded her of *La Dame aux Camelias,* known to film
fans as *Camille.*

It wasn't easy to get Tallulah to sit still in those days, but
artist Augustus John did a quick sketch of her while she was
carousing in a Soho restaurant, the Eiffel Tower. He showed
it to her and persuaded her to pose for a soulful-looking painting in his studio. She sat, consuming cigarettes as if they were
as necessary as oxygen, as Lawrence of Arabia watched.

Lawrence had artistic yearnings, and the price he paid to
watch John at work was to go off on his motorcycle, whenever Tallulah exhausted her supply of cigarettes, and bring
back more. It was something to have the uncrowned king of

Arabia as your messenger boy. No doubt he got a kick out of it too.

Probably because of her political family in America, Tallulah was a pet of British politicians. Ex-Prime Minister Lloyd George, World War I equivalent of Winston Churchill, invited her to his home in Surrey, cut a rose in his garden and handed it to her. Prime Minister Ramsay MacDonald went one better and had Tallulah to lunch at the House of Commons and afterward he drove her to the theatre. He accepted her invitation to see her in *Mud and Treacle,* a political play which the citics had damned as being even more boring than a parliamentary debate. But MacDonald went and after the show shared a bottle of champagne with Tallulah in her dressing room. He brought his rather strait-laced sister with him and it was just too tempting for Tallulah. She introduced her to a doctor friend, adding: "And you must remember his name, darling. He's wonderful at abortions."

Another member of parliament, Sir Patrick Hastings, wrote a play which Basil Dean decided to produce. Feeling he'd goofed in not persuading Somerset Maugham to accept Tallulah in *Rain*, Dean gave her a part in Hastings' *Scotch Mist*. In it she played the frustrated wife of a cabinet minister, who tries to seduce an old flame, played by Godfrey Tearle.

Tearle was married to Mary Malone, a beautiful Irish actress. She was so jealous that she attended every rehearsal to make sure that her husband was safe from Tallulah. The rest of the cast watched with amusement, aware of what was going on and that Tallulah in fact had no interest in Tearle. He just wasn't her type. Not enough of a cad perhaps. Tearle's wife made sure he had a dressing room at the very top of the theatre, next to the wardrobe room "where he can get fresh air." It was as far away as was possible from Tallulah's star dressing room on the ground floor. At the dress rehearsal Mary stationed herself in the middle of the front row of the stalls with the absorbed concentration of someone trying to catch a magician at his tricks. When they reached the seduction scene Tallulah pulled out all the stops and played it with such abandon that Mary began to cry. It was as if she was seeing her husband raped before her eyes.

When the curtain fell, Basil Dean got up to give the cast notes. But before he reached the stage, Tallulah poked her head around the corner of the pass-door, glanced at Mary wiping away her tears, and then, chuckling gleefully, said to Dean: "All right, Basil? Good thing I had me drawers on, wasn't it?"

Another woman was added to the small group that would have considered Tallulah's murder an act of charity.

The critics damned *Scotch Mist* and so did various religious bodies, which saved it from the extinction it deserved. But it was Tallulah alone who assured its financial success. "She was given a rapturous reception by the gallery at every performance," says Basil Dean, "as she blew them repeated kisses, ending with what was fast becoming her signature tune: 'Bless you, darlings.' "

Dean was grateful for Tallulah having kept *Scotch Mist* alive long enough to make a profit. He repaid her with the best part she'd ever had, in Sidney Howard's *They Knew What They Wanted.*

Though Dean had a reputation among actors for being a monster, Tallulah took his dictatorial directing without a murmur. She played the role of a poor girl discovered in a Chicago spaghetti joint, who eventually appears onstage in a wedding dress. It was anticipated that fashion-conscious Tallulah would go all out in that scene and demand an expensive gown. Instead she bought the cheapest clothes she could find for three pounds ten shillings, approximately ten dollars. But she wore it with such flair that a woman's magazine accused her of overdressing the part.

"I was a little anxious as to how her noisy followers would take Tallulah's attempt at a character part of such serious intent," says Dean. "I need not have worried. Her performance was restrained, sincerely felt and accurately characterized throughout. The audience rose to it with surprise and delight, while the fans, taken aback at first, gave a riotous reception from which the usual hysterics were notably absent."

Napier Alington was in and out of Tallulah's life like a lightning storm in the tropics. It was always exciting when he was around, but his mysterious, unannounced disappearances enraged and perplexed her. Goddammit she was the one to be unexpected and unpredictable. He had been out of her life for months when she fell for Wimbledon tennis champion Bill Tilden. She went with him to Paris for the Davis Cup matches. And while other spectators were going left, right, left, right, to watch the contest, Tallulah would vary the rhythm to left, right, left, right around—just in case that infuriating Napier was somewhere back there watching the whole thing.

Tallulah went from her summer idyll with Tilden to rehearsals for *Her Cardboard Lover* with Leslie Howard, which opened at the Lyric Theatre in London on August 21, 1928. Tallulah now almost made it a droit de senorita that she should have her leading men before they went home to their wives. Howard had a wife who was aware of this and was vigilant. Howard was fond of Tallulah but went from the play, most nights, straight to the home of John Balderston where the two men prepared a production of *Berkeley Square* while drinking beer and eating chunks of ripe Stilton cheese.

The behavior of the audience during *Her Cardboard Lover* is an indication of the impact she had on her fans. Leslie Howard entered and received a round of applause. Tallulah entered and the gallery sprang to their collective feet and screamed. As the screaming died words could be heard: "Marvelous! Ravishing! Exquisite! Tallulah you're wonderful!" This was before Tallulah had opened her mouth. When she did, every line got a response of approval. After the play ended, two thousand fans waited for Tallulah at the stage door. Leslie Howard shut himself in his dressing room until Tallulah had gone and with her the screams.

Reviewers and critics were put on their mettle to describe the woman they saw on the stage without getting swept into the general hysteria. One woman journalist wrote of Tallulah in *Her Cardboard Lover*: "Down go the lights and up goes the curtain, and in a few minutes Tallulah—in a sheath of ebony ring velvet, shoulder-strapped with diamante—insinuates herself onto the stage. The famous husky voice with the break in it is there, the swift, lithe movements of the body, and the rapid and disarming changes from hair tossing and tearing, to chuckling, wheedling tenderness. As a vivid, irrational emotional Frenchwoman she carries the vein of unrestrained farce without a moment's departure for subtlety. Beautiful? Oh, quite! Feline? Yes, with the broad languorous movements of a blue Persian kitten whose claws are never far concealed. She can scream, too, not unlike the wail of a cat in the night."

Arnold Bennett worked on a film script the evening of December 3, 1928, then dashed out to see Tallulah in *Her Cardboard Lover,* a French farce by Deval, anglicized by P. G. Wodehouse and another writer. He recorded in his diary, "This was quite a good boulevard farce in the traditional manner, well played by Tallulah and Leslie Howard. The rest very mediocre. Wodehouse had handled it with some skill. Tallulah has great resource, and so has Leslie Howard."

But no play could hold Tallulah's enthusiasm for long, and she spent most of her energy on romances with men and women and parties of every description. She liked best the parties Lord Beaverbrook gave to just a dozen or so guests. They'd include Lord Ivor Churchill (Winston's cousin), Lord Brownlow the Prince of Wales' equerry, and Michael Wardell. When Beaverbrook wanted to make a bigger splash he hired rooms at the Savoy Hotel and kept the entertainment going with an orchestra and Rudolph Valentino. At such parties Tallulah met people of achievement as well as the titled, and the tipsy.

One otherwise empty afternoon in October, 1928, Tallulah went with Beatrice Lillie to watch Aimee Semple McPherson hold a revival meeting at Albert Hall. Tallulah viewed her as a fellow-actress and although she considered Aimee's eyes to be beautiful and her skin lovely, criticized her badly dyed hair and said she had the body of a peasant. A few nights later, after playing *Her Cardboard Lover*, Tallulah invited Aimee home to meet her chums. Cellist Gwen Farrar was there with Leslie Howard and Audry and her brother Kenneth Carten. They tried to get the evangelist to admit she was human too by confessing their own sins, some invented. She didn't fall for the trap, and said that as long as they didn't hurt others, she didn't mind what they did.

Tallulah was in three plays in 1928—which shows that though none of the plays had a long run she was in constant demand. Aside from *Her Cardboard Lover* Tallulah romped through *Mud and Treacle* (a title that begged for sticky treatment from the critics), and *Blackmail*, a melodrama by Charles Bennett. Actor Raymond Massey, appearing in another play, was doubling as director for this production. The producer was Al Woods, a stocky man with a walleye and a no-nonsense approach. He would have made a great lion tamer, but now he had a tougher task, to tame Tallulah.

Tallulah was "starring in her sixth play in London and at the height of her solid success there," writes Raymond Massey in his autobiography *A Hundred Different Lives*. "Tallulah was hugely talented but at this stage of her career, brash and undisciplined. She was not yet twenty-five and she was having fun. The crowd of sycophants who surrounded her offstage and who had nothing to do with the theatre, had slightly turned her head, which, fortunately, was not an empty one. Tallulah had been prone to express her opinions about scripts, casts, and other production affairs with undue emphasis in previous plays, but in the English theatre, which was a little

more easygoing than the American, it hadn't disturbed anyone too much.

"In the *Blackmail* job she was dealing with a different
manager, and Al Woods began to bristle. [His nickname was
Sweetheart because he called everyone "sweetheart," regard-
less of sex.] Tallulah's frequent suggestions about improving
the script had irked 'Sweetheart' and a few days before rehearsals started he told me to see Miss Bankhead and reassure
her about the healthy state of the script. His words, as I recol-
lect, were like this: 'Get that Bankhead broad off my back—
you're the director of this play, not her. Tell her to learn
her jokes and not bump into the furniture.' This made sense
to me.

"Accordingly, I arrived at Tallulah's house in Farm Street
by appointment, armed with the script of *Blackmail*, and was
immediately taken upstairs by her maid and shown into her
bathroom, where her lovely head and shoulders were dimly
visible through the dense steam and soapsuds. I sat on a
stool and for about ten minutes listened to Miss B.'s views
on the care and feeding of theatrical managers and dramatic
authors. These indicated that far from dismounting from
Mr. Wood's back, Miss B. would use spurs in future. When
I left Farm Street, my script a mess of pulp, and dizzy with
the heavy scent of bath salts, I realized that I had scarcely
uttered a word.

"I reported my failure to Al Woods, and the next day,
Saturday, I had some minor surgery on an infected toe done
after the show Consequently I had to play Austin in *The
Second Man* for a few days with one foot in a black felt
slipper. I got through the Monday-night performance fairly
well.

"The reading of *Blackmail* the following morning was
plain sailing but I didn't look forward to being on my feet
all afternoon blocking out the first act. I was sitting in the
aisle stall with Tallulah next to me, an open script on my
knees, when Al Woods appeared.

" 'Well Miss Bankhead, can we go ahead with the rehearsal?'

" 'Buzz off, Sweetheart, I'm talking to the director.'

"That was more than Al could take. He grabbed my cane, which was hanging on the seat in front of me, and in making a violent gesture at the script on my lap he brought the weapon down on my bad toe. I yelled. Tallulah leapt at Al across me, stepping on the toe in the process. Another yell, and Tallulah shouted, 'You walleyed old bastard, you've hurt him!'

"She followed Sweetheart up the aisle and they disappeared into the lobby. She returned shortly and handed my cane back to me, murmuring, 'All right, darling'—the Bankhead equivalent of the Woodsian 'Sweetheart'—'let's go. Sweetheart will be quite tame tomorrow.'

"He was, we did go, Tallulah was impeccably professional throughout rehearsals, but despite an excellent performance by her and the cast, *Blackmail* failed.

"I asked Tallulah what she had said to Al Woods in the lobby after the fight. Without batting an eye she told me. 'I just said to the old pirate that I was young and inexperienced, that I couldn't stand violence, I just wanted peace and love and understanding, and would Sweetheart please for God's sake leave me alone and let me work it out with you, darling!' "

When she wasn't too involved with a play, Tallulah pursued a life that attracted eccentrics, for which England is a haven and the theatre a magnet.

Sir Francis Laking was one of the most eccentric. His grandfather, surgeon to the Royal Family, had whipped out King Edward VII's appendix when he was Prince of Wales. Francis, of neuter gender, according to Tallulah, was malicious, spiteful, jealous, and witty.

An example of his wit:

TALLULAH: I'm dining with the Earl of Lathom and Gladys Cooper.

FRANCIS: They're no good to you. One's got consumption and the other's got a matinee.

After going on vacation with her to Venice, he had lisped his way into Tallulah's Farm Street home. When he arrived all the servants left. If Tallulah showed an interest in men he became violent. Although he liked to start fights at parties by calling men pimps and then ducking, Tallulah took an almost sisterly interest in him and more than once bailed him out of Bow Street after a cop had found him stoned in the street.

Laking's sense of humor survived him. He died on August 4, 1930, at twenty-six years of age, after drinking an overdose of yellow Chartreuse, and in his will he left Tallulah all his cars. The joke was that he had none to leave. Not one of his best. His sister claimed he died of a broken heart because of a frustrated love for Tallulah. But Tallulah's sister Eugenia says: "I was told that his liver just blew up from drinking too much."

Tallulah had wanted to become a star before getting married. She was a star now. But the only man she wanted was God knows where.

Then one afternoon in Paris she saw him again. They fell into each other's arms. He told her that he had to catch the midnight train to Geneva. They were together until it was time for him to leave—and then Napier couldn't do it. Five nights running he missed the train to stay with Tallulah. On the sixth night he caught the train but as it started, he saw Tallulah's expression of anguish and affection, and jumped off. The seventh night he again caught the train, but got off, saying: "It doesn't go to Geneva. It goes to Genoa." They spent most of that night at Bricktop's restaurant at Montmartre, and Napier took her back to her hotel at dawn.

"Before he left, Napier had made me promise I'd spend two weeks with him at Evian-les-Bains, on Lake Geneva, where he was taking the cure, before I went into rehearsal," wrote Tallulah in her autobiography. "I was to wire him the time of my arrival. To facilitate travel in a strange land I borrowed Sister's French maid. On my arrival at the hotel I went at once to my suite after telling the clerk: 'Let Lord Alington know Miss Bankhead is here.'

"Miss Bankhead was there, sure enough, but Napier wasn't. He was registered but not in. Where was he? Perhaps in Montreux, across the lake. I was blazing with indignation. For forty-eight hours I never left my rooms. My insistent phone calls had no result. I would stand on my terrace for hours, awaiting the arrival of the small boats from Montreux—forty-five minutes away—in the hope that Napier might step from one of them.

"Then a Belgian, whom I remember only as The Fox, called on me to say he had been sent by Napier. He offered a lot of fantastic excuses which added up to the suspicion the fugitive was on a monumental spree. My Lord would be back tomorrow, he said. Glad to escape from my rooms, I accepted this emissary's invitation to go to the casino. Crushed and humiliated, I gave no sign. We went to the chemin de fer table and as I sat down I looked across the green board and there sat Napier, calmly saying 'Banco! Banco!' When our eyes met, he casually said: 'Hello, Lulas,' and calmly continued riffling his chips.

"I decided to blast him then and there, but when he approached my rage vanished. In a few minutes we were laughing and drinking together. I spent two magic weeks with him. Memories of the gin fizzes I drank with him at the Sporting Bar in Geneva still linger. My holiday over, we caught a night train for Paris, leaving Napier behind for God knows what adventure. The French maid and I went on an emotional binge. She sobbed for her lover killed in World War I, while I cried my eyes out over Napier the whole night long. I knew he was doomed. I had a feeling he welcomed that doom."

Tallulah admitted that she was happiest with Napier, even

when his conduct was outrageous. Whenever they were to-
gether there was always laughter. Napier was with Tallulah,
Princess Natasha Paley, Cecil Beaton, Oliver Messel, and a
few others at a performance of the Russian Ballet in London.
They decided to celebrate afterward at Tallulah's home on
Farm Street. They roused Beatrice Lillie (also known as Lady
Peel) from a deep sleep in the Savoy Hotel and she put a
coat over her nightdress and joined them. At six that morning
Tallulah noticed Lady Peel was missing from the party and
found her upstairs, sloshed. Napier, two other men, and
Tallulah took her back to the Savoy in a cab. Believing she
had the edge on Lady Peel, now being held on her feet by
two of the men, Tallulah said to the hotel clerk: "Give me
Lady Keel's pee, please!"

The clerk froze with astonishment.

Tallulah tried again: "Lady Keel's pee, please!"

Lady Peel came to for a moment: "My pee, my good man,
my pee!"

They eventually got what they wanted.

What was Napier Alington's attraction for Tallulah? She
admitted that he wasn't all that sexually attractive, and when
they were apart she wanted to avenge her humiliation by
doing something cruel to him. She knew he was a sick man
and that he knew it. Was her love partly pity?

It was a big blow for her when Alington, after giving
her an expensive necklace as an engagement present, disappeared. He hadn't paid for it. To save face, she footed
the bill.

She had little time to brood, with a new play to rehearse
and thousands of adoring fans to take her mind off Alington.
Arnold Bennett went to the first night of *The Lady of the
Camellias* in 1930 and filled several diary pages with his impressions. He notes that 'the auditorium is crowded. And
the price of seats has been doubled. . . . Until she comes the
play is reduced to a mere prologue, has no general interest.
Tallulah, and nobody and nothing else, is the play. . . . Ordi-

nary stars get 'hands.' If Tallulah get a 'hand' it is not heard. What is heard is a terrific, wild, passionate, hysterical roar and shriek [as she makes her first appearance]. Only the phrase of the Psalmist can describe it: 'God is gone up with a shout.' The play stands still. Tallulah stands still. She is a little unnerved, and to be unnerved becomes her. . . . The play is not bad. It is merely dead. It is one long demonstration that Dumas fils was was not a patch of Dumas père. . . . What is Tallulah's secret? If she is beautiful, and she is, her beauty is not classical. How many wayfarers would look twice at her in the street? Her voice is not beautiful. It has, however, the slight seductive huskiness which lent so much enchantment to the acting of Pauline Lord. . . . Then the end of the show. The loudest roar and shriek of all. Storms. Thunder and lightning. Gusts. And Tallulah, still virginal, withstanding everything with a difficult smile.

"I looked up at the gallery. Scores of lusty girls hanging over the rail and tossing their triumphant manes and gesticulating and screeching . . . I reach a landing and see an open door and a dressing room and a hot crowd within and Tallulah in the center. She breaks through the cordon and dashes out onto the landing.

" 'Are you coming to my party tonight?'

"After all the terrible strain of rehearsals, of frock-fitting, of the dress rehearsal, of the first night, of the thunder and lightning and roaring of her reception, this astonishing, exhaustless creature is giving a party! Even now the hour is within a quarter of midnight, and she is still in her paint and her dying white nightgown. A difficult moment, for I am not able to go to the party; I am only able to go to bed. But she is full of tact. I love her. She returns to her worshipers . . ."

Tallulah's real-life performance in the Savoy Grill that same year gave Bennett something more to write about.

She was dining with Sir Gerald du Maurier on November 27, 1930, in the crowded, fashionable restaurant overlooking the Thames. A young woman stormed up to Tallulah and slapped her in the face. There were the customary gasps and then a shocked silence from the other diners.

Tallulah's normal reaction would have been to swing at her attacker with everything to hand including Sir Gerald and two wine waiters. But she unconsciously mimicked people she was with—and Sir Gerald was the master of understatement. She now out-du-Mauriered du Maurier, ignored her attacker and coolly continued the conversation: "As I was saying, dahling . . ."

It was characterized in one gossip column as "Scandal at the Savoy Grill."

Tallulah was playing in her last play in England called *Let Us Be Gay*—the title might symbolize the entire history of the twenties. Rachel Crother was its author. Tallulah had appeared in another play of Miss Crother's in New York ten years before called *Everyday*. In it Tallulah had a line: "Kings and queens are really kind of a joke. The most interesting person I met was a prostitute." Tallulah refused to say the line until she was told that if she failed to say it once more, her understudy would replace her. But she again balked at saying it. Before she could be replaced the play closed. Now ten years later, Tallulah told Rachel Crother why she wouldn't say the line.

"It was out of loyalty to Napier," she explained. "He had great respect and affection for the Royal Family and I thought that maybe he would be in the audience the night I said the line. So I never said it just in case."

"Why didn't you tell me?" Miss Crother asked. "I would have understood."

The reason Tallulah didn't tell her was that she was too self-conscious about her feeling for Napier.

While she was playing in *Let Us Be Gay* Tallulah signed a contract with Paramount Pictures.

Eight years, sixteen plays, and one silent film after landing on English soil, Tallulah, now just twenty-nine, returned to America.

When she left England in January, 1931, the Depression hit it and the country was never again the same.

VI

Exile's Return

1931–1937 Tallulah had encouraged the wild, scandalous stories about her in the past by going more than halfway to proving they were true. But now her pride was hurt. The rumor spread that she was being deported from England for all manner of evil, from tempting Eton schoolboys to hefty income-tax evasion. Fact and fancy joined in a no-holds-barred fandango. The funny stories that had been made up about Tallulah now came to life again with knobs on. True, she had left without paying her bills; true, she did owe some income tax. But with the fifty thousand dollars Paramount Pictures had promised her for ten weeks' work, Tallulah planned to hotfoot it back to Britain, pay up all her debts, and outface her critics.

Her big fear was that the ugliest rumors would reach her father, even though she knew he wouldn't believe them.

He was waiting for her as she stepped off the gangplank in New York. Her stepmother, Florence, was there too.

They thought she looked haggard. She thought they looked wonderful. And from her father's first few words she sensed that the rumors had not crossed the Atlantic. Her parents went with her to the Lombardy Hotel and shared eight years of memories in as many hours.

There wasn't much time to look up her old friends because in less than a week she had to report for film tests at the

Paramount Studios in Astoria, Long Island. She used the time to play-hop on Broadway. It was the start of a new era. Broadway theatres were just being equipped with air conditioning, which promised that they'd stay open through the hottest summers provided there was an audience.

Noel Coward was rehearsing his *Private Lives* with Gertrude Lawrence, Katharine Cornell was having the success of her career in *The Barretts of Wimpole Street,* and Tallulah's friend Clifton Webb was starring with Libby Holman and Fred Allen. Tallulah went to see them in a musical, *Three's a Crowd.*

Backstage, afterward, she was introduced to Tamara Geva, a young Russian actress who was making her debut in the play.

Tallulah's reaction to people was chemical and her reaction to Tamara Geva was prussic acid. She greeted Webb with an embrace and "Hello dahling!" She greeted Tamara with an "Ugh!" and a short time later was saying of her: "I HATE this girl. She has this face that doesn't say anything!"

Tamara felt on that first meeting "a strange, almost instinctive, kind of extrasensory dislike."

They were both proud, volatile, ambitious women. And before long they would have good cause to hate each other.

That first brief, abrasive encounter led to a second. Tamara had made a test for a part in *Tarnished Lady*, the first film Tallulah was to star in after her arrival in America. Early reports had been promising, there was enthusiastic talk of a contract for Tamara, and then suddenly it fizzled out.

A few evenings later she arrived at the Lombardy Hotel for a party. Tallulah was sitting at a table near the entrance. She hailed Tamara right away and as she came close, grabbed her and sat her in her lap. "You know, my dear," said Tallulah, "I threw you out of the picture. I'm no fool. I wouldn't have you around me."

"Bullshit!" says Cukor who directed that film. "Tallulah had no power to hire or fire anybody on *Tarnished Lady*.

She might even have been trying to make Tamara Geva feel good, as if to say: 'You're too dangerous a rival, too good an actress for me to risk as competition.' "

It's probable that Tallulah, hearing that Tamara was not going to play in the movie, pretended that she had wielded the axe—a little ego trip.

Tallulah got fifty thousand dollars out of *Tarnished Lady*, a talkie that lived up to its name. She also got a lifelong friend in director George Cukor. He really had a ball directing her. He found her very grateful, very sensitive, and ready to try anything to make a scene go, on or off camera. "I have a very warm and loving feeling about her," he says. "And I'm very grateful for the ENORMOUS amount of fun I had with her. She was enormously diverting and touching, too. Tallulah would do anything to get a laugh."

Tallulah didn't go back to England after the film as she had intended. She got caught up on the Paramount assembly line. Her next director was George Abbott, a tall, frank, businesslike man. He was scheduled to see her through *My Sin* and *The Cheat*. Tallulah surprised him at her home once when she asked him to pour a huge can of milk into her bathtub and told him that she loved only cads. Feeling he didn't qualify, Abbott left. But on the set she rested on his lap between scenes and behaved with little whispered confidences and warm chuckles just as if they were lovers. The moment they were alone together, Tallulah kept her distance.

At first baffled, Abbott later decided that Tallulah was a flamboyant woman who wasn't sure of herself and behaved amorously or hit out in all directions to attract attention and seem important.

"She was a wild creature," says Abbott. "She had a background but she was not what a lady would call a lady."

Paramount decided to transport Tallulah from their Long Island studios to Hollywood for three more movies.

On the train from New York to Hollywood she met Joan Crawford and her new husband, Douglas Fairbanks, Jr. The fat little boy at the Algonquin had grown into a slim man-about-town with a friendly grin and the hint of a moustache.

Crawford was unsure of herself and straining to be sophisticated.

Tallulah said to her: "Darling, you're divine. I've had an affair with your husband. You'll be next."

Crawford looked at her husband for support, but he was gasping for air and trying to smile at the same time.

"It scares the bejesus out of me, if you want to know the truth," said Joan Crawford. "I wasn't mature enough to take it in my stride and I didn't have a sense of humor then. I just looked up at her and said: 'I'm so sorry, Miss Bankhead, but I just love men.' "

Tallulah was quite often lighthearted about her love affairs with women. Psychiatrists say such love was a form of emotional immaturity, that it was almost self-love. Friends say that she was sexually omnivorous, eager for every experience. Others believe that her drinking and especially her use of cocaine were partly responsible for her lesbian affairs. As she grew older they became less frequent until her romances were entirely with men. Her father's warning to beware of men and her failure to find any man who could measure up to him may have had some effect on her. Into the equation too must go her lifelong attraction to and for homosexual men; though she also had heterosexual friends of both sexes. The "why" of Tallulah will get a different answer from almost everyone who knew her.

Joan Crawford recovered from Tallulah's onslaught and found her one of the delights of Hollywood. "We all adored her," said Joan Crawford. "We were fascinated by her, but we were scared to death of her, too. She had so much going for her. Very few people had that kind of queenly attitude toward people. She should have been born in Antoinette's time. She loved to tease and taunt people. Somebody said she was the female equivalent of John Barrymore and I thought that was a brilliant observation: she was. I've met other peo-

ple who were just as shocking as Tallulah was, but they don't
have the flair or the gift of gab. And she had such authority,
as if she ruled the earth, as if she was the first woman on the
moon. She behaved like a lord and a lady at times. I can't
tell you: I never knew which she was going to be. I think
she was one of the most exciting actresses we've had."

Tallulah rented the Hollywood home of William Haines,
an actor turned interior decorator. "It was a divine home,"
Tallulah told an interviewer. "And one evening I had six
guests. We had finished dinner and had gone into the next
room for coffee—intending to play bridge afterward. I suddenly looked around and saw the ghost of a horse walk by.
I wasn't frightened. I was sitting there in bright light with
six people. I could see right through the horse, it was quite
transparent. I saw it for about three seconds and then it suddenly disappeared. No one else saw it. Now the funny thing
is that in the same area in Hollywood during a rainstorm
several people had heard the noise of frightened horses. They
thought perhaps they were from a traveling circus and maybe
something had happened to frighten and stampede them.
The noise was so disturbing that the people called the police
and the police came and investigated. It had been raining,
the ground was muddy, so that if there had been horses they
would have seen their hoof prints. But the police found absolutely nothing."

Tallulah saw no more ghosts in Hollywood though her first
director there, Richard Wallace, had worked as an undertaker's assistant while at medical school. When Tallulah had
a trying day on the film *Thunder Below*, Wallace invited her
out for the evening and took her to the morgue. "This should
cheer you up," he said. "See how peaceful they are." That
incident was more memorable to Tallulah than the film
itself.

It's extraordinary that Tallulah could find herself so con-
sistently in bad movies even when the cast was outstanding.
Her next bomb was *The Devil and the Deep* in which

Charles Laughton, Gary Cooper, and Cary Grant shared the blame. The film puts in a not-infrequent appearance on late-night television. That's where actor Tony Randall, who idolizes Tallulah, saw it. His review: "If you want to see how bad Tallulah could be, see *The Devil and the Deep*. Gary Cooper was all right in it. The film introduced Charles Laughton. Of course he was a genius, but he was often bad. In this, it wasn't merely that he was hammy: he stank! Cary Grant had a small part in it and was simply beautiful. He was always good. Nobody had anything to do in the film. Cary Grant didn't try to do anything: he kept it as simple as possible. But the others, Tallulah included, went ape."

In her film performances Tallulah gave no indication why the English audiences had almost canonized her. She hadn't yet learned to modify her exuberant stage acting, and when she tried to throw away a line or underplay a scene, she went overboard and the line was swallowed and the action too sketchy. In either event she looked like an amateur, over- or underdoing it.

Tallulah finished up her year in Hollywood playing *Faithless* with Robert Montgomery. On the next set were all three Barrymores starring in *Rasputin and the Empress*. It was twelve years since John Barrymore had chased her around his dressing room. Now all he did when they met between scenes was roll his eyes and show her his best profile (the left). But Tallulah still found him and his sister Ethel fascinating.

The biggest shocker on the sets in those early thirties was Carole Lombard. She used to unzip men's pants while they were taking a film test, just to throw them. Tallulah kept her hands to herself, but between films she had a ball. One of her gambits, when she was sitting with a group of men and another one entered the room, was to say: "Hi there! I've slept with every man at this table, and now I'm going to sleep with you." It was a sure way to separate the unwilling from the ever-ready. At one party Tallulah met Greta Garbo and succeeded in thawing the Swedish actress by clowning around.

And she soon collected a little coterie which included Laurence Olivier and his wife, Jill Esmond. "She was great fun to be with and had more glamor than almost anybody alive," recalls Sir Laurence. "She was unusually attractive with overtones of sensuality and she had a very catchy voice. She excelled at all party games and we would sit gurgling at her feet with shining eyes."

Olivier had turned down Tallulah's offer to star with her in England when she performed in *The Lady of the Camellias* because fellow actors had warned him his part would be swamped by Tallulah's. Now that he saw her often at close range he realized his advisers had been right. In those days he would have been no match for her.

In her autobiography Tallulah tells how she spent an evening at the theatre with Gary Cooper but, she said, "He never opened his trap throughout the evening."

"He might have said 'yup!' " suggests Tallulah's friend Ruth Hammond. "I know he didn't say 'no.' "

But Tallulah the catalyst, Tallulah the shocker, was also Tallulah the chameleon. Anita Loos' mother recalls Tallulah as a demure young lady who spent her Hollywood evenings quietly knitting.

The year in Hollywood gave Tallulah her independence. She left with $200,000 and the resolve to return to the stage. There she might face cheering fans instead of yawning electricians. And she wouldn't have to get up at godawful hours to act.

Hollywood had given her something else. She now could add to her repertoire of imitations. At her almost nightly all-night parties in the Hotel Elysee in New York guests would be silenced by a Tallulah roar. And then, "Now dahlings, this is Greta Garbo: 'Tallulah you're wonderful.' This is Marlene Dietrich: 'Tallulah you're wonderful.' " In fact she gave imitations of everyone saying, "Tallulah, you're wonderful."

Ethel Barrymore came to one party and Tallulah, hearing

she was tired, had planned for someone to escort Ethel home fairly early. Then Ethel began to say: "Tallulah, you really know how to walk across the stage darling. . . ." A few more such compliments followed and Tallulah turned on the other guests and bawled: "Everyone else go home! Ethel stay! Now tell me more, tell me more!" She was just avid for praise— but she could also get a laugh while asking for it.

When Tallulah was sloshed at a party, she wanted everyone else to be sloshed too, including her two dogs. She'd put a glass of whatever she was drinking—champagne or brandy— on the floor for the pooches. And when they keeled over she'd laugh hysterically.

Her kinkajou monkey seemed to be kept mainly to torment Joan Crawford. Tallulah made it a ritual when Joan arrived for a party to put the monkey on Joan's shoulder. "It would curl its tail around my neck and promptly do large bits of things down my back. I threw more dresses away . . ." said Joan Crawford with a sigh and a laugh. "And one day I said: 'Miss Bankhead, I don't think that's funny any more.' It took me years to call her Tallulah."

But a few words overheard could turn Tallulah from a practical joker to a crusader. If she heard of some injustice, she'd be on the phone to her uncle or her father in Washington, demanding they go into action and right the wrongs. "She carried a very clean banner," says Marc Connelly, who saw Tallulah in action.

Despite Tallulah's instant-hate reaction to Tamara Geva, the two met at parties quite often—and stayed. And that's when Tamara saw Tallulah the stripper. At a certain time of night, no matter who was there, Tallulah would strip, "She would get plastered drunk and later on, for no reason, for no REASON, whatsoever, she started to take her clothes off," recalls Tamara Geva. "And then she'd laugh like a loon. It just made me embarrassed for her."

Was this just showing off, trying to live up to her reputation for daring? Or had it a deeper origin?

Most of her friends see her as a lady, and say that she carried off everything, even the outrageous, with a flair.

"A flair she had," agreed Joan Crawford. "A lady? Not always." And she laughed affectionately at the memory of Tallulah.

When Tallulah strode the Broadway stage again on March 1, 1933, she had been away for ten years. She was thirty-one. And she was scared. Tallulah was financing as well as starring in *Forsaking All Others*, a light comedy by Philip Barry. New Yorkers could do with a few laughs, she thought. That very morning the banks had closed and the government had run out of answers.

Would anyone turn up for the play when their minds were on their pockets?

Then she got the news. The house was packed. Tallulah was on the edge of panic. She had electrified the British audiences. Broadway must now be saying: "Show me."

When frantic, Tallulah always looked at the photograph of her mother for comfort. Now she looked and found it missing. "Quick," she told her maid, Rose Riley, "go back to the hotel and tell Edie to bring mother's picture." But Tallulah's secretary, Edie Smith, had already left for the theatre. It was raining hard. There wasn't enough time for a messenger to get through the theatre traffic and bring the picture back

And then there was a knock at Tallulah's dressing-room door and the stage doorman brought in a package. There was a letter with it: "Dear Miss Bankhead: I knew your mother well. Noting that you are opening in a new play it occurred to me that you might like to have this picture. It's possible you may not have it." The note was signed by a stranger to Tallulah.

Sentimental, superstitious Tallulah, who adored the mother she had never known, now felt completely calm and protected. It was as if the stranger was divinely inspired, or at least a messenger from another world.

Unafraid, Tallulah made her first entrance, and the audience drowned the sound of the pelting rain in a storm of cheers and applause.

Critic Brooks Atkinson described her as dynamic and amusing. Gilbert Gabriel wrote: "There is no withstanding her vitality, humor and her half gamin half ladylike loveliness." And Walter Winchell, guru of the gossip columnists, called her his favorite valentine. But there were empty seats after the first night. Pride, hope, and the gambler in her kept Tallulah from closing the play. Reason took over after fourteen weeks when she closed the show she was financing at a loss to herself of forty thousand dollars.

A month later producer Guthrie McClintic, husband of Katharine Cornell (she and Tallulah acted together as girls in *Nice People*), bagged Tallulah for *Jezebel*. McClintic regarded Tallulah with the fascination of a rabbit for a cobra, attracted yet almost repelled. This is no reflection on McClintic's courage, but the effect Tallulah had on him was titillating and traumatic. He talked about her endlessly, yet when a friend suggested they'd be perfect desert island partners, McClintic protested so vigorously he looked like a man in the throes of hara-kiri.

With several weeks free before the first rehearsal of *Jezebel*, Tallulah took off for Hollywood to look up old friends and to relax in a bungalow at the Garden of Allah Hotel.

For a few hours she listened to Vincent Youmans play his own *Tea for Two* and *More Than You Know* from a nearby bungalow, counterpointed by the friendly chink of a bottle on glass in Robert Benchley's place and the half-hearted scream of a starlet being immortalized by a falling star.

Then Tallulah decided to join the action.

Sheila Graham witnessed the aftermath of "a hell of a party." Tallulah joined Olympic swimming champion Johnny Weissmuller on the top board of the swimming pool. He was fully clothed, in a tuxedo. Talullah wore a heavily beaded dress and diamonds. Johnny took a dive. Tallulah jumped and sank to the bottom like a stone. "Having an instinct for survival, she shed her clothes and jewels while weaving at the bottom of the Black Sea," writes Sheila Graham in her book *The Garden of Allah*. (When movie star Nazimova owned the property she had the pool made the shape of the Black Sea to remind her of her homeland.) "Tallulah came out of the pool naked. 'Everyone's been dying to see my body,' she croaked. 'Now they can see it.' Johnny took to the hills after dragging his intoxicated companion out of the pool. . . . Dredging operations to recover Miss Bankhead's jewelry took some time, while Tallulah removed Gar from the big sign on the outside wall, leaving it The   den of Allah."

While Tallulah was dunking her diamonds, Guthrie Mc-Clintic was having qualms about casting Tallulah. A psychic landlady of his young days had called him out of the blue and said: "It's too bad you cast Tallulah Bankhead for the part. Because she'll never play it." This landlady had impressed McClintic, when he was her youthful lodger, with her ability to go into a trance and bounce a table around the room just by putting her hands on it. Her phone call had really worried him.

Tallulah came back from her Hollywood rest raring to go, then suddenly collapsed and was hurried to a hospital, her stomach strangely swollen. She was drugged with codeine to ease the pain. Could it have been something she caught from the Black Sea? The cast of *Jezebel* came to her bedside to rehearse the play. "Is Tallulah pregnant?" a reporter inquired, not unreasonably. Tallulah was so ill she couldn't even laugh when she heard the question. She got worse. Mystified doctors decided they'd have to operate. She was on the operating table for five hours—for a hysterectomy—and recovering in the hospital for five weeks. By an odd coincidence the sickness cost her another forty thousand dollars.

The psychic landlady was right. Tallulah never played in *Jezebel*. Miriam Hopkins replaced her. It ran for a month in 1933.

Tallulah tottered down to Jasper, Alabama, to spend Christmas with her father and stepmother, and made a personal appearance at the local movie theatre, ending her speech with: "Daddy has never let me forget I am still an Alabama hillbilly." Her father had just suffered his second heart attack, and they each expended a lot of energy trying to persuade the other to rest. "Take it easy, dahling." "No, you take it easy." "No, you . . ."

That Christmas Tallulah sang carols with her father, keeping her language weak because he didn't like it strong, and just sipping at her bourbon, as if it didn't agree with her.

The next Christmas she was sloshed and had to be put to bed by her friend Glenn Anders. As is the form when putting a drunk to bed, he whispered consoling little phrases: "Now be a good girl Tallulah and in the morning Santa Claus will have left something nice in your stocking." Tallulah didn't feel like being a good girl and roared ribald threats about what she would do to Santa Claus if she got hold of the old gentleman.

During that period Tallulah was engaged to a wealthy publisher and at the same time was having an affair with another man. "Tallulah was always saying funny lines," he recalls. "And they weren't always meant to be funny. One of the funniest lines was during a wild kind of affair which we were having—and it had gone to an extent which you can't imagine—when she said to me: 'Please stop now, stop now! I'm engaged to George!' "

Tallulah's night on the town with Robert Benchley, when he returned from Hollywood, lasted thirty hours, and even then she didn't want to break up the party.

Her energy astonished everyone, especially Burgess Meredith, who in 1935 became Broadway's newest star through his performance in Maxwell Anderson's *Winterset*.

Burgess had recently celebrated his twenty-first birthday when he got a note from Tallulah inviting him to her St.

Regis Hotel apartment after his show. He could hardly wait. He went up there with great expectations, but he wasn't prepared for the reception he got. He rang the bell of the suite and the door immediately opened and there was Tallulah. She grabbed him and kissed him passionately. Then she gripped his hand and took him around the room full of people. "Dahlings, this is the young genius of the time. He's a great, great actor."

Meredith recalls: "In a few minutes she was saying there was no question at all that we were going to mate. It was all very gay and wild. And later—and nobody seemed particularly startled by it—she was wandering around stark naked. She had quite a good figure in those days. Then it was an eye-popping thing. But what was funny to me, is that her friends paid almost no attention to her when she was naked. They went on playing their games or just talking.

"In those days I think she'd experiment sexually with anything and she was absolutely open about it. I don't mean to say this in any deprecating way. She was way ahead of her time in being almost sexless in a sense: hedonistic is the word that applies to her. That will put her down in certain people's eyes, but she wouldn't care. She would have been more at home in this generation. She was taking the same kind of dope that the young kids take today. She was on cocaine. She'd pass it around and she'd be drinking at the same time."

In 1936 Tallulah was cast as an actress torn between the urges for fame and for marriage and a family, in George Kelly's *Reflected Glory*. Kelly was one of the few men she admired wholeheartedly, and his impression of her was of a convent-bred girl whose gift for comedy had never been truly exploited.

Tallulah was rehearsing *Reflected Glory* in Los Angeles when she met John Emery, then playing the Earl of Warwick in *Saint Joan* at the Biltmore Theatre. She had seen him once before as Captain William Henry O'Shea in *Parnell* and had liked the look of him.

But nothing seemed to get Napier Alington out of her system, not stardom, drugs, drinks, other men, women, nor the knowledge that Napier had run out on her.

Then *Gone with the Wind* came into her life. It began life as a thick novel that threatened to topple the Bible from its bestseller position. And so, like the Bible, it was bought for the movies. Seventeen screenwriters, including Scott Fitzgerald, labored to make it screen material. David Selznick was to produce it and George Cukor to direct, at least for a while.

It is safe to say that almost all the leading actresses in the Western world who were not in alcoholic or maternity wards—with the exception of Zasu Pitts and Marjorie Main— begged to be tested for the leading role of the Southern belle, Scarlett O'Hara, in *Gone with the Wind*.

It is even safer to say that those who weren't invited curled their lips over "l'il ole me, honeychile" phrases for hours, after snarling at their agents: "Get me a test, buster, or find yourself another goddam client!" Floods of them got tested.

Tallulah's test came by invitation. She was resting in her hotel before a performance of *Reflected Glory* in Los Angeles when her maid said: "Mr. Cukor on the phone."

The message from director Cukor was exciting. He told Tallulah: "David Selznick, who's producing *Gone with the Wind*, saw you in *Reflected Glory*. He immediately phoned me and said: 'I've found our Scarlett.' "

Tallulah's play headed cross-country for Broadway. The critics mauled *Reflected Glory* but they and the audience were wild about Tallulah, and that gave the impetus to take it from town to town and to fill the seats with paying people.

The thought of playing Scarlett O'Hara gave Tallulah more of a lift than a glass of ammonia. And she needed it. Five years of futile films and plays were enough to disenchant anyone. Wasn't she almost custom-made for the role? Like Scarlett, she was a Southern belle and with the same volatile temperament. Both director Cukor and one of the major financial backers, Jock Whitney, were her close friends. That didn't hurt.

When *Reflected Glory* reached Broadway and looked like running, Tallulah got a second call from Cukor. "When can you make a test?"

She couldn't leave the play. The best thing she could do would be to take the first plane after the last show on Saturday night and spend a hectic twenty-four hours in Hollywood.

To make the test Tallulah flew through an electric storm and the plane made an emergency landing. Frantic, Tallulah called Cukor: "I'm in Lincoln, Nebraska, darling. A storm forced us down."

"Don't worry, Tallulah," he reassured her. "We'll shoot one test tonight and another tomorrow."

Someone was listening to Tallulah and the storm cleared.

She was ready for action that same evening and, following a massage and a strong drink, she made the first test. That night she lay awake, reliving the terrifying flight, reliving the flops and fiascos of the last few years, thinking of John Emery, thinking of Napier Alington. "My God, four o'clock!" She took a couple more sleeping pills. They just made it more difficult to think.

Next morning, exhausted, jumpy, her eyes bloodshot, she did another test with a different cameraman. And then a third in color. Cukor ran the tests for her to see for herself. In the first, made while she felt at her best, she looked tired, old, and haggard. In the second, when she felt whacked, she looked wonderful. Tallulah learned from that how the camera can lie—thank God—and began to study the secrets of angles and lighting for her own advantage.

She knew the part wasn't in her pocket yet. Hadn't she been fired by "that bastard Maugham" after two rehearsals of *Rain*? She went back home to pray and throw parties. She needed the part. Pride alone demanded it. But she was as good as broke too, after debts run up while enduring five successive flops.

As months went by and ninety other actresses were tested for the part of Scarlett, Tallulah's intuition told her she'd lost it. And with that feeling, she stopped hoping and almost relaxed.

Then she heard that Vivien Leigh, fiancée of Tallulah's old chum Laurence Olivier, was to be Scarlett.

Why did she lose it? Both Olivier and George Cukor agree that at thirty-four Tallulah was rejected because she was too old. Vivien Leigh was ten years younger.

Reflected Glory ended after sixteen weeks. For that time she'd been debating in George Kelly's words—before a sympathetic audience—whether a woman is more fulfilled as an actress or as a wife and mother. Maybe it got to her.

She had only just turned thirty-five when she went back to England to give Napier Alington one last chance to marry her. Very few of even her closest friends knew of this trip and she concealed it so well that some deny it took place. But Cecil Beaton was there when it happened, and he recorded it in his diary for May, 1937. Beaton had been to the Chelsea flower show in the morning and was impressed by the remarks of the crowd there. They seemed to him to represent the soul of England speaking. That evening he had a quiet dinner at Sybil Colefax's and he records: ". . . followed by Tallulah's Walpurgis night. Marian Harris mad as a march hare, sang. Tallulah danced frenziedly, throwing herself about in a mad apache dance with Napier Alington. After he left, she wept and bemoaned the fact that he had never married her, then she threw off all her clothes, performing what she called 'Chinese classical dances.' In the midst of these outrageous situations, one had reluctantly to drag oneself away."

Napier became entangled with another woman and Tallulah was in the Café de Paris when he came in with his new interest. Napier tried to ignore Tallulah.

"What's the matter?" Tallulah called out. "Don't you recognize me with my clothes on?"

Why did they never marry? Estelle Winwood, who knew

them both, believes that Napier was shocked by something
outrageous Tallulah had done. Although he was generally
an easy-going man, Napier had a granite sense of right and
wrong, according to Beaton. But if she knew what it was
she had done to shock Napier, Tallulah never told.

Napier was a lost cause. In July of 1937, back in America,
Tallulah invited John Emery to spend a weekend at the home
she was renting near Westport, Connecticut. He went.

"And she never let him out," says Tamara Geva.

Estelle Winwood says: "Tallulah used to get violent crushes
on people and she got one on John Emery—a terrible crush.
And she was going on the road and he was going to be in a
play with her, so I said: 'Why the dickens don't you marry
him, Tallulah? I'm sick of you going on journeys and having
affairs with these men and everybody talking about you. Why
don't you get married? You've always said you want to try
everything once.' So she told him the next day that she was
going to marry him."

Emery had been married once before and had led a Hollywood star to believe that she might be his next wife. When
she wasn't, she made sure he never acted in her films.

Tallulah became the wife of John Emery ("a road-company
John Barrymore," says Orson Welles), a competent actor of
great charm, on August 31, 1937, three months after she had
been weeping because Napier Alington wouldn't marry her.

VII

Tallulah Marries

1937–1938 There are some who think that by marrying Tallulah, John Emery revealed himself to have been in the wrong profession—he should have been a kamikaze suicide pilot. Who else but a man bent on destruction would tie himself to a volcano? There are others who say that he was down on his luck, in need of ready cash, and not the first man to marry a woman wealthier and more successful than himself. A few believe he married her for the most unfashionable reason of all—because he loved her. Who knows? Did John Emery himself? He told friends, "It was a challenge." In fact, at the time she wasn't wealthy. She was down on her luck, too. A string of stage failures and monumental doctors' bills had eaten into her film earnings. Maybe having played Horatio he now fancied himself as Mercutio. But from all the evidence at hand, it seems that he was in love with her, in the marrying mood, and available.

They were married in the home of Tallulah's father in Jasper, Alabama. She was thirty-five, he was thirty-two. The state of his nerves can be judged by his greeting of Tallulah's father, Speaker of the House. Said Emery: "How d'you do Mister Squeaker?"

When Tallulah went upstairs to powder her nose, her father and husband tried a little Shakespeare on the lawn with Bankhead as Antony and Emery as Cassius—not bad casting. Shakespeare was very much in the air as Tallulah and Emery were to act in a production of *Antony and Cleopatra* that fall.

They drove back through a rainstorm to Birmingham hoping to catch a plane to New York, but the flight was canceled and they spent their honeymoon night at the Tutwiler Hotel in Birmingham.

Next day they reached the Long Island Sound home where Tallulah had first invited Emery for the weekend. And there they shared their two-week honeymoon with an avalanche of reporters, many of whom came to shake the hand of a brave man.

"Does this mean you plan to retire?" asked one reporter of thirty-five-year old Tallulah.

"If I wanted to retire, you idiot, would I marry an actor?" The idiot accepted a drink, toasted the couple, and fumbled for his next question.

"Why did you marry him?"

"Oh," said Tallulah, "because he looks like a Greek god."

The reporter scribbled this down in shorthand.

"I'm only joking," Tallulah said. "He reminds me more of John Barrymore."

Another reporter got that down.

Tallulah soon learned that a joke often arrives as a stone-sober statement in print.

Practically the only time Tallulah and Emery were alone on their honeymoon was in bed or at breakfast. And at breakfast she tried to act the dutiful wife and greeted him with a glass of Planter's Punch.

He did a double take.

"But dahling " Tallulah cooed. "It's full of nourishment, loaded with orange and pineapple slices. Look. There's a couple of cherries. It's rich in food value and a tonic besides."

She astonished him with her ability to talk, drink, read a book, and do her hair at the same time.

On one occasion she persuaded him to go with her to watch the famous Joe Louis–Max Schmeling fight, a German versus a Negro, in the days when Hitler was boasting of the superiority of the Aryan Germans and the inferiority of other races. Four men sitting behind Tallulah were loudly pro-Schmeling. When Louis knocked Schmeling cold in the first round, Tallulah sprang to her feet, turned to the four men and screamed: "I told you so, you sons of bitches!"

It was then Emery should have taken the hint to get into training fast. Fortunately the four pro-Schmeling men had seen enough action. Tallulah enjoyed a good fight in or out of the ring and was disappointed that Emery tried to avoid them.

Tallulah's marriage had caught practically all their friends by surprise, among them Burgess Meredith. He says: "I asked Tallulah shortly after her wedding: "Why did you get married?' And she said: 'Why not?' And I said: 'Why didn't you tell me you wanted to get married? I'd have married you.' She thought that the funniest thing she'd ever heard. She told everyone, treating it in a way as a joke. I had meant it as a joke in a sense, but partly because she never wanted to take anything seriously.

"Theirs was a stormy marriage. I knew Emery very, very well and I was there quite a bit during their marriage, because I was fond of Emery and fascinated in some curious way by the fact that they were together.

"And of course it never changed anything. When they got back from their honeymoon to the apartment in the Elysee Hotel the parties went on just the same, except now he was there. But rather than settling down after the marriage, it increased the tempo of her wildness.

"She made the decisions in their marriage. I don't think there could have been any other way."

Some describe Tallulah as a ball breaker and Robert Ryan, in different words, agrees: "John Emery was a competent but not exciting actor. He was a wonderfully kind and nice man.

I never understood how an essentially gentle man like him could get mixed up with a dreadnought like Tallulah."

On first acquaintance, John Emery didn't impress Mrs. Alice Roosevelt Longworth, daughter of President Theodore Roosevelt, famed for her put-downs of the pompous and her pain-provoking wit. Having known Tallulah as a teenager, Mrs. Longworth was curious to meet the man she'd married. But it was a disappointment for her. "John Emery was dreadfully unattractive," she says. "It was the time when John Barrymore's looks were considered enormously desirable, I gather—and he was a sort of third print Jack Barrymore to look at. He tried to talk in whatever was the current slang of the period. He was straight through and through, a second-rater, to my way of thinking. I knew and liked Jack Barrymore and I was very fond of his sister, Ethel. Jack was a show-off, you know, but he had quality. And Emery, I shouldn't think had any quality."

Mrs. Longworth must have caught Emery at an off moment, because several women of distinction found Emery to be a charming, thoughtful, and witty man and not only Burgess Meredith and Robert Ryan were fond of him.

Orson Welles says: "Emery was a darling, sweet fellow. He was a wild man, a sort of road-company Jack Barrymore, who was a great love of Tallulah's. And that's what she saw in him. Emery was very dominant at all moments except maybe in public where he felt like he was nobody, because she was such a big star."

When Tallulah and John Emery had satisfied the reporters' curiosity about their marriage they buckled down to learning their parts for *Antony and Cleopatra*. It was Tallulah's first attempt at Shakespeare. She was to be Cleopatra; Conway Tearle, Antony; and John Emery was cast as Octavius Caesar. This enterprise seemed to Tallulah to be the possible start of a wonderful partnership. "Tallulah Bankhead and John Emery in *The Taming of the Shrew*." "Tallulah Bankhead and John Emery in *The Merchant of Venice*." The list could be almost endless: the world's immortal plays. She could redeem herself for all the years of inconsequential little plays and films, and have the man she loved on stage with her, working together at rehearsals, waiting eagerly for the notices afterward and celebrating their triumphs.

Ten weeks after her marriage Tallulah opened in *Antony and Cleopatra*. Next morning, Armistice Day, 1937, Tallulah and Emery read the notices. The critics had a playful time searching for funny ways to say she stank. She was called "a serpent of the Suwannee, the Queen of the Nil, not more dangerous than a garter snake." The hisses were unanimous. That morning Emery found he needed a second Planter's Punch for breakfast.

"When Tallulah appeared as Cleopatra," says her friend, theatrical attorney Arnold Weissberger, "it was the time that Orson Welles had just opened in *Julius Caesar,* at the Mercury Theatre. Orson's production was an enormous success. It was done on a bare stage and the theatre wall was the background. As soon as Tallulah's play closed, which I'm afraid was the following Saturday (after five performances), she went to see *Caesar* and was very impressed by it. Orson was a great friend of hers and she went backstage to see him and said: 'Darling, how much did this production cost?' And Orson said: 'Eight thousand dollars.' Tallulah said: 'Eight thousand dollars! That's less than one of my fucking breastplates!' "

That year, English playwright Terence Rattigan, in town to launch his *French Without Tears* on Broadway, got his first glimpse of Tallulah at one of her parties. The games had started when he arrived. The idea was to act out play titles by using mime. "In one room a girl had put up an umbrella and everybody guessed *Rain*. In another room Tallulah was still going on acting Sadie Thompson for hours and nobody guessed it. They were guessing *Jezebel* and I don't know what. And she got very angry."

That memory stayed with Rattigan and, when he wrote the

script of *Goodbye Mr. Chips* for the movie musical version thirty years later, he included a scene in which Sian Phillips gives a not heavily disguised imitation of Tallulah playing the acting game in which she had to do "the part is greater than the whole."

Rattigan's play opened in New York with Frank Lawton and Penelope Dudley Ward, and Tallulah attended the first night. Rattigan was afraid that Tallulah and his mother, a little old-fashioned English lady, would collide during the interval and that his mother would be startled by Tallulah's free speech. At the first curtain as Tallulah was weaving her way toward Rattigan and his mother was sticking close to his side, Rattigan managed to get a quick word to Tallulah to be on her guard. Tallulah could be marvelous with little old ladies, and for the ten-minute interval she was the epitome of the congressman's charming daughter from Alabama. And then, just as they were going back to their seats, Tallulah said, right in his mother's ear: "There you are darling, I didn't say 'fuck' once."

Despite that, Rattigan remembers her as generous and sweet to strangers. "Most people thought her outspokenness was a pose," he says. "I thought it was absolutely genuine."

Tallulah and Emery spent a lean Christmas in 1937. Both were out of work. Then they were invited to a party at "21" on New Year's Eve. It was a chance to have fun, to show their faces and show too that *Cleopatra* was only a technical knock-out.

The first person Tallulah saw there was Frank Hunter, wealthy tennis-playing partner of Bill Tilden. Tallulah had lent Hunter a thousand dollars during the depression in 1931, when his fortune had been wiped out, and hadn't seen him since. He was now agent for all drinks sold at "21" and doing well.

"Come here you bastard," Tallulah shouted across the room. "Where's that thousand bucks I loaned you? I could do with it right now."

"My God, Tallulah," he said, "don't tell me I never paid it." And he handed her two five-hundred-dollar bills.

Whether in order to stick the pace, or through osmosis, Emery began to booze his way through the nightly parties where Tallulah was making more impact than on the stage. Underneath the Emerys' thirteenth-floor apartment in the Elysee Hotel, Marc Connelly and his wife often woke in perfect unison at three in the morning. "What the hell is that noise?" Connelly mumbled. "It sounds like another heavy safe being dragged across the room," said his wife. "What can they be doing up there?"

Joan Crawford laughed when told of this: "About three in the morning is when the parties started," she explained. "Every night that Douglas Fairbanks and I went to the theatre, we'd always end up at Tallulah's. We'd arrive about three and leave about seven in the morning. And they were always noisy parties."

In those early months of their marriage Tallulah clung to Emery as if she were afraid he'd make a break for it. Tamara Geva noticed this when they came to a party in her apartment on the fifth floor of the Elysee Hotel. Ironically, with all of New York to choose from, Tallulah and Tamara, instinctive enemies, wound up in the same hotel. "They came down together," says Tamara, "and I have never seen a woman holding onto a man like that—like a leech. And all night they were making telephone calls to Hollywood. Just a short while before, John Emery had made a terrific hit in a picture called *The Road Back*."

But the excitement faded. John Emery was not going to be another John Barrymore. Not even a Lionel. His film career would be limited to supporting roles in mostly forgotten movies.

People who loved Tallulah could forgive her almost anything—in fact they applauded her most outrageous behavior. Vincent Price was one of those. As a junior at Yale he had a crush on her and on a handful of other actresses. In the spirit of the times he sent telegrams to all of them to be his guest at a football game. Tallulah was the only one who replied. She couldn't come but she answered. The fact left a warm glow in Price which burst into flame one evening in 1938. Vincent Price had become an actor and was in his dressing room at Westport making up for a play in which he appeared with Anna May Wong. There was a knock on the door and Tallulah came in. It was a basement dressing room with dirt floors, more appropriate for the set of *Tobacco Road*. Price was bowled over by her being there and then, after a while, "she was sitting on my washbasin," says Price, "and suddenly I realized that she was taking a leak. You know, if she hadn't been, I'd have been terribly disappointed. Because that was part of the Tallulah legend."

Tallulah was a ravishing beauty. Everybody says so. But Price saw that it wasn't a simple matter of flesh and bone. "She had that magnificent beauty that is ugly in a funny way. Judith Anderson and Laurette Taylor had it too. They came off as being the most beautiful women in the world through an illumination of their own personality. I've seen Tallulah look absolutely dreadful, then take a shot of ammonia and Coca Cola and turn into a beauty."

Vincent Price became a close friend of both Tallulah and Emery and thought theirs was a marvelous marriage. He considered John Emery one of the nicest men that ever lived, just the kind of man Tallulah needed, because he had a marvelous sense of humor and a great spirit of fun.

But other friends saw the marriage as a short course in guerrilla warfare, with Emery the recruit and Tallulah the marine sergeant. At times Tallulah's home life was like a hysterical dress rehearsal for a French farce, with overtones of Noel Coward and undercurrents of Tennessee Williams. Burgess Meredith says: "It was a very stormy marriage. Emery was a whipped boy and he was lashed by her tongue and probably physically by flying objects." Orson Welles disagrees: "Emery kept belting Tallulah and she loved it. He could be pretty rough. I know some people say that she hit him, but it's like a lot of those happy marriages, there are two sides to it."

Tallulah the ball breaker had moments when she'd have driven a bishop to blasphemy, and it isn't surprising that Emery sometimes let rip. Nothing Tallulah did was ever half-hearted: a punch and an embrace were equally ferocious. "When we first kissed," said Emery, "she damn near knocked my tonsils down my throat!" And Vincent Price remembered the bruise still, when she spotted him in a New York bar one night and suddenly tackled him and threw him to the floor. That was just a Tallulah "hello!"

But strangely, although she often came on like a football team, she hated to be touched, even by her friends and especially by surprise. And the echo of her scream, "Don't touch me!" rings in many a head. This almost terror of contact is one of the extreme contradictions in her personality, because, on the other hand, she was sexually amoral, both sensuous and sensual. None of her friends' explanations— running from "She had fragile bones and they'd often been broken," to: "It was the only way she could protect herself from the crowds who wanted to maul a famous star"— completely explains her reaction. It may have reflected another imperious facet of her personality that, like a tyrannical ruler, she could touch but no one was allowed to touch her. But unquestionably this dread of being touched was genuine.

The newspaper headlines were becoming more arresting than even the most provocative Broadway dialogue. If there was any light on the horizon, its batteries needed recharging. In Spain people were killing each other, and reporter Ernest Hemingway spoke of "the carnival of treachery on both sides." Hitler had occupied Austria and was shaping up for a try at surpassing Napoleon and Genghis Khan. He was threatening the lives of Jews in Nazi-occupied territory and among them were relatives of stage director Otto Preminger.

Tallulah knew Preminger slightly and heard that he was

desperate. His father, his brother, and his brother's family were trapped in Austria. Preminger had tried in vain to get them out to safety. He spent the entire night of March 11, 1938, phoning from his New York home to Vienna, trying to reach friends who might help, but no one was able to offer any hope. He turned to the friends he had made in America. He had been in the country only three years and his circle of close friends was small. They told him that it was impossible to get his relatives into the United States because the quota for Austrians was filled. He was in a panic. He didn't know what to do or to whom to turn.

And then his phone rang. It was Tallulah.

"She told me to go to Washington to meet her father and uncle," recalls Preminger. "One was in the Senate and the other in the House of Representatives. Without my knowledge she had appealed to them. There was only one possibility to get my relatives into America—by bringing in a special Bill. And they brought this Bill into Congress and it became a law. And that is how she helped to get my family in. Naturally what she did made me forever very grateful, or committed, or bound, whatever you like to call it, to Tallulah. I'd probably have loved her anyway, because her personality appealed very much to me."

In the spring of 1938 Tallulah and Emery—the new husband-and-wife team—played in Somerset Maugham's stylish comedy *The Circle* for nine weeks. *New Yorker* critic Wolcott Gibbs described Tallulah as "a brilliant and turbulent actress." It was soothing to the spirit, but Tallulah wanted something to pay for the groceries, especially when the nine weeks were over. Any money she made disappeared to pay debts. She had to keep working to feed her creditors. "I have been frequently racked with terror and despair, often hungry, often broke," she once admitted. Now she was broke again. She and Emery took the next offer and toured in *I Am Different,* which opened in Chicago in August and expired in Washington a few days after Thanksgiving.

VIII

Triumph

1939–1940 Lillian Hellman wrote a drama about a Southern family tied up in knots with bitterness and hatred, and was searching for an actress to play the biggest bitch of them all, Regina Giddens.

"Tallulah Bankhead?" suggested producer Herman Shumlin.

"Too young," said Lillian Hellman. "Regina has a teenage daughter."

"Tallulah's almost thirty-seven," Shumlin pointed out. "She could be the girl's mother. Let's try her."

"All right," said Hellman. "Let's. She's a damned good actress."

So Tallulah got the call. When she read the as yet untitled play, she saw Regina as a totally unsympathetic character: "a rapacious bitch, cruel and callous, a frightened opportunist who stopped at nothing to further her prestige and fortune." Tallulah was a bad judge of plays, but she realized that the part of Regina, although it was short, had guts. By comparison, the odious Regina Giddens made Goneril and Regan seem like sedate members of the D.A.R.

Tallulah said yes. She'd given audiences enough chances to giggle at and with her. Now she'd make them hold their breath.

Lillian Hellman's friend Dorothy Parker watched rehearsals. On the second day Parker suggested a title for the play, from the Song of Songs: "Take us the foxes, that spoil the vines. For our vines have tender grapes."

So it became *The Little Foxes,* with Tallulah Bankhead as Regina Giddens.

Shumlin was a good, driving director, and Tallulah worked hard to please him. He persuaded her that a "Tallulah" performance would wreck the play, so she made an effort to submerge her personality and project another.

The Little Foxes opened on January 30, 1939, the day before Tallulah's thirty-seventh birthday. Her performance was uncanny. For the first time on any stage, Tallulah enthralled, not only her fans, but the most discriminating of critics and colleagues. She was the embodiment of an evil, grasping monster. And even when she wasn't on stage, her invisible presence haunted every scene. The reaction was overwhelming. Tallulah Bankhead became a name that took its place among stage immortals, after almost twenty-two years of mostly messing around.

All who saw her were astonished.

Says Dore Schary, playwright and movie mogul: "Tallulah was absolutely wonderful in *Little Foxes.*"

Lee Strasberg, director and leading light of Method acting, agrees: "The earthiness of the character as she played it was extraordinary."

A representative of the younger school of directors, Arthur Penn, called her: "Quite compelling and rather majestic and stately."

Otto Preminger described her as "tremendous," and Lillian Hellman says: "It's the best part she ever had."

Joan Crawford went to see the play four times and thought Tallulah was "absolutely, sensationally beautiful and strong. I can't tell you how great she was." Another actor, Robert Ryan, rated it one of the greatest things he ever saw and said:

"Tallulah was extraordinarily beautiful and yet she conveyed that sinister quality marvelously, and another quality: of being a lady." Novelist Norman Mailer considers it "one of the two best performances I've ever seen on the stage. The other was Laurette Taylor in *The Glass Menagerie.*"

And even her rival Tamara Geva says of Tallulah as Regina: "She was superb."

There was something almost supernatural about Tallulah's appearance in the play. Although a small woman, she seemed to dominate the other players not only by the impact of her personality but as though she had grown tall for the part.

Years later she explained her secret to a friend, Gene Coffin.

He said to her: "When I was about seventeen my mother and I saw you in *The Little Foxes* and you seemed so tall. And then when I first met you at the Hotel Elysee I was surprised to find you were only about five feet."

Tallulah raised her shoulders as only she could do and said: "You son-of-a-bitch: I THINK tall. You know, backstage just before the curtain goes up and everybody's pacing back and forth and saying their first line over and over? Well, darling, I know my first line. And I'm saying: 'Tallulah you're tall. Tallulah you're tall.' And when I walk out I AM tall."

Only a few days after Tallulah opened on Broadway in *The Little Foxes,* John Emery opened in Boston in an amalgam of Shakespeare plays called *Five Kings.* Orson Welles had done the editing and cast himself as Falstaff. Emery was Hotspur. And here was his chance to show what he could really do with a classical role. But the Theatre Guild would finance the play only as far as Philadelphia. There was no money to bring it in to Broadway. Orson Welles and Emery got together. They needed twenty-five thousand dollars in a hurry. Who could raise that kind of money? They looked at each other and nodded and that night they were in New York with Tallulah, pacing the floor of the Elysee Hotel apartment, name-dropping with a purpose.

Tallulah was up to her eyebrows in debt or she would have gladly given it.

"Now who in the hell can we find in New York," asked Tallulah, "who not only has twenty-five thousand dollars handy but is also awake?"

While Welles and Emery thought, she dialed the phone.

At two-thirty a.m. in the apartment below them Marc Connelly and his wife were woken by the phone. "It's Tallulah," Connelly whispered to his wife. "Some problem. They want my advice." He dressed and went to the apartment overhead.

Connelly expected to have at least to referee a marital fight.

But to his relief there appeared to be complete amiability between Tallulah and Emery. He glanced at a young man in his twenties slumped in a corner chair and they nodded at each other.

Tallulah said: "Darling, you've got to help us. This is Orson Welles . . ." the young man nodded again ". . . and he's in an awful jam. We've got to see what we can do about it." Connelly quickly got the picture and then there were four of them puzzling over what millionaires they knew with insomnia.

"The only person I can think of who might have twenty-five thousand dollars and still be awake is Sherman Billingsley, who runs the Stork Club," said Connelly.

"Marvelous idea, darling," Tallulah said, sprinting to the phone. "Oh, Sherman darling, get over here quickly. It's something very, very important."

Billingsley showed up soon afterward with a bottle of champagne. As Tallulah opened it she explained the problem. "It's a wonderful, wonderful production. Orson and John are simply marvelous in it and it'll be a tragedy if it has to close out of town just because of a measly twenty-five thousand dollars darling."

Tallulah's enthusiasm at past three in the morning was

extraordinary: it might have been noon on a very happy spring morning.

But when Billingsley realized they were putting the squeeze on him he went into shock.

Welles said: "To insure you against loss, I promise to turn over my father's estate to you, as soon as it's settled. He died recently."

Billingsley began to regain his color. "How much would that amount to?"

"About eighty thousand dollars."

Tallulah poured another round of champagne. Billingsley furrowed his brow. Tallulah predicted the glory and fortune that would be Billingsley's if he'd just part with a little of his money for a few weeks. She damn near promised him immortality if he said yes. But Billingsley was more the hardheaded businessman than a patron of the arts and there was just too much risk involved. He said no.

If 1939 had been a time of peace the run of *Little Foxes* might have been peaceful too, but the Civil War in Spain and the Russian invasion of Finland spilled over into the theatre. Tallulah and Lillian Hellman were more or less on opposite sides.

Says Tallulah in her autobiography: "I thought the Russian invasion (of Finland) on November 30, 1939, the brutal act of a bully. The people of the theatre, their emotions inflamed by this wanton assault on a small and peaceful neighbour, were quick to volunteer aid for the victim. I protested at the top of my lungs. Miss Hellman and Shumlin thought otherwise. Challenged, Miss Hellman said: 'I don't believe in that fine, lovable little Republic of Finland that everybody gets so weepy about. I've been there and it looks like a pro-Nazi little republic to me.' Shumlin concurred. Eager to do my bit I announced that I would give a benefit performance of *The Little Foxes,* the entire receipts to be used for Finnish relief. Miss Hellman and Mr. Shumlin promptly vetoed this proposal. As author and producer of the play there was no appeal from their decision. I raged with anger. I expressed my scorn for their attitude in no uncertain terms. Our entente cordiale was scuttled forthwith, our conversation reduced to nods."

Says Lillian Hellman: "She'd also met the Finnish ambassador. She thought he was charming. She sat next to him at lunch and saw him a couple of times. It was his job to get support for the Finns during the Finnish-Russian war. Nobody could blame him."

Tallulah and Lillian Hellman later burst into print, sniping at one another over the Spanish Civil War. Although by then the Spanish War was over, theirs wasn't. Miss Hellman felt that Tallulah was indulging in Red-baiting, and Tallulah was incensed that her sympathies for refugees and underdogs—whatever their politics—could be doubted. "She was in many ways very good-hearted," says Miss Hellman. "People can have many sides. And they don't intellectually always fit." She chuckles.

The Little Foxes lasted a year on Broadway. Tallulah agreed to join the road tour starting in September, so she was free for the summer of 1940. But instead of taking a rest she chose to tour the summer theatres in *The Second Mrs. Tanqueray* by Pinero.

She was sitting in the dressing room of her Dennis, Cape Cod, dressing room when a young man knocked on the door. "Come in darling." It was Tennessee Williams, a self-mocking, insecure twenty-nine-year-old, out of breath, having bicycled forty miles to see her. He wanted to know if Tallulah would play in his *Battle of Angels*. He had written the part of Myra Torrance for her.

"No, I'm not going to do it," Tallulah said. "It's an impossible play. Quite dreadful. You can't mix sex and religion. It just doesn't work. You've written a dirty play and I wouldn't touch it."

She demolished Williams, then, taking pity on the dejected wreck, tried to revive him.

"But you write very well, darling. You very definitely have talent. And when you're not being filthy, there's quite a lot of poetry there. Have a drink."

Williams was moved by her effort to console and encourage him and warmed by the drink, and before he had emptied the glass he was determined to tackle her again—maybe with his next play.

He had seen Tallulah in many films before he first met her. On the screen he found her startling and astonishing—and he found her no less so in the flesh.

It was raining heavily and he faced a 40-mile ride back on his bicycle. "Just a minute, darling," Tallulah called, and she persuaded her friend and manager, Stephan Cole, to put Williams' bicycle in the trunk of his car and drive him home.

Miriam Hopkins played the part of Myra Torrance in *Battle of Angels* a few months later. It ran for a week.

By that time Tallulah was touring in *The Little Foxes* and when it reached St. Louis, Tennessee Williams again tapped at her dressing-room door. "Come in. Oh, it's you darling. Well I'm luckier than Miriam Hopkins who lost her mind and actually appeared in that abominable 'Battle of Something' you had the impertinence to write for me! Have a drink. What are you writing now?"

A hint of what they were to mean to each other is given by Peter Pell, a friend of both: "The relationship between Tallulah and Tennessee was one of the most incredible—two titans—one of the greatest actresses of our time encountering one of the greatest authors. So much of Tennessee's thinking is geared to a Tallulah-type performance. His fixation with a certain type of woman is the Tallulah kind of woman. Tallulah and Tennessee had a deep rapport, they had an understanding that was beyond all the fights and articles in *The New York Times,* and opening night, or good performances, or bad performances."

They also shared an appetite for booze and barbiturates.

And the two ostensibly belonged to the same church, which prompted Tennessee to say at one party: "Tallulah, you and I are the only two constantly high High Episcopalians I know."

Her father had warned her against the dangers of drinking; in fact, one of his conditions for allowing her to be an actress had been that she wouldn't drink. She hadn't been able to live up to his expectations. But where her father had failed to influence her, World War II succeeded. She had been following with passionate concern the trials of the British in their war with Hitler's Germany since September 3, 1939. When it seemed that the British army would be trapped and destroyed at Dunkirk, *The Little Foxes* had reached Chicago.

There, in her Ambassador Hotel bedroom, she fell to her knees and prayed for a miracle.

Then she drank three tall glasses of a mixture of champagne, gin, and brandy.

Before blacking out she announced: "I'm on the wagon. I'm staying on the wagon until the British are back in Dunkirk!"

Tragedy

1940 Tallulah was about to go on at the Mc-Carter Theatre in Princeton, on September 15, 1940, when her Uncle John phoned from Washington to tell her that her father was dying.

She decided to play that night, convinced he would have wanted it. After the performance the express train to Washington made a special stop at Princeton to pick her up. She arrived at Baltimore at three in the morning, and her family told her that her father had died in the night after a series of heart attacks.

Politicians of all persuasions lined up to express their grief, and Secretary of State Cordell Hull, tears on his cheeks, said: "I loved him so."

After the funeral Tallulah's friend, Dola Cavendish, said to her: "You need a drink. At a time like this you should not hold yourself to your vow. Circumstances alter things."

But Tallulah refused: "I'm not going to break it, darling. Of all times, not now!"

She had once described her father as a fusion of "Santa Claus, Galahad, d'Artagnan, and Demosthenes." He had been an unfailing source of love, pride, and encouragement. In her autobiography she wrote: "He was something more than a gentleman. He was a MAN. His place will never be filled in my heart or in my mind."

There is no doubt he was one of the greatest loves of her

life. Another, Napier Alington, a man she loved perhaps only
less than her father, was killed in action as a fighter pilot
during the Battle of Britain.

Tallulah doesn't mention Napier's death in her autobiography. But his friend Cecil Beaton, who attended his funeral,
found the same rare, elusive quality in the man that both
attracted and infuriated Tallulah. Beaton writes in his diary
that a portrait of him "conveys Napier's spirit. It is a portrait
to inspire a novel—a portrait of someone who spells a distinct
mystery. Napier died at forty-three, a boy. A tired boy in appearance, but essentially young, with the willowy figure of a
bantam-weight champion, a neat head covered with a cap of
silken hair, pale, far-seeing eyes and full Negroid lips. He
made life seem almost bearable to a large number of people,
many of whom will be hard put to continue without him."

During her greatest triumph in America Tallulah lost the
two men who meant most to her. At times of personal tragedy
some actors find consolation in the demands of their work, the
concentration needed to repeat the same role with renewed
zest for every performance. Tallulah was not of that breed.

In a way the theatre demands the impossible: it encourages
unique personalities and then it requires them to give rubber-
stamp performances. Some take drink or drugs to provide the
nightly spark. Others practice auto-suggestion and try to kid
themselves that each performance is a first. The dreamers
imagine a big movie producer is out front for every show.
Quite a few tell themselves that although their words and
moves are the same, each audience is different. But only a
brainwashed actor could convince himself that his two-hun-
dredth rendering of "To be or not to be" is a suicidal thought
that had just occurred to him. And Tallulah was not inclined
to practice that kind of self-delusion.

If things onstage were tedious by repetition, offstage Tallulah searched for the unexpected like a child let loose in a toy
shop. Bored with the same faces at nightclubs, she frequented
night court to see how the other half tried to live. She con-

tinued to indulge in cocaine. At one shindig in her apartment during this period, Melvyn Douglas caught her putting nose drops in her nose.

"What have you got there, Tallulah?" he asked.

"Cocaine, darling."

"Oh, sure," he scoffed. "Give me some. My nose is stuffed."

It cleared his nose and passages he didn't even know he had. Other guests wondered why he suddenly acquired a most peculiar glazed expression.

Tallulah refused all offers of bourbon, brandy, gin, and vodka with an expression that would have suited Joan of Arc on hearing her voices.

"No, darling, I've made a vow not to touch a drop of drink until the British win the war—and I'm sticking to it. A Bankhead never breaks a promise."

And with that she would raise a glassful of spirits of ammonia—which looked just like water—and gulp enough down to rot the insides of a boiler.

When someone challenged her she said: "Darling, it's not a drink. Southern ladies often take a few drops of it at funerals. It's medicine. I ought to know what drink is. When did you last hear anyone order a round of spirits of ammonia?"

But the effect on Tallulah was indistinguishable from bourbon. A few glasses and she wanted to do something to shock.

In those days anyone who made it big on Broadway discovered that Tallulah went with the territory. Danny Kaye and his lyric-writer wife Sylvia Fine were part of the whirl and then the whirlwind.

"Have you seen me in *Little Foxes*, darling?" Tallulah asked Sylvia. "You haven't? I'm at Newark next week. You must see me there."

Sylvia went and joined the ranks of the astonished and worshipful and followed Tallulah around like a puppy. Tallulah took Sylvia to the Cub Room of the Stork Club and to night court and to parties, and Danny Kaye eagerly joined them whenever he could get away from the show he was starring in with Clifton Webb.

Then Tallulah started to target in on Sylvia's mother.

"She specialized in shocking my mother," says Sylvia. "She used to stand on her head and say: 'You see, I have no underwear on,' no matter WHO was in the room—if my mother was there. Mother used to turn absolutely white and was afraid to react too much because she thought I wouldn't want her to. And Tallulah just kept doing it. And one night Tallulah got under the bed and came out dressed in a sheet, and making terrible noises, hoping that my mother would faint. Once mother reacted very satisfactorily: she turned very pale and started to shake. I guess mother thought it was part of my wild Broadway life.

"She really was very hard to be with after a while because she kept shocking people and saying dreadful things. It got to be embarrassing and so we had a short-lived friendship. Whatever she thought would get under somebody's skin, she would do. It seemed sort of pranky at first, but then when she continued to do the same thing to shock new people, I was a very poor audience for it.

"Finally I said: 'It's terribly distasteful.'

"And she said: 'You come from Brooklyn. How would you know?'

"She would dig out whatever she thought would draw blood. I thought that sometimes her behavior was an attention-getting device, a substitute for how things had been in the early part of her career when she was so successful.

"Clifton Webb was a great friend of hers and when we had that fight and I said to him I'd never, never have her in my house again, he said: 'You must be more tolerant of Tallulah. That's just her way.' And I said: 'I don't like her way, Clifton.' And he said: 'You must be more forgiving.' And I said, 'I would be if she had her human moments, but if she has them, they're not apparent. She has them in private.'

"She would be absolutely wonderful with poor people in

low-income brackets, people who were destitute, people who were obviously in need of help. But with her peers she was impossible. She was an odd one."

After a year on Broadway and the best part of a year on tour, Regina began to fade and Tallulah to intrude. Her performance lost its cutting edges, as she entertained herself as well as the audience.

Playwright-critic George Oppenheimer heard that "Tallulah was behaving abominably, pulling up her skirts, putting in lines, saying 'damn' and 'hell,' which in those days were considered a little shocking. I think she was fed up with the part and was probably tight."

Lillian Hellman, staying in California, hadn't seen the play for some time. When she caught up with it she was incensed. "It was just an unspeakable performance. Tallulah was throwing everybody else and it looked like a performance of animals. We didn't talk by this time and her maid came to see me afterward and said: 'Miss Bankhead took a purgative last night and doesn't feel well.' And I said: 'Yes, tell her it's onstage.' And I called up Herman Shumlin and said it was an unspeakable performance and we decided not to extend the run of the show."

Probably just what Tallulah wanted.

Divorce for Love

1940–1941 John Emery barely survived his marriage to Tallulah. She had not destroyed his spirit, but she had given him a hell of a jolt. One evening he telephoned their mutual friend Burgess Meredith to give him the news: "I'm leaving Tallulah."

Burgess Meredith recalls: "I was astonished that John seemed to be rather broken by it; because I don't know how anybody could have taken what he took. I didn't have much to say to him except, 'I don't know how you can remain in love,' because he still seemed to be in love with her. I said to him: 'I can imagine that as a whirl—marriage to Tallulah—but I'm sorry I didn't really consider it anything that was going to change her.'

"I have no idea why the marriage occurred. It was one of those things that you almost knew from the beginning was doomed."

Now the situation took a turn that you'd expect in a Noel Coward play. John Emery left Tallulah and went to live with Tallulah's bête noire—Tamara Geva, the woman Tallulah had hated on first sight, the woman who had watched Tallulah clutching Emery when first married, as if afraid someone would snatch him from her. And now . . . Too farfetched for Coward. Make it real life.

When the news reached the outside world that Emery had

left Tallulah for Tamara, one of Tallulah's friends said: "Tallulah tried to marry a copy of John Barrymore when she married Emery and it was a great ego-buster for Emery when she found he wasn't. So he went out and got a copy of Tallulah—Tamara Geva."

But in the early days of their break-up, Tallulah didn't know that there was another woman in Emery's life, least of all THAT woman. Emery asked for a divorce and Tallulah agreed.

She was in Reno going through the motions when she heard of the new setup.

Tamara Geva recalls: "John and I were 'living in sin' waiting for Tallulah to give him a divorce. The telephone rang one morning and it was George Cukor, the director, who said: 'John, will you come for lunch? I've got to talk to you.' So John went to his place and I stayed home. John rang me later to say: 'What do you suppose? I walked into the room at Cukor's place and there was Tallulah with four or five other people and she started yelling at me: "NOBODY in the world is going to do that to me! No woman is going to step on my toes! If you don't give me your word as a gentleman and get Geva to agree, that you won't get married for a year after the divorce, I'm going right back to New York and I'll NEVER give you a divorce." ' So John said: 'What do I do?' And I said: 'Tell her okay. If our relationship isn't worth a year, it isn't worth a cent.' " So Emery agreed to Tallulah's terms for a divorce.

It isn't surprising that those at the center of a storm view things differently fom those on the outskirts. Cukor remembers the occasion when he called Emery to lunch to meet Tallulah and discuss their divorce, and Cukor's response to Tamara Geva's version is: "Bullshit! Tallulah and John Emery were on very friendly terms even then."

Tamara Geva believes that "Tallulah nearly destroyed John and the fact that he never got where he should as an actor was partly her fault. Before he married her he was going great guns. He had everything to become a star: he was handsome, he had talent, a magnificent voice, he was marvelous in comedy, in Shakespeare he was unbeatable."

In the after-shock of marriage to Tallulah, something happened. Emery floundered about like a man up from the count.

Whenever there was something that would bring him recognition as an actor, he was so accident-prone at that moment that he always did something to himself. The first night of *Angel Street* he hurt his knee. He always got hoarse just as he was about to go on. He broke his ankle when he did *Royal Family* as he was walking down the stairs.

Tamara Geva said to him one day: "You've got to get rid of this thing. This is not an accident anymore, John. You're bringing it on yourself. Unless you go to a psychiatrist and talk this out, I'm leaving you."

He did go to a psychiatrist, who helped him a great deal. After that he played *Coriolanus* with Robert Ryan, and there was something of the old Emery on stage.

Still Tallulah's influence lingered. Her ability to see ghosts rubbed off on him. He awoke one morning to see a woman sitting at the side of his bed. He sat up, lit a cigarette, and pinched himself. She was still there, looking like the British Queen Alexandra and wearing a red dress. He smoked that cigarette and lit another. After a while the apparition got up, walked away, and vanished. Not wanting to seem out of his mind, it was three days before he told Tamara about it and she recognized the woman as someone she'd known in her young days.

John Emery and Tamara Geva were eventually divorced (after almost twenty years of marriage), and Emery was going to marry Joan Bennett, but he died on November 16, 1964. Joan Bennett says: "John never had a bad word to say about Tallulah. They were friends until the end."

Why did Tallulah marry Emery? "Because I loved him," she told a friend. And the divorce? "Because I loved him."

XI

Tallulah Buys
a Playmate

1941 On June 13, 1941, Tallulah got her divorce on the grounds of mental cruelty.

Tallulah lost a husband in Reno and gained a lion. She fell in love with the eight-day-old creature, all eyes and paws, and paid the circus one hundred dollars for him. At least she wouldn't return to her old haunts empty-handed. She named him Winston—after her hero—and bottle-fed him.

Back at her New York hotel she carried Winston past the sign NO PETS with her usual panache and slammed the door on her past.

Late that summer she began a tour of *Her Cardboard Lover*, a frothy comedy she'd starred in with Leslie Howard in England. She played the opening night at Cedarhurst, Long Island, in a rage. The first act had sagged because the young man playing the croupier had been unsure of himself and the play never picked up.

Back at her hotel she paced the floor while Winston tried to nip her heels. Another actor had to replace the croupier, she decided. But where the hell do you get an actor at two-thirty in the morning? She phoned around a few nightclubs. No luck. Then she remembered her friend Lyman Brown, an agent, who used to hang around all-night Broadway cafes. She called a few cafes on the off chance. And then he was on the line.

"It was terrible, terrible, darling. I've NEVER been so angry. It was a fucking disaster in fact. I need another young man to play the croupier, tomorrow. No, not tomorrow goddamit, tonight. You must find me someone. I know you can do it. Now don't let me down, will you darling?" And she hung up.

Brown went back to the teenage young man he'd been drinking coffee with.

"It was Tallulah Bankhead," Brown said to Ricardo Montalban. "And she's madder than a hornet. I don't know what to expect but you come with me."

Tallulah opened the door to them and the first thing they saw was the Lion.

"Winston won't hurt you," she reassured them. "He's just been fed. I've told you about my fix, Lyman, what are you going to do about it?" She waved them to seats.

The lion started to lick Montalban's shoes, and then to bite them.

"Ignore him, darling: he's only playing," Tallulah ordered.

"Well, what about Ricardo here?" Brown said.

"What have you done, darling?"

"Nothing professionally, yet."

"But he's very promising," Brown said.

"Well, as long as you don't forget your lines," Tallulah warned, handing the script to Montalban. "It has to go very fast. If it drags the whole play goes down with it."

Tallulah pulled Winston off Montalban and wished him and Brown good morning.

Montalban had no rehearsals. When he arrived ahead of time, the stage manager said: "I'll push you each time you have to go on. And when you make your first entrance, I'll call out 'George' and that's your cue to turn around. Don't worry about it."

When a very worried Montalban reached the dressing

room, he had a tussle with the actor he was to replace. The man hadn't been told he was fired and was dressed, ready to go on. He eventually surrendered his body-warmed clothes.

Montalban stood in the wings, the stage manager suddenly pushed him and said in a hoarse whisper "NOW!" and Montalban was onstage. Then he heard "George!" and turned around to meet the gaze of Tallulah Bankhead, standing in the wings.

She was looking open-mouthed with expectations as if to say: "Now what can this Montalban do? Is he going to ruin the play, too?"

And staring back at Tallulah, Montalban went blank.

It was only for a fraction of a second. The lines he'd repeated a thousand times came back to him. He said them with extra speed to make up for lost time. And he got laughs where they were intended. When he made his first exit soon after, Tallulah was waiting. She hugged him and said: "Marvelous darling. It was the way they'd play it in France. It was done with dignity. You'll be with us for the rest of the tour!"

Montalban had made it. He was one of those who saw only the sweet side of Tallulah. He'd heard many of the wild stories about her but never saw any of them confirmed. She obviously took him for what he was, a rather innocent young man who admired her extravagantly. The greatest shock he ever got from working with Tallulah was to have her lion treat him as if he were a prospective snack.

Tallulah felt guilty about Winston. She didn't think it fair to coop him up in the apartment day and night. So she took him with her to the theatre and he made his stage debut at the Westport Playhouse.

The play was now zinging along at the speed she wanted. At the first-night curtain call Tallulah faced the audience alone in an alluring negligee. The audience called for more. So she scooped up Winston from her dressing room and took him on for the second curtain call. The applause doubled.

For curtain call three she had him on her shoulder. The applause tripled. Curtain call four: under her arm. The calls ended when she ran out of ideas for new tableaux.

Winston grew during the tour until toward the end he was over thirty pounds and almost as large as a St. Bernard, and Tallulah had to quit carrying him. Instead she led him on a leash for the curtain calls.

Producer Cheryl Crawford also had a traumatic encounter with Winston, when Tallulah played at Maplewood, New Jersey. "All the companies who played [there] were well behaved, although Tallulah Bankhead tried some mischief," she writes in her autobiography.* "She invited me to drive back to New York in her car one evening. She put me in the back seat. I didn't know she had also put her lion cub there.

" 'Darling,' she called back as we drove, 'you don't mind sitting there with the cat, do you?'

"Cat! The cub had already begun to prowl behind my head with a low, hungry growl.

" 'Why should I? Is he edible?'

"She laughed. I didn't.

"She looked back several times saying, 'Everything all right, darling?'

" 'Of course,' I said each time with a rigor mortis grimace. In the dark she took it for a smile. I was sweating when I finally reached home in one piece, but I was damned if I would give her the satisfaction of my showing it.

"I never heard of anyone beating Tallulah to a punch line. Much has been written about her, but I remember one anecdote that has not been told. A young student at Yale was enamored of Tallulah, after seeing her performance many times and listening avidly to stories of her wild sexual activities. Eventually he found a friend who knew her and insisted on being taken backstage to meet her. 'By God,' he told his

* Cheryl Crawford, *One Naked Individual* (Indianapolis: Bobbs-Merrill, 1977.)

friend, 'I know how to shock her.' When they were introduced, he announced proudly, 'Guess what, Miss Bankhead, I am going to fuck you tonight.'

"Without a pause she volleyed back, 'And so you shall, you dear old-fashioned boy.' "

Back in New York there were more plays waiting for her to read. One from Lawrence Langner and Theresa Helburn of the Theatre Guild appealed to her, so she asked them tô come and talk about it.

They immediately saw the lion lying outside on a small balcony separated from them by French windows. And he immediately saw them.

"I love having Winston here," Tallulah said. "We understand one another. But the hotel people are so damned silly. They don't even like him traveling in the passenger elevator."

Tallulah broke off to go into her bedroom to get a manuscript.

Winston pushed open the windows and bounded into the room. He started to paw at Langner's legs. Theresa Helburn sat up straight and pulled her legs in. The noise attracted the lion, who was then intrigued by the glint of her spectacles. He left Langner and leaped into Helburn's lap.

Tallulah came in at that moment, saw her two horrified guests, grabbed Winston by the tail, dragged him slithering into her bedroom, and locked the door.

"Don't pay any attention to him," Tallulah said breezily as she straightened the shambles of tumbled chairs and tables. "He loves to do that to people. It's his way of having fun."

Winston's fun began to get a little more furious and after he'd bitten two reporters and nipped a howling hotel porter, Tallulah listened to the pleas and threats of the hotel manager and gave Winston to the Bronx Zoo.

XII

Clash by Night
and Day

1941 As Regina in *The Little Foxes* Tallulah
proved herself to American audiences, after
ten years of effort. She had given a flawless,
arresting performance, one that would be remembered as
great.

Fame was fine but life was lousy. Her father and her lover
were dead, her husband an ex, and her only close friend,
Estelle Winwood, was often away in plays or Hollywood films.

Tallulah filled the void with frenzy and her home with
friends, strangers, and enemies, subjecting them to endless entertainment in which she acted out glories and gaieties of the
past. Even with pills she had difficulty sleeping. The more she
needed it, the more sleep eluded her until bedtime was something to be dreaded, like a dangerous journey not to be endured alone, and she begged others to stay with her until she
was out.

She rarely woke before noon and then she glanced at scripts,
all of which seemed anemic imitations of *The Little Foxes*
or thin comedies with the characters created only to spout the
playwright's gags. She rejected them with a little qualm each
time, knowing her own judgment of plays was poor to terrible.
Then one arrived that seemed a wonderful challenge. In it
she would play a bored Staten Island housewife, a poor,

slovenly woman of Polish origin. It was called *Clash by Night* and was written by Clifford Odets, a Group Theatre product who wrote passionate, poetic, left-wing plays. The producer was Billy Rose, a five-foot showman who coveted and quarreled with tall blonde show girls and only saw eye-to-eye with them in bed. The cast included Lee J. Cobb and Joseph Schildkraut, two actors of consequence. It was a challenge just to stand on the same stage with them.

Rose took Tallulah across the Hudson River to Maplewood, New Jersey, to watch Robert Ryan in James Barrie's *A Kiss for Cinderella*. Luise Rainer (Mrs. Clifford Odets) was also in the play. Did Tallulah think Ryan right for the juvenile in *Clash by Night*? Tallulah thought he was a beautiful hunk of man and said yes.

The director of *Clash by Night,* Lee Strasberg, was a quiet-spoken man who believed in and practiced the Stanislavski method—that is, to encourage the actor to use any tools he can, mainly imagination, to believe himself to be the character he's playing. But Strasberg knew that Tallulah had her own technique of acting and didn't attempt to reeducate her.

Strasberg had seen and admired her in *The Little Foxes.* He wondered why she accepted the part in *Clash by Night.* He guessed that she hoped to make a tour de force out of it. In other performances he noticed she gave a comic overtone to everything she did—Regina was a magnificent exception—but he kept a fairly open mind and wondered how she would respond to the other actors.

At first rehearsals were uneventful enough to give a press agent heartburn. Robert Ryan's wife came to one of the rehearsals and was introduced to Tallulah. "Oh, you're Mrs. Ryan, huh?" said Tallulah. "Well I want to tell you something. If I was fifteen years younger I'd take him away from you."

Ryan and his wife chuckled. It was just a pleasant compliment and very mild considering Tallulah's reputation for le mot devastating.

Schildkraut didn't join the laughter. He was rehearsing in a fog, utterly lost by what he felt were Strasberg's well-meant but vague stage directions.

As rehearsals progressed, the fog cleared and the atmosphere became feverish. Tallulah hated almost everyone with the exception of Robert Ryan and Lee Strasberg.

Her biggest hate was for producer Billy Rose. He had reached Broadway via spectaculars with show girls as the chief attraction. Now he behaved as though he could produce the world, if someone else hadn't beaten him to it. Tallulah thought he knew nothing about the theatre and frequently told him so in four-, five-, and six-letter words. Rose considered Tallulah was box office, and tolerated her tantrums and derision for the sake of the property.

She treated Rose as if he were a pocket version of the devil. "You're not putting on a rodeo now, goddammit!" she roared at him.

Playwright Clifford Odets next tangled with Tallulah, and all five feet of her roared at him: "Take your glasses off! I can't hit you with your glasses on!" But that fight faded gradually into tolerance and even friendliness.

Not so with Lee J. Cobb or Joseph Schildkraut. Tallulah complained to friends that Cobb was picking his nose, mumbling, and scratching his ass during rehearsals. ("It was part of the character," says Strasberg. "I wish Tallulah had done more of it!")

And she just didn't like anything about Schildkraut, probably sensing rightly that the feeling was mutual.

But despite all the screaming and threats and shaping up for fights, no blood was spilled and Tallulah began to face the real fight of giving a performance to match the other giants on the stage. Cobb was obviously going to be magnificent, even though he swallowed every other word. And Schildkraut, still perplexed about exactly what Strasberg wanted, was shaping up for a performance that would bear comparison with Cobb's.

Tallulah knew her lines before anyone else, she turned up early and left later than any of the other performers. By putting herself into Herman Shumlin's hands she'd been a superb Regina. Now she wanted to do the same with Strasberg.

But Strasberg was afraid that would lead to a mechanical performance. He resisted her appeal for detailed instructions and decided to keep her as flexible and natural as possible through every scene. She was fighting one of the worst cases of type-miscasting in theatre history. Although her emotional scenes during rehearsal lacked the genuine passion she displayed when cursing Billy Rose, Strasberg gambled that when Tallulah faced an audience, it would be the catalyst that would produce fire.

The play was to open in Detroit. When Tallulah saw the sign on the theatre the day before the opening, it nearly closed in Detroit. The sign read "BILLY ROSE PRESENT" (the final s was missing), and Tallulah's name was under his. There was no mention of Cobb or Schildkraut.

Tallulah commanded Rose's manager to tell his boss: "Unless that sign comes down immediately, there'll be no performance tomorrow night. If your foul employer insists on 'Billy Rose Present' then you need only add, 'Tallulah Bankhead Absent.' Who does he think they're coming to the theatre to see? Fannie Brice's ex-husband?"

The sign was changed.

Next she decided that the audience wouldn't be able to see the stage from some of the seats and demanded that they be removed. Rose refused. Tallulah insisted. She called him a "bastard" and a "bully." "Who can bully Niagara Falls?" he responded almost plaintively. The seats stayed but he didn't— because Tallulah threatened not to go on if Billy Rose appeared in any part of the theatre.

Backstage was so taut with tension you could almost play a tune on it. Strasberg went there to wish all the actors a broken leg—the strange superstitious way theatre people have of wishing each other well. Tallulah bawled: "Come in."

Strasberg went in. She was stark naked. He was taken aback, for a moment. "I was embarrassed, she wasn't," recalls Strasberg. "Tallulah was just a little ahead of her times. Today she would be behind the times." He wished her well, and hoped to God the audience would give her the spark she needed.

The audience was waiting, noisy with expectation, then hushed. The curtains opened. The fight was on.

And it was a fight in that each major performer was struggling to enhance his own reputation, each feeling animosity for the others, and yet the demands of the theatre required them to play as a team, to cooperate and even support each other. A play in which one of the major actors gives a selfish performance, taking an interest only in the moments when he is the focus of attention, is like a sore thumb on a body; a play in which a minor actor turns in a self-centered performance is like a body with a sore thumb: in either event it's the bad that sticks out and the good that's ignored.

Schildkraut avoided the sparring during rehearsals but had merely been hiding his emotions. He had been irritated by what he felt was "Mr. Cobb's introverted and monosyllabic approach to his role." He had forced himself to be polite to Tallulah, though incensed by her "obstreperous and condescending manner." He controlled himself because he felt if he once lost his temper, he'd have killed her.

Fortunately all this passion could be employed onstage, especially by Method actors. Tallulah played Cobb's wife. Schildkraut was her lover. When Cobb found out, he tracked Schildkraut to his job in a projection booth—and strangled him.

Strasberg watched from the back of the theatre. Would his gamble come off? Would Tallulah take fire from the audience? Lee Cobb and Joseph Schildkraut would be fine—they were more used to creating characters than Tallulah was. Could she convince the audience that she was a Staten Island housewife living on relief?

Strasberg felt his gamble had come off. Tallulah was giving

a remarkably good performance. "The stimulus of the audience was creative incentive for Tallulah," he said.

Onstage, Ryan watched her too. She was good, he thought, although she was having a hard time turning into a Staten Island housewife. Her manner was too big for the part, too big for almost any part—unless she was playing herself. He admired her as an unselfish actress who allowed other actors to have their moment in the sun. Tallulah in performance and Tallulah in rehearsal were two different women.

According to the reviews next day, Lee J. Cobb ran away with the play.

When the company reached Philadelphia, Tallulah fainted. But she played the first night there. And then she gave, says Strasberg, "not a good performance, but a superb one. Maybe, because she was ill, she was quite relaxed in a strange way. But that performance was wonderful and quite startling."

After that first night she was taken to a Philadelphia hospital and put in an oxygen tent. She had double pneumonia and a temperature of 105. Billy Rose registered her under an assumed name, afraid that news of her sickness might kill the play. For three days she was on the danger list. For two weeks she lay in the oxygen tent.

She came out to resume her part, and the play reached Broadway. But no performance ever came near the one she gave when she was dangerously ill.

Among the Broadway audience was actor Tony Randall. It was an unforgettable experience for him. Lee Cobb's was one of the best performances he'd ever seen in his life. "He's never been as good since," says Randall. "Joseph Schildkraut up until then had seemed to be a florid ham, capable of nothing but narcissism, but in *Clash by Night* he gave a real, genuine acting job. Robert Ryan's was a small part, but he was very, very good. And Tallulah was trying to be a character and was very fine indeed. Strasberg was able to shape and dominate Cobb and no one has ever been able to do that with him since.

I think the same was true of Bankhead. Strasberg was able to force her to give a submerged performance."

If he forced her, by his own admission it was by leaving her to her own devices, and letting her fight the competition.

The fights offstage continued and, if anything, got more strident. Overshadowed by Lee J. Cobb, Tallulah was anything but sunny. Strasberg defends her: "She was a woman who got over things quickly. After she had quarreled with Lee Cobb she went to my wife Paula, and said: 'I've bought presents for everyone and I don't know whether Lee will take his.' She had a fight with the author, Mr. Odets, and they almost came to blows, but those are par for the course with people who feel things intensely at the moment. Many times if you paid no attention to Tallulah and didn't react to what she'd said, you got along very well. Odets and Tallulah were both very passionate people and they felt very strongly, which you have to do in the theatre. I wouldn't blow up at Tallulah normally. I liked her. But once I blew up and told her she was wrong about something, when she was taking exception to Billy Rose. And strangely enough she took it from me. Later I found out that whatever it was she said, she was right about it: I was wrong."

Silently suffering through it all and, as he says, "behaving like a lamb," was Joseph Schildkraut.

Clash by Night closed after eight weeks on Broadway, and Schildkraut congratulated himself on avoiding a murder rap: Tallulah was still alive. Just before the last performance he sent a box of roses and a polite goodbye note to Tallulah's dressing room. His motive was perplexing to say the least. But Tallulah's response wasn't.

On stage, after the last curtain call, she turned to him and said: "Thank you for the roses. You're a gentleman, but I don't like you. I still like your wife." And she walked off the stage leaving him gaping.

The only one who came away from *Clash by Night* without

scars was Robert Ryan. To him, "Tallulah was a stereotype of what the public thinks star actresses are like: they really aren't except in her case. She liked some kind of excitement going on and didn't much care where it came from. She was a great experience and she came at a most important time in my life, when I was just starting out as an actor. She was one of the most exciting human beings I've ever met in the theatre. Most of them aren't, you know. We're people who try to be exciting when we're in front of the public, but we're working people. And most actresses, oddly enough, are quite lonely. Their marriages don't seem to work out. They're in a presumably envied position, but they sit home a lot of nights with the phone not ringing.

"Tallulah used to call Billy Rose 'a son of a bitch,' " Ryan said with a laugh, "and I'm inclined to agree with her. I didn't think much of him either."

If Tallulah was sitting at home, she wasn't lonely. She was still groggy from her bout with double pneumonia, Billy Rose, and her struggle with the part (because she knew in her heart she couldn't play a "common" woman). At least now she could choose the fights on her own ground—where she made the rules.

XIII

The Skin of
Her Teeth

1942–1943   "Ouch! What the hell?" Estelle Winwood cried out. She'd been playing bridge with friends, when one of them suddenly grabbed her hair and pulled.

"Just trying to find out if what Tallulah says about you is true," explained the friend.

"You're the second one to pull my hair this week," Estelle complained. "What the dickens has Tallulah been saying about me?"

"That you're completely bald."

The card game broke up for a while, while everyone laughed. "Just like Tallulah," Estelle thought. "It's her exaggerated way of saying my hair's thin. You can't take her at face value when she's being funny. She colors everything."

Late that night Estelle finished reading the manuscript of a play Tallulah had sent her for an opinion. Tallulah had been offered the chance to play in it as an Ice-Age housemaid, a beauty contest winner, a bingo-parlor hostess, and an actress. Should she accept? The play had had a hard time finding a producer, although Thornton Wilder had written it. Thirty-seven producers had turned it down. But Michael Myerberg, the thirty-eighth, had imagination and decided to have a go.

Estelle read the play, *The Skin of Our Teeth,* and loved it. She phoned Tallulah.

"Take it," she said. "You'll be an awful idiot if you don't."

"But it's already been turned down by a producer who graduated from Harvard—because he didn't understand it," Tallulah objected.

"It's different," Estelle admitted. "A sort of comic-strip history of man's fight for survival with one family enduring down the ages. If you don't play Sabina, some new girl will play it and become a star overnight. The part is that good."

"Howard Cullman thinks it's too like *Life With Father.*"

"Tallulah, listen to me. It's a great play. You made an enormous hit in *The Little Foxes,* and now to have a chance to follow it up with a part like this is too much happiness for anyone. You take my tip and play this part. You'll be a damned fool if you don't."

So she did.

Fredric March was to play the father; Florence Eldridge, his wife; Montgomery Clift, their son. Elia Kazan was to direct fresh from his first Broadway experience directing Ruth Gordon in *The Strings, My Lord, Are False.*

Tony Randall arrived on the first day of rehearsal to understudy Montgomery Clift and to play a broadcast announcer.

"I was so in awe of these great stars," he says. "On that first day Tallulah Bankhead came up to me and said: 'I know your name. You may not know mine. You're Tony Randall. I'm Tallulah Bankhead.' "

Randall stood there thunderstruck. He'd seen her in *Reflected Glory* and thought her devastating, and brilliant, as well as in *Clash by Night.*

She said: "I understand the army's gain is going to be our loss." And she shook his hand.

Randall no sooner had the job than he was drafted. He rehearsed that one day and left for the army, to carry with him the memory of a handshake and a smile from one of his idols.

Also caught up in the war was the playwright, Thornton

Wilder. So his sister, Isabel, represented him at rehearsals. If the play was a version of man's struggle against Nature that was trying to obliterate him, the rehearsals were another version of the struggle to survive. Kazan had that same year made his not-too-successful Broadway bow as a director and had yet to prove himself. March and Eldridge were stars of the first magnitude, a husband-and-wife team who must have made Tallulah nostalgic for what might have been. It was her chance to reveal what she could do with comedy, to prove that she could match her dramatic performance in *The Little Foxes*, after botching *Clash by Night*.

Again Tallulah had incredibly bad luck with her producer. Michael Myerberg grated on her from the start. She called him erratic and tactless. Isabel Wilder, who takes a generous view of everybody, describes him as "difficult in his own way beyond the wildest dreams," and she sets the scene for the fights that were to follow.

"Elia Kazan was really on trial with *Skin of Our Teeth*. It was one of those front-page productions and Kazan was then a dark horse. He was on his mettle. It wasn't easy with a barrage of four major not only actors and actresses, but temperaments. And the author, my brother, wasn't there to back him up and give him moral support. So it was a sticky passage and things like that take a couple of years off your life. No play goes easily, but this one broke all records."

Despite Tallulah's fights with Kazan over interpretation of Sabina, and because she wanted to replace him with her friend Orson Welles, the play opened in Baltimore.

The audience hated it. They walked out puzzled, bored, angry.

Crushed, Tallulah phoned Estelle Winwood, who was in Washington playing in *Lady Windermere's Fan*.

"Estelle, why the hell did you talk me into playing in this farce! You were all wrong about it!"

"What do you mean?"

"They hate the goddam play and they don't understand a

goddam word of it. There's a big line at the box office now—
of people asking for their money back. I should never have
listened to you."

Estelle kept her cool: "My dear Tallulah, this is no road
play. This is a New York hit."

"Not judging by this audience. They were ready to riot."

"Tallulah, I'm telling you straight, you've got a New York
hit."

The play came to New York and they had a preview. Tallulah phoned Estelle. "Well here it is in New York and the
audience hates it even more than the Baltimore audience.
You're wrong Estelle."

After a few questions, Estelle discovered the audience had
been foreigners—many of them refugees—who didn't understand too much English!

When the play opened in New York on November 18, 1942,
the critics vindicated Estelle Winwood. Wolcott Gibbs of
The New Yorker described Tallulah's Sabina as "the most
brilliant and certainly the most versatile performance of Miss
Bankhead's entire career." Louis Kronenberger of *Time* magazine wrote: "Tallulah Bankhead played Sabina with brilliant
verve and vivacity."

The *Newsweek* critic was bowled over: "It is with the casting of Tallulah Bankhead as Sabina that the producer becomes
inspired. As the French-farcical maid of the first act, the
mincing bathing beauty of the second, and the enthusiastic
camp follower of the third, her perennial 'other woman' is a
superb comedy performance. Whether she is confiding to a
fascinated audience that she doesn't understand a word of the
play, and only took the part because she was starving; or,
finally, advising the customers that it is time to go home,
please, the ex-villainess of *The Little Foxes* sustains *The Skin
of Our Teeth* with a gutsy, irresistible humor that is almost
sufficient, in itself, to justify Wilder's theatrical jump over the
moon." Alexander Woollcott was completely absorbed and en-

tranced with the play and with Tallulah: "Wilder's dauntless and heartening comedy stands head and shoulders above anything ever written for our stage . . . the nearest thing to a great play which the American theatre has yet evolved." Woollcott went back to see the play several times and he stood to watch half a matinee the day before he suffered a fatal heart attack.

Tallulah fought for those she liked with as much energy as against those she loathed. She liked Morton Da Costa, who, as a broadcast official in the play, never stepped on stage but spoke through a microphone for each performance.

When, after a quarrel about salary, producer Michael Myerberg tried to fire Morton Da Costa and replace him with a recording, Tallulah heard the record, rushed out of her dressing room and shouted: 'If that thing goes on again I'm not going on."

But Myerberg ignored the threat. The record played for the evening performance—and stuck in the second groove.

Tallulah and Da Costa were unjustly accused of collusion with an electrician but Da Costa's job was saved. And the record (of the voice of Alexander Woollcott shortly before he died) wasn't used again.

But three months later Myerberg fired Da Costa again. When Tallulah heard of it she said to him: "Unfortunately there's nothing I can do. I have approval of contract but I have nothing to say about dismissal."

But she immediately contacted her doctor and got a letter from him saying that she had a duodenal ulcer, that she followed Mr. Da Costa on during the play and unless he was rehired she felt that she would be too upset to continue in the role. Da Costa was rehired.

Tallulah's fights with Kazan died down once the play was underway and a success. She outwitted producer Myerberg without too much effort, at every turn. But what smarted was criticism from Florence Eldridge—Mrs. Fredric March.

Florence had a big speech with the whole company onstage, during which she threw a bottle into the ocean while Tallulah held Fredric March's arm.

The curtain fell and Florence said: "I wish you wouldn't move during that speech, Tallulah." Tallulah ignored her. The second time Florence said it, Tallulah replied: "I haven't been moving"—which was the truth. Finally, one night, the curtain came down and Florence said: "Tallulah will you stop moving on my speech." And Tallulah snapped back: "I haven't been moving on your fucking speech."

Florence: "Now Tallulah, be a good girl."

Tallulah: "I'm sick of being a good girl and I'm sick of your frustrations."

From then on the only words they exchanged were in the play.

The Skin of Our Teeth won the Pulitzer Prize for Thornton Wilder, the critics' "best actress of the season" award for Tallulah, and an assured future for Kazan. His fights with Tallulah couldn't have been as bitter as legend made them, because he wrote a letter to her two months after the play opened on Broadway: "Thanks for being right those times when I was completely wrong. . . . And thanks above all for a thing no one can thank you for—for your gift akin to genius."

The popular picture of Tallulah as a wildcat who fought with everyone in range just for the hell of it is not upheld by Isabel Wilder, who, sitting in for her brother Thornton, had watched the action from early rehearsal, all through the rocky tour, to New York.

It's reasonable to suppose that she should have the interest of her brother's play at heart and that if Tallulah's behavior had jeopardized its success, she would have said so. She says, instead: "I had great affection and love for Tallulah although it wasn't always easy. She was a warm, outgoing woman. Everything she did was from the toes up—with a full honesty that could be overpowering. Her real personality was warm and generous. She was really interested in people, and she didn't count the cost of her giving when she was involved. There was an aura, a shining light around her: and yet, the other side of the coin, it took such patience and it took real love to accept and endure.'

None of the stars agreed to tour with the play after the Broadway run. Without them it lasted just one week on the road.

Tallulah was eager to go home. She'd bought a house in the country after falling in love with it on second sight and had called it "Windows." She moved in on April 1, 1943. Now she wanted to enjoy the first real home of her own she'd ever had.

XIV

At Home with
Tallulah

1943 Grab *Hellzapoppin* or any crazy farce, add *Hay Fever* and *You Can't Take It with You*, stir into that a synthesis of Tennessee Williams' plays in which a princess or fading star has a young man in thrall, add plenty of liquid, season with pep pills and tranquilizers, and stand back. See what you've got? It's Tallulah's place in the country, called "Windows" because her life is an open book or window, take your pick, on eighteen acres, surrounded by five thousand daffodils and the ear-aching detonations from the blasting of rocks needed to make a swimming pool.

Without a husband or a lion cub for company, Tallulah was lonely. She had a myna bird who said "Birds can't talk" and a carpet full of dogs and a parakeet, but they weren't enough.

Estelle Winwood was always welcome and often at "Windows." It was a pleasant twist. Estelle had sheltered Tallulah in her apartment twenty-five years before, when the Algonquin became too expensive for Tallulah. Dola Cavendish, the youngest of thirteen sisters and sole survivor, was often there to be bullied. "But she asked for it," said a mutual friend. Dola, a wealthy Canadian, behaved as though Tallulah was the Empress of the British Empire and she, Dola, a humble and adoring subject. It seemed to work well.

The staff at "Windows" included Rose Riley, the perfect maid; a cock; and Robert Williams, the butler, who had the same birthday as Tallulah's father—April 12. Very soon Robert was taking over the role of a father, telling Tallulah when she'd had enough to drink and refusing to give her any more. Tallulah obeyed him like a dutiful daughter. Robert had first arrived at "Windows" as a guest of a friend and Tallulah liked him so much, she said: "You're not going home."

A typical Tallulah day lasts thirty-six hours. The cast consists of Tallulah, Estelle, and Dola, a couple of men who wandered in and found the entertainment and refreshment to their liking, a poet, a young actor and actress, a playwright, and a businessman who came to the wrong house but prefers it to the right one. There's a glass in every hand and Robert is refilling the dry ones. A French poodle and a Maltese chase each other around the furniture, and a piano tuner who finished tuning two hours ago is now playing background music from Puccini. Tallulah is imitating Marlene Dietrich crooning, "See what the boys in the backroom will have," and if it's any indication of present company, they'll have another one. One guest finds a parakeet in his large brandy glass. "It's only Gaylord," Tallulah reassures him.

Then Tallulah walks to the library and comes back with the Bible. "Hold it! Hold it! Everyone." Tallulah's going to preach. Time stands still as the sun goes down. The piano goes pianissimo and the guests freeze. Tallulah holds them transfixed while she orates her favorite lines for forty-five minutes. Then she opens the Bible at random to tell the guests their fortunes. "Don't move, darling! Robert will get you another drink." And from the Dietrich imitation and the Bible, Tallulah goes to the time she greeted the stuffy English lord when she was having a bath in a bathroom where every wall was a mirror, and in his confusion he took her soap-sudded hand and apologized for not being dressed.

Someone recalls when Lawrence of Arabia accepted an invitation to Tallulah's party in London. She'd invited him because, she said, "I adore brave men."

"What if he doesn't turn up?" a friend had asked.

"Darling, he's not that brave," replied Tallulah.

And someone else tells of when Tallulah and Estelle were in a play together. Shortly before curtain time, there was a phone call for Tallulah. The stage doorkeeper tapped on her door: "Call for you Miss Bankhead." Tallulah stepped out to get to the phone and she was completely naked. She walked past the doorman and Estelle Winwood. As she went by, Estelle called out, almost plaintively, her much-repeated comment: "Why do you do that, Tallulah? You have such pretty frocks."

Estelle Winwood has remained her best friend, partly, perhaps, because she responds to Tallulah's tricks with the affectionate patience of a mother. And, by playing it straight, her reactions to Tallulah are as funny as Tallulah's antics. From their accounts life in England seemed to be one long laugh.

Then suddenly, as startling as a thunderclap in a clear sky, Tallulah is fighting with Robert. She slams the bedroom door in a fury. Robert can hear her laughing behind the closed door and he's laughing too, but not loud enough so she'll hear. Tallulah comes out from her bedroom imitating Ethel Barrymore, and day passes into night, night into day and again into night and Tallulah is still on her feet—the champion through a series of knockouts.

But still Tallulah was lonely, and so, into this Bedford Village, New York, five-bedroom, five-fireplace house with a library, she brought a string of captives—one at a time and sentenced to terms ranging from one year to eighteen months, seldom more or less. The captives were always young men, usually actors in the plays she was then starring in.

First prisoner, in 1943, was Morton Da Costa. He played the broadcast announcer in *The Skin of Our Teeth*. Da Costa had been terrified and in awe of her at first meeting. He kept his distance until, after a couple of months in the play, they found themselves face to face offstage. He mentioned his interest in antiques. That did it. "Darling you must come antique hunting with me tomorrow." Da Costa obeyed her royal decree and the trap began to close. "You must come back to see 'Windows,' " she said. "I've just bought it." They went that night when it was too dark to see anything, and Da Costa stayed to wait for daylight. He rarely got out of the place for the next year.

When Tallulah awoke on that first morning in "Windows," she gave him a guided tour of her kingdom.

Suddenly she had her mule off and was waving it in the air, shouting.

"What is it?" he asked, baffled.

"A hill of ants! Are you blind? Here, use this."

She watched him at work, then shouted: "Oh you bloody fool! That's not the way."

Da Costa straightened up. "Look," he said. "There are two ways to kill ants: your way and mine. I prefer mine."

Da Costa the ant killer had found the right response to keep Tallulah in check. She never lost her temper with him again. "Because I wouldn't take a lot of her crap, I think that's one reason she sort of clung to me."

Tallulah tried all her tricks on Da Costa. When she couldn't scare him into submission, she tried her strip strategy.

One moment she was dressed: next moment she wasn't. Da Costa summoned all his Broadway Theatre bravado to keep the ice from chinking against the side of his glass.

He survived that and she never shocked him again. He felt, contrary to all the stories and some of the evidence, that Tallulah was essentially pollyanna. The shocking things were done just for effect, to be outrageous.

Da Costa quickly learned the danger of saying "goodnight" to Tallulah. Because she'd immediately reply: "Just have one more drink darling." Or: "But it's only two." Or: "Don't be an unsociable bastard. Get me a cigarette and sit down." If he wanted to get any sleep, he slipped quietly away with no "goodnight."

But more often than not Tallulah held Da Costa there until she was ready for bed. She went to her room with a jigger of bourbon in one hand and her sleeping pills in the other. Da Costa followed and stayed at her bedside until the pills knocked her out.

"Estelle Winwood and Paula Strasberg were also living in her house then," says Da Costa. "Tallulah wanted people around her all the time, because she was desperately lonely, and it was murder to get away.

"She had more adrenalin than ten human beings put together. I would be a physical wreck and say, 'Tallulah, we haven't read a book for ages. Why don't you lie on that sofa, I'll lie on this. And let's read.' She'd say: 'Marvelous idea, darling.' And I hadn't turned the first page before she'd say: 'Let's move the piano.' I taught her, unfortunately, 'I'll Be Seeing You.' She had me playing it fifty times one night until the piano bench broke, thank God. She was loaded by that time and it didn't occur to her we could pull up another."

Da Costa stayed because he loved her and pitied her and, when he tried flight, found her pleas for him to stay irresistible.

One visitor who got away was Cleveland Amory, perhaps because he said "goodnight" when Tallulah wasn't listening.

Amory was just out of school and armed with a letter of introduction to Tallulah from their mutual friend, Katharine Hepburn. Kate had told him his education wasn't complete until he met Tallulah. So, his face stinging from too much aftershave, Amory approached "Windows" to graduate.

Amory rang the bell. Robert the butler opened the door, to what sounded like the third act of an orgy. The butler took the note and although he closed the door Amory could still hear the noise inside. Then there was silence, broken after seconds by Tallulah's voice: "Goddammit, I can't see every last damn one of Kate Hepburn's friends!" and then the orgy resumed.

The butler opened the door again, handed the note to Amory, saying: "It doesn't seem to be a good time, sir."

"What does he look like?" Tallulah bawled.

Robert retired discreetly, leaving the door open and Amory on display. There was a hushed discussion among the guests. "Not bad." "A trifle young." "He looks sober." "Throw him in the pool and see if he floats." And then: "Come in, darling!"

Amory had passed muster. As a Boston-bred boy he thought he was entering the depths of Bohemianism .

Amory slept in his own home that night—a feat in itself. But he went back for more and grew to know and adore Tallulah. "She was capable of the most incredible kindnesses," he says. "She was really one of the great-hearted people of all time."

Jacqueline Susann, a young actress—not yet the best-selling author of *Valley of the Dolls* and *The Love Machine*—also arrived at "Windows." It was at the height of Tallulah's singing craze, when she broke into a song at the drop of a glass. Jacqueline Susann walked in while Tallulah was into "Don't Throw Bouquets At Me," and when she left forty-eight hours later, Tallulah wasn't out of it.

"Hello darling," Tallulah greeted her. "This is my dear friend Dola Cavendish, those young men over there came to deliver the TV set . . ." she waved at five other guests around the room. "Just people, darling. Robert will get you a drink."

At two o'clock Sunday morning, someone was snoring on the sofa. Dola had gone to bed and Tallulah was entertaining the survivors. 'I was having an affair with this Englishman, can't tell you his name. And the first time I byzed with him . . ." she was saying.

"Byzed with him?" someone interrupted. "Is that anything to do with Byzantium?"

"No, darling. Byzed. Beddy byze. I went to bed with him. Didn't your daddy or mommy ever tell you to go to 'beddy byze'?"

Future author Jacqueline Susann was amazed and amused that Tallulah, who normally used longshoreman language, never even "slept" with men: she "byzed" with them.

"I was also amazed by her enormous energy," says Jacqueline Susann. "I went to sleep at night and when I got up in the morning Tallulah was still holding forth with a glass in her hand. She had the most enormous capacity for drinking and living of anyone I've ever seen. I went home thoroughly exhausted and Tallulah was still wide awake—and she never slept the entire weekend."

On Mother's Day, Mary Chase arrived and, with Tallulah, took turns making up poems to suit the occasion. Mary Chase, who wrote about an imaginary rabbit in her play *Harvey*, found Tallulah more entertaining than any make-believe character. "Tallulah was in great form," says Mrs. Chase. "And we were having a marvelous time."

One of the guests that day had come to call and three months later was still there. Another man, a stranger to Tallulah, had walked in just to say "hello" and was reluctant to say "goodbye."

"Whoever wrote the play *You Can't Take It with You* must have heard of Tallulah first," says Mrs. Chase.

Anyone who did think of modeling a stage character on Tallulah must have been discouraged by the thought that she wasn't believable.

Mrs. Chase had arrived with her children, and normally Tallulah would have played with them. But now she had launched into imitations of celebrities and didn't want to lose her audience.

"Our youngest boy was five," says Mrs. Chase, "and he watched Tallulah for a few moments and then turned back to his toy train. Tallulah stopped and did a slow take and looked over at him saying: 'How DARE you, while I'm giving an impression!' And he looked at her, and turned right back to his train She roared with laughter and said: 'See, I don't impress him a bit.' And she gave him a kiss."

Strong men had failed and found themselves trapped by Tallulah because they didn't know the secret of handling her. But the five-year-old boy hit on it right away—don't let her scare you.

The days and nights floated by with never-ending house-guests, TV repairmen, TV performers, poets and parasites, people and pets of all pedigrees and persuasions. But the money was floating by, too. And Tallulah had to provide.

Over in Hollywood, director Alfred Hitchcock was casting for a movie to be called *Lifeboat* in which the action would be confined to a forty-foot boat holding a handful of the crew and passengers from a ship sunk by a U-boat. He needed a hardy bunch of spartans as they'd be doused by water to simulate hurricane-tossed waves, and they'd require enough charisma to hold an audience with only salt water as scenery.

Hitchcock remembered Tallulah. He'd first seen her in Gerald du Maurier's *The Dancers* in 1922. Thought she was marvelous then. He offered her a leading role in *Lifeboat* for seventy-five thousand dollars. Tallulah had been warned about playing opposite children and animals but hadn't been told of the hazards of playing in a boat. "Darling I'll do it," she told Hitchcock.

XV

Fifteen Weeks of
Water Torture

1943 In the movie *Lifeboat*, Walter Slezak played "the enemy," a Nazi sea captain sharing a lifeboat with other torpedoed survivors. Tallulah treated him as though he personified the whole Nazi breed. She called him a "goddamned Nazi" many times between the shots. "The poor man didn't have an easy trip," says the director, Alfred Hitchcock. "Talullah was so vehement against the Germans in the war that she took it out on Walter. But she wasn't serious: only semi-serious."

Semi was enough to give Slezak a severe case of disenchantment. He'd seen Tallulah in *The Little Foxes* and thought her wonderful. He realized she was giving an excellent performance in *Lifeboat* though he considered her the triumph of personality over acting.

What got him was that he was trapped with her in the lifeboat for hours at a time. He wasn't a man who made many friends or enjoyed the outgoing exuberance of fellow actors. He tried to control his anger by counting the number of names she dropped in an afternoon. "Winston Churchill called me from London," she said (One). "Last time I saw him was with Lord Beaverbrook" (Two). "I suppose you'd be more impressed if it was Hitler, you goddamned Nazi" (Could Hitler count as Three?).

"Listening to her constant talk was like a Chinese water torture," recalls Slezak. "She told us she'd given up drinking for the duration of the war about seventy-two times a day."

Slezak was surprised that Hitchcock seemed to enjoy Tallulah so much. Of course Hitchcock could walk away any time he wanted to.

"Once Tallulah tried to play a scene her way," says Slezak, "but Hitchcock said, 'No, no,' very quietly with that wonderful dead-fish face of his, and she suddenly turned to us and said plaintively, 'He won't listen to me.' And, of course, she did it his way."

But Tallulah wasn't plaintive for long. She taunted and tormented Slezak as if he were a real-life Nazi war criminal and she was a partisan whose family had been destroyed.

What also soured Slezak was Tallulah's startling entrance into the lifeboat every morning.

"In order to step into the boat we had to go over a little ladder," says Slezak. "The first day she lifted her skirt to under her arms—with nothing underneath. She carried on that tired joke for about fifteen weeks, while I was on the picture. Every day, three, four, or five times, she showed she wasn't wearing panties. Maybe I'm a prude, but I don't like vulgar women."

Behind the camera Hitchcock was having the time of his life. There was nothing he didn't like about Tallulah. What pleased him more than anything was her "tremendous sense of humor." He enjoyed her "healthy" four-letter-word language. And when a woman journalist complained of Tallulah's antics on the set that were also annoying Walter Slezak and boring Hume Cronyn (who, at first, thought she was like a naughty fourth-former), Hitchcock decided something would have to be done.

The unit manager took Hitchcock aside and said: "A woman on the set is complaining that Tallulah's getting in and out of the boat with no panties on. Should I talk to her?"

Hitchcock said: "Well, I wouldn't if I were you. You know

she's a bit of a firebrand. Don't think she's too keen on you."
Hitchcock thought for a while and said: "Anyway I'm on loan
from Selznick. I don't work for Twentieth Century–Fox. It's
a matter of protocol. You'd better go up front and find out
for yourself what to do."

The unit manager went to Darryl Zanuck, who instructed
him: "You tell Tallulah."

Worried, the unit manager came back to Hitchcock and
said: "Zanuck says I've got to tell her."

"I wouldn't if I were you," Hitchcock advised. "It's not
your department."

"Whose department is it?" the unit manager asked.

Hitchcock thought for a while: "Either hairdressing or
makeup."

Tallulah's companion, Paula Strasberg, finally told her of
the no-panties problem. "What's all the fuss about?" Tallulah
asked; after all there was a war going on. Opinion is divided.
Some say she wore panties on the set from that moment on.
Others say she triumphed over criticism and remained panty-
less, striking a blow for democracy and freedom.

"The whole point about Tallulah," Hitchcock sums up,
"was that she had no inhibitions. Now some people can take
this, others can't."

Playing in *Lifeboat* nearly cost Tallulah her life. "She stood
up to being doused by 5,400 gallons of water," says Hitchcock,
"and got a round of applause from the stage hands."

But those 5,400 gallons, the hot studio lamps, the wet, dry,
wet, dry treatments hit Tallulah at her weakest spot. She got
her second attack of pneumonia. Her temperature hit 104,
but a studio doctor brought it down with drugs, and after
three days' rest Tallulah was back under the lights and in the
water-swamped lifeboat. She got pneumonia again. There was
only one shot needed to complete the film, and Tallulah was
in it.

Tallulah was so anxious to finish the film and get home

that she pleaded with the doctor to let her do that one shot even though her temperature was back at 104.

The doctor told Tallulah she was the most defiant, contradictory patient he'd ever encountered. He thought she must be part yogi. He didn't think anything could kill her. In the interests of science and his own peace, Dr. Fox let Tallulah go back to the studio. The last shot was in the can in December, 1943. Tallulah proved her immortality by surviving and was soon home at "Windows"—but not for long. She had yet to endure her biggest humiliation in Hollywood.

XVI

Otto Preminger
to the Rescue

1944   *A Royal Scandal* was a lighthearted film script about Catherine the Great of Russia. She had lax morals, legions of lovers, and a lust for literature. So who should producer-director Ernst Lubitsch, master of the sophisticated comedy, want for the part?

He offered Tallulah $125,000 for fifteen weeks' work and she signed.

Then Lubitsch had a heart attack. He survived, but was warned by his doctor to rest completely and not to excite himself in any way, or the next attack would be the last.

Lubitsch half-obeyed his doctor by hiring Otto Preminger to do the donkey work: directing. But, unable to keep away from his baby entirely, he haunted the set and the screening room as the film's producer.

"Lubitsch should really have retired when he had his heart attack," believes Vincent Price, who also played in the film. "He invited me into his office one time to tell me how *A Royal Scandal* should be filmed and it really was hysterical. Otto didn't have that kind of sense of humor. As good a director as he is, that isn't his flair.

"It was the most frustrating thing in the world to see Lubitsch almost having another heart attack every time

anybody played a scene. It was an impossible situation because he sat on the set the whole time and yet he couldn't do
anything. It was difficult for Otto and the actors."

By doing what they thought he wanted, Preminger and the
cast tried not to give Lubitsch another heart attack. But the
instructions not to excite Lubitsch were especially hard to
follow because he was very easily excited.

Then one morning Lubitsch asked Preminger to come into
his office. He was excited. Preminger was worried. "Don't
excite" were the watchwords. But it soon became clear that
Lubitsch was excited in a positive, health-sustaining way.

"Something terrific has happened," he said in his pronounced Berlin-German accent. "I had dinner last night with
Greta Garbo. We ate in a little Italian restaurant. And I told
her the story of *A Royal Scandal,* the treatment I was giving
it and described the part of Catherine. And Garbo said: 'This
is the part that I want to play.' "

But Preminger wouldn't go along with the plan to replace
Tallulah with Garbo. "It's your film, Ernst, and I can't stop
you from doing this," Preminger replied in his pronounced
Viennese accent. "But count me out. I won't do anything that
would in any way hurt Tallulah. I'm a friend of hers."

"Garbo is offering to come back to work! Don't you understand what that means?" Lubitsch asked, looking as though
Preminger was the excitement the doctor had warned him
against.

"I'd have been very delighted if you'd asked me to direct
the film with Garbo at the beginning," explained Preminger.
"But not now If you change to Garbo now, I can't partici-
pate."

"Nonsense!" Lubitsch said. "Anyway, come with me to see
Zanuck."

Zanuck solved problems on the move. Now he walked up
and down the room carrying a polo mallet. If only the problem had been a ball he could have driven it straight through
the window.

"It would be double-crossing," insisted Preminger, "to take an actress of Tallulah's standing and replace her without good reason. If she had given Ernst or me any trouble that would be different. I know I am simply a hired director and I have no power to persuade you. But if you do go ahead and replace Tallulah, I'll quit."

Zanuck stopped walking. "We'll call New York," he said. And did. He discussed the situation with the salespeople who were supposed to be experts on who was and wasn't a box-office attraction.

"At that time it was still the star era," says Preminger. "It is difficult to realize now what it meant then—that Garbo might return to the movies. Only people who knew her personally, like Lubitsch who directed her in *Ninotchka*, could even talk to her."

Eventually the whole thing petered out. Tallulah stayed with the film, and so did Preminger.

But from that moment, Lubitsch was so unhappy at the thought he'd lost Garbo that he couldn't stand Tallulah. Playwright George Oppenheimer has called Lubitsch "one of the loveliest men that God created." He showed another side of his nature to Tallulah. He kept away from her whenever possible. If he saw her approaching down a corridor, he'd walk into the nearest room. Having haunted the set to start with, he only visited it now when Tallulah wasn't in a scene.

He continued to see her screen performance in the rushes, however, at eleven every morning. Preminger saw the same scenes after lunch and then they discussed them.

Several weeks after the Garbo affair, Tallulah was on the set, waiting for Preminger to return from seeing the rushes, when Lubitsch came in and, quivering with anger, cursed her in front of crew and cast for every crime in the book, from scene stealing up. He left her humiliated and shattered, and hurried out, to collide with Preminger coming in.

"I told her off!" he said. "I told her just what I thought about her behavior!" He was in an incredibly excited state, more like a man who'd just killed a dragon than the producer of a comedy, and using language that shocked Preminger.

"Tell me what it is?" asked Preminger, trying to calm him.

"In the rushes today, in the scene with Anne Baxter, didn't you see what Tallulah tried to do to her? It says she closes her eyes while Anne Baxter speaks to her. And she kept them open all the way through!"

"But Ernst, that's what I told her to do. I don't go by the script verbatim."

But Lubitsch wouldn't concede. "Anyway, the way she behaves! Impossible, simply impossible!" And he stormed out.

Preminger walked on the set. Tallulah wasn't there. The cast and crew were standing around like spectators at a fatal traffic accident. Somebody pointed to the tent where Tallulah changed because her voluminous dresses were too wide for the normal portable dressing room.

Tallulah was lying on the floor, crying. She'd taken off her costume. Her makeup was destroyed. When she saw Preminger she sobbed: "Darling, nobody in my whole life has ever done this to me! You must take me right now to Zanuck and I'm going to quit this picture. Lubitsch accused me of stealing the scene. I would NEVER do such a thing! I wouldn't try to steal a scene from the greatest actor on earth! I wouldn't steal a scene from Barrymore. But from this little thing! Why should I? Who needs it? I don't. I'm going back to New York TODAY! I'm going to give them back the whole money. I don't want any part of it."

Preminger, with Zanuck's help, finally persuaded Tallulah that Lubitsch was not really responsible for his actions, that he was overexcitable because of his heart condition.

"She agreed to stay," says Preminger. "She went back to the set and made up again, put on her costume and finished the day's shooting.

"And now comes a point I want to make. After we were through shooting, and I went into her dressing-room tent, I told Tallulah: 'I'm going to ask you something which I know will be very difficult for you to do, I want you to come with me to Lubitsch's office and tell him that you feel that, while perhaps he was wrong, you want to make up with him in the interest of our collaboration, because otherwise he won't be comfortable to come on the stage or talk with you.'

"You know, without hesitation, she answered 'Yes.' And she went with me. She didn't make any qualifications. She went to him and said: 'Ernst let's forget the whole thing.' And they shook hands—and it was really a wonderful thing to see how generous she was. Because one of the great assets or virtues that she had was her incredible generosity. And the matter was forgotten. She never referred to it again. It was really one of the additional reasons why I really loved this woman.

"I think Tallulah gave a great comedy performance in *A Royal Scandal*. I think she was much better than the film. Instead of character comedy, it was situation comedy, which Lubitsch liked, which was his strength. And situation comedy started to be old-fashioned at that time.

"Darryl Zanuck, Lubitsch, and I went to the preview, and after, sat together in the car. And the preview had seemed like a tremendous success. The laughs came, you know. Terrific. But there was a feeling of coldness in the audience. Nobody seemed to feel it, except I.

"Zanuck asked me: 'What's the matter? Aren't you happy about the preview?' I said: 'I don't think it went as well as you think.' He said: 'But there were many laughs.' And he got very excited and enthusiastic and he said: 'This is the greatest preview. . . .' But it was not as big a success as they hoped. And I, for some reason, instinctively more than intellectually, didn't hope. In hindsight, in analyzing, I felt, between you and me, that Lubitsch blamed Tallulah. He said that if Garbo had played it, it would have been different. I don't believe that. I think Garbo could also have played the party very well. But I believe Tallulah's performance was tops. And I think that if the financial success was not as great as the studio hoped for, it was really because this type of comedy—it was very funny but it twisted situations for laughs, twisted characters for laughs instead of being comedy based on characters. It was a farce."

In her autobiography, Tallulah writes simply: "In *A Royal Scandal* Lubitsch said my Catherine was the greatest comedy performance he had ever seen. Otto Preminger, who directed the picture, can so testify under oath."

Shortly after her return from Hollywood, Meyer Berger decided to profile her in *The New York Times*. Tallulah invited him to "Windows." With some trepidation he made the trip, and in his February 27, 1944, article, recalled what it's like to experience Tallulah in full flower.

"The uneasy feeling that you've stepped suddenly into a Fortress' propeller wash starts after you've toiled up the long hill to the sprawling white-washed brick house. Your finger's hardly off the bell when five dogs—a lumbering sheepdog, a Sealyham, a wet-nosed Peke, a kind collie, an Irish terrier—swoosh between and around your legs in a charge for the great outdoors. This sets the tempo. The Tallulah is in the doorway and you're overwhelmed by the hoarse cataract of her speech . .

"Standing still, The Tallulah somehow gives the impression she's at a destroyer's prow, knifing into a howler. Her long, tawny hair whips into her face with every gesture. She flips it back impatiently every few seconds with a motion almost as regular as breathing. Her speech is a racing torrent, the whisper-in-a-rain-barrel sound of it curiously hypnotic.

"She paces like something wild that's caged, chain-smokes, drains off Cokes as fast as her maid snatches empties from under her restless fingers. When she's really fervent—and that's no trouble at all—The Tallulah lids close like a china dolls, and you stare at a pair of inverted teacups that quiver with intensity.

"Up in the living room and back. Flop into a chair. Bounce out of it. Stand staring into the fireplace. Whip around and warm the other side. The telephone barely indicates ringing pains: The Tallulah's off in a flash. Back again, her speech still an unrestrained torrent, she takes up exactly where she left off. Another cigarette, another Coke. The visitor weakens under the impact.

"Brooks Atkinson summed it up when he described The Tallulah's arrival one night at the Stage Door Canteen. He wrote: 'She arrived with a gusto that must have been felt in Java.'"

Why *The* Tallulah? Meyer must have seen her as an institution, like *The* Louvre.

When *The New York Times* wanted an official biography of the paper,* whom should they choose to write it but Tallulah's interviewer—Meyer Berger. Any man who could bring Tallulah back alive, so to speak, was a cinch to write a lively account of history in the making—the sinking of the Titanic, Lindbergh's solo Atlantic flight, and the dropping of the atom bomb.

---

* Meyer Berger, *The Story of The New York Times: The First One Hundred Years* (New York: Simon and Schuster, 1951.)

XVII

Peace—and Chicken
for Breakfast

1945   With the Allies victorious and the war in
Europe over, Tallulah was free from her
vow. In her fashion she'd kept her promise
not to touch alcohol again until the British won. She didn't
count spirits of ammonia, that was just a pick-me-up. And
the whiskey she drank during *Lifeboat* was strictly on doctor's
orders, because of pneumonia. So that was medicine.

Now the Theatre Guild gave her the chance to play in
Foolish Notion, with Donald Cook as her leading man, and
ex-husband John Emery in a supporting role. Tallulah and
Emery had remained friends. Tallulah and Cook were to become close friends.

Rehearsals were as deceptively peaceful as the moment before an ambush.

Foolish Notion opened in Baltimore, and the audience
spotted the weakness in the defense. The third act was no
good. Playwright Philip Barry gave up his sleep to put it right
and next day, bleary-eyed, handed the cast the new version.
Tallulah read through a few of the new lines, muttering to
herself, then flung the pages to the floor as if she'd been bitten
by a snake. Barry watched her make an angry exit breathing
heavily.

The producers gave Tallulah a few hours to cool off, then

knocked nervously on her hotel-room door. She was pacing up and down, talking and looking like Catherine of Russia in a homicidal mood, while her friend Dola Cavendish filled the moments when Tallulah gasped for breath, with murmurs of approval.

Tallulah snorted at the producers: "You ought to have a great playwright like Noel Coward write you a great play! The trouble with all you Theatre Guild people is you're too damned normal. All the great writers from Shakespeare on down were peculiar, to say the least."

The original, weak version of *Foolish Notion* was played that night, and the next morning the producers tried to console and inspire playwright Barry. But each time they mentioned Tallulah his face grew a shade redder until, finally, he burst a blood vessel. A key down his back, cotton wool up his nose, he was rushed to Johns Hopkins Hospital.

Told Barry was in the hospital, Tallulah agreed to continue the pre-Broadway tour "as is," until Barry could get back to his typewriter without bleeding on it.

But when she read an item in the New York *Daily News* reporting that Philip Barry had been taken to the hospital with internal hemorrhages brought on by a Tallulah tantrum—she nearly burst a blood vessel.

She pounced on the nearest phone and called the publisher of the *News*, Joseph Patterson, whom she considered a friend. "Darling you know I loathe the repulsive editorials in your paper, and consider its attacks on Franklin Roosevelt beneath contempt. They didn't sway the vote of one cab driver, did they darling? And I'm well aware that your paper is only read by followers of 'Dick Tracy' and 'Little Orphan Annie,' but now your paper has gone too far. Danton Walker has libeled me in his column."

Patterson laughed. "Tallulah, you actresses are always working yourselves up into a tizzy. Cool off. These column writers have to do their job."

"Their job?" she yelled. "Are you implying their job is to

At 5, bright-eyed, chubby Tallulah imitated a risqué singer she'd seen in a vaudeville show, and her father loved it. (*Wide World*)

Profile in 1956, age 34. She was proud of her bone structure, complexion, hair, and much else. (*Wide World*)

ABOVE LEFT, Tallulah's beautiful mother, Adelaide Eugenia Sledge, at 21.

ABOVE CENTER, Tallulah's father, William Bankhead, on his election to the House in 1916.

ABOVE RIGHT, Lord Napier Alington, Tallulah's great love, as painted by Ambrose McEvoy.

BELOW LEFT, as Charles Laughton's wife in the 1932 movie *The Devil and the Deep.*

BELOW RIGHT, abandoned at the altar in *Forsaking All Others,* Tallulah is comforted by her rival, Ilka Chase.

One that got away. Although Tallulah's marriage to Count Tony de Bosardi was announced as a *fait accompli* in 1928, she suspected his motives, called the whole thing off, and returned his engagement present—a Rolls Royce. (*Wide World*)

Tallulah the temptress, as the whore Sadie Thompson in a revival of Somerset Maugham's *Rain* in 1935.

Ever superstitious, Tallulah makes up for George Kelly's *Reflected Glory* with a rabbit's-foot powder puff given to her by the man she idolized—her father. (UPI)

With husband John Emery shortly after their August 31, 1937, marriage. Divorced June 13, 1941, the relationship really lasted less than three years, although they were lifelong friends. She said: "He went into the maelstrom with his eyes open but overestimated his recuperative powers." (UPI)

In her greatest stage success, as the bitch Regina Giddens in Lillian Hellman's *The Little Foxes*—title thanks to the Bible and Dorothy Parker. It was 1939, Tallulah was 37. "One of the two best performances I've ever seen on the stage," says Norman Mailer.

Alfred Hitchcock, the master of mystery and mayhem, dines with Tallulah in 1942, the year before he directed her in *Lifeboat*. She called Hitchcock a genius but suffered three bouts of pneumonia before completing the film. He enjoyed her "tremendous sense of humor." (*Wide World*)

RIGHT, Tallulah comforts a survivor in Hitchcock's movie *Lifeboat* (1943), in which she played a sophisticated journalist. The film was based on a John Steinbeck story. (Peter Stackpole, *Life* magazine © 1943 Time Inc.)

Worshiping Ethel Barrymore at a Hollywood party in 1950. (Ed Clark, *Life* magazine © 1950 Time Inc.)

With pals Laurence Olivier and his wife Vivien Leigh at a Hollywood party in 1950. (© 1950 Time Inc.)

Tallulah's imitation of the classic Durocher-versus-umpire stance for a skit in the New York baseball writers' show, 1953. (*Wide World*)

"I love you . . . I hate you." Tallulah and Tennessee Williams at a play, 1955. He didn't realize that she couldn't bear to be touched unexpectedly. Tallulah was soon to suffer on- and offstage as Blanche in his *Streetcar Named Desire*. (UPI)

Hug for her hero. Tallulah shows her feelings for former president Harry Truman at a Democatic luncheon in 1958. (*Wide World*)

JFK supporter Tallulah helped entertain the waiting crowd for five hours when John Kennedy was late. She's sitting on his right. To her right are Henry Fonda, Otto Preminger, and Eva Marie Saint. (Walter Sanders, *Life* magazine © 1960 Time Inc.)

Masks off, Tallulah and Adele Astaire (Fred's sister) arrive at
Truman Capote's masked ball at the Plaza Hotel in New York
City, 1967. It was called the party of the century. (Henry Gross-
man, *Life* magazine © 1966 Time Inc.)

libel? Did Barry say I put him in the hospital? Did I say it? No! Only Walker said it. Gossip columnists have no concern for facts. They thrive on suspicion, touched up with malice."

Patterson's laughter lost some of its impetus.

"What if Barry dies in Johns Hopkins?" Tallulah roared. "Your readers will think I've committed murder. I've been libeled and I demand a retraction and if I don't get it I'll sue!"

Patterson stopped laughing, but Tallulah never got the retraction. Danton Walker reported a few days later that Barry was recovering at the hospital, and that was all.

The play had reached Washington the night Barry was expected to return. And then Tallulah found she had a high temperature. "It's nothing to worry about," she told the harassed coproducer Lawrence Langner. "As a matter of fact, darling, I give my best performances when I'm ill, because then my diaphragm is not quite so powerful." Langner nodded his head like a man on the end of a rope.

Tallulah went to the doctor to okay her for the performance, but returned with bad news. "Sorry I can't go on tomorrow after all. The doctor tells me I've a temperature of 102."

Next morning Langner was about to cancel that night's performance when Dola Cavendish phoned. "It's all right. Tallulah woke up feeling much better. But she hasn't eaten for ages. We've been trying to get chicken, but there are none on account of rationing."

Langner's wife and coproducer, Armina, made a frantic search of Washington stores and came back triumphantly with a roast chicken.

"Tallulah ate it for breakfast," writes Langner in his book about the Theatre Guild, "and thereupon behaved like an angel, accepting her new lines without any comment and played out the Washington engagement in the most beautiful manner."

However, Tallulah had one last shot at getting her own way. Washington law wouldn't allow a child under fourteen to appear in the play, so a woman midget had been hired to play a child. Tallulah hated the idea and was all for breaking the law. "By the time the police come after us, we'll all have left town," she said.

"But, Tallulah, the Bankheads are famous for making the laws, not breaking them. Don't you want to continue the family tradition?" asked the manager, Peter Davies. It was a masterly approach.

"You're quite right, darling," she answered. "Daddy certainly wouldn't want me to break the law."

Although *Foolish Notion* was only a moderate hit on Broadway, the Tallulah–Donald Cook combination was a wow, and they decided to act together again as soon as they could find the right play.

XVIII

Tallulah Lays
an Egg

1946–1947 Tallulah now made one of the big mistakes of her life, turning down Tennessee Williams' *A Streetcar Named Desire* to play in Cocteau's *The Eagle Has Two Heads*, more aptly described as "The Eagle Lays an Egg."

Why did Tallulah reject *Streetcar?*

According to her friend and secretary, Ted Hook, it was because the play had the word nigger in it. He says she turned down *Sweet Bird of Youth* for the same reason. Tallulah was raised by mammies, was on the original board of directors of the NAACP, was the first white woman to appear on the cover of *Ebony* magazine; her maid, Rose Riley, was the first Negro maid allowed into the White House as a guest. Tallulah, as one of the greatest supporters of the Negro cause in America, says Hook, would not dream of appearing in a play in which the word nigger was used.

But apparently Tallulah would not have got the part even if she'd wanted it, and for that Williams blames himself.

He wrote in a *New York Times* article: "It is the winter of 1946–1947 and as always while writing a play very close to my heart, I think I am dying. My work-table is beneath a New Orleans skylight and beside it is the spectral figure of a lady and a star, impatiently keeping watch over my last agony at the typewriter. She is not still for a moment. She is sweeping all about me as I work, crying out, laughing, sobbing, but never losing the arrogance of a lady descended from a queen of Scotland. It is duly submitted to my agent, Audrey Wood, and after a short time that seemed like a century to me, Miss Wood dispatches a wire, mysteriously summoning me to a conference in Charleston, S.C. In the wire she mentioned that I would there be introduced to a person so important as to be called a personage, and since I have always been hooked on mystery and importance, I pulled my dying body together and caught a plane to the designated place of top-level consultation.

"The personage was a lady whose father was a Hollywood monarch and whose husband was another. (Obviously Irene Selznick, daughter of Louis B. Mayer, wife of David Selznick.)

" 'Whom do you have in mind,' asked this lady-producer, 'for your fantastic Blanche?'

" 'Well,' said I, 'while I was writing this play, all of the speeches seemed to be issuing from the mouth of Miss Bankhead.'

"The lady-producer said that she admired that inimitable voice as much as I did but that she feared that Tallulah would have such power in the part of Blanche that, if she consented to play it, the moth-like side of Blanche would be demolished at once by the tiger-like side of Blanche. And I must shamefully admit that, being a 'dying man,' I lacked the strength to oppose this strongly stated opinion, being not only a man who thought he was dying but a playwright who had entered that phase of a playwright's remorseless cycle of existence when he may even suspect that unanimous 'Yes' notices can add up to a sweetly disguised obituary to his professional being."

So Tallulah traveled by Eagle instead of Streetcar.

Playing opposite her was Marlon Brando, a young unknown who had to stand onstage for one scene doing nothing but listen to Tallulah talk nonstop for twenty-five minutes. Brando already showed signs of his future greatness, but one thing he found beyond his powers was to do nothing.

According to Tallulah's press agent, Richard Maney, Brando squirmed, picked his nose, adjusted his fly, leered at the audience, cased the furniture, and finally fixed his gaze, not on Tallulah, but on an offstage property man.

The play was meant to be a romantic melodrama. Brando turned it into a farce. In a nutshell the play was about a revolutionary (Brando) who turns up to assassinate a queen (Tallulah). Instead, he falls in love with her. She scorns him, so he shoots her and drinks a cup of poison. But once Brando had plugged Tallulah and had the stage to himself, he refused to give up the ghost. With a stomach full of poison he staggered about the stage, looking for a final resting place like a car in midtown Manhattan looking for a parking spot. The audience roared. Tallulah, spread out on the stairway, was raging. With half an eye she could see that Brando was stealing her thunder and lightning. The audience were in hysterics when Brando decided to fall and stop twitching. So was Tallulah.

She demanded a replacement—at once.

Martin Manulis, assistant to the play's producer, John C. Wilson, hurried to New York to rehearse the new man, Helmut Dantine.

Dantine watched Brando give his last three performances and thought he had a magnificent presence. "Basically," says Dantine, "I felt that he didn't believe in the play, didn't like his part and didn't like playing opposite Tallulah. His instinct told him that 'the play ain't no good.' It was colorful and amusing and old-fashioned—it wasn't 'with it' even at that time. Brando was very courteous and wanted to know if there was anything he could assist me with. He was very civilized and wished me good luck. On my opening night with it, he was sitting in the front row center wearing tennis sneakers. After the second act I saw him shuffling out the center aisle, but that was not a demonstration against me or the play. I think, being a totally honest human being, his curiosity having been satisfied, having lived with the play, why the hell should he sit through the third act? He knew what was going to happen. It was one of those uninhibited acts about which you would say: 'It isn't etiquette, but free spirits don't live by etiquette, as imposed by so-called normal people.' "

Dantine gave an accomplished performance and died on cue. The play reached Broadway and expired shortly after.

Meanwhile Brando had gone from the *Eagle* to *Streetcar*— from a bomb to the most important play of 1947. It won the Pulitzer Prize and established Tennessee Williams as one of the greats.

Tallulah went back home to "Windows" to plan her next move.

XIX

Private Lives
Gives Noel Coward
Public Shudders

1947–1948 Actor William Eythe had appeared with Tallulah in the traumatic movie *A Royal Scandal*. Now he was driving near her country home, "Windows," with a young actress, Buff Cobb. He stopped the car and said: ' That's where Tallulah lives. She eats young actresses alive, she's so rude to them. Want to meet her? I'd better go and see if I can bring you in. Just stay in the car until I find out."

Buff waited and listened for screams. Moments later she heard: "Bring her in, darling." The coast was clear.

"Hello darling," Tallulah greeted Buff Cobb. "Did you know that my father once saved your grandfather [Irvin Cobb] from drowning? They'd been off fishing together. Your grandfather fell in and my daddy pulled him out."

With the Cobb connection, says Buff Cobb, she was immediately "one of Tallulah's kind." That afternoon she remembers how Tallulah dropped names. "It was funny. Other people would name-drop Tallulah's name. She would name-drop the English nobility and her lovers—sometimes the same names."

Tallulah was looking for a cast to tour with her in a revival of Noel Coward's *Private Lives*. She'd already recruited Donald Cook to play opposite her. Their partnership had flared into romance after their meeting in *Foolish Notion*. Would Buff like to join them? The answer was yes.

Tallulah set out for the opening performance at Westport with her maid and her traveling companion, Dola Cavendish. Tallulah never traveled with a pocketbook—emulating the Queen of England—but had Dola trailing after her carrying the petty cash.

"You can choose all your own clothes," Tallulah told Buff, but when she saw her, exclaimed: "What kind of damn fool would let an eighteen-year-old go on in white tulle? I'm crazy to allow it, but you look so cute, I'm going to."

The tour was to turn out the longest, most rewarding, and most exhausting of Tallulah's career. During one heat wave the cast took salt pills to survive. Tallulah asked Buff her secret of looking fairly cool when there was no air conditioning in the hotel bedrooms.

Buff explained that she was living on cold lobster and daiquiris and Château d'Yquem and sleeping in the air-conditioned pump room.

"Tallulah was a tremendous extremist," recalls Buff Cobb with a laugh. "She ordered herself two cases of Château d'Yquem, a blender, and daiquiris and she existed on them for the next month. Naturally she got sick. She had vitamin deficiencies and such painful bursitis in her arm she was in traction for a week."

The play got stuck in Chicago. Playgoers crowded in week after week and it seemed as though the tour would never move on as planned.

Tallulah was often ill and in agonizing pain from neuritis. Radio interviewer Mike Wallace told her of a hypnotist with a remarkable reputation as a pain-killer. "Why don't you try him, Tallulah?" Wallace suggested. Wincing with pain, she answered: "Nobody can hypnotize me. I'm much too strong-willed." But she decided to give it a try. She desperately wanted to cooperate, but the hypnotist wasn't able to put her out.

Although Tallulah and Donald Cook played lovers with exuberant abandon on a stage sofa, offstage their romance had lost its spring. They were still friends, but there were other men in her life.

"Dave Garroway and Tallulah had a marvelous relationship," says Buff Cobb. "And they were a very odd couple indeed. But they had fun! Garroway used to end his radio show with 'Goodnight tiger,' which he changed to 'Goodnight Tallulah.' Later Tallulah took up with Bill Langford, who was an understudy with the show."

There wasn't much difference between the lighthearted, wacky play *Private Lives* and Tallulah's own private life in those days. During an after-theatre party at Mike Wallace's, Buff Cobb heard a tremendous row going on between Tallulah and her latest man. They were arguing over whose apartment they were going to, his or hers. Tallulah was wearing a dress with nothing but buttons down the back and she yelled: "Who the fuck is going to do it up in the morning if we go to your place? Any damn fool could get me out of this, but who's going to get me into it in the morning?"

Donald Cook was fighting the heat and humidity with drink and conviviality so Tallulah warned the company: "If you go out with Don, for Godsakes don't let him drink!"

Buff went out with him one night after this warning, but "how do you keep a grown man from drinking if he wants to? He started this toot and it ended up in a piano bar where he drank heavily. When he got back, Tallulah was furious with him and threatened to call Equity. He went on that night a bit groggy, but he got through his part. Tallulah was trying to find out who had been with him when he drank so much. I finally confessed. I said there wasn't anything I could do about it. She was in a towering rage. Although she drank a lot too, it never affected her performance."

It was twenty-five below zero when they played Minneapolis, and Buff Cobb was so ill that she suddenly went stone deaf on stage and had to lip read.

The night Noel Coward came to see what they were doing with his play, Tallulah knew he was out front.

"She gave a marvelous performance that night," says Buff Cobb.

Coward didn't think so. He had never intended that Tallulah should respond to almost every line of Donald Cook's with a gurgling laugh, or make double takes triple takes. "If I'd been Cook I'd have killed her," cracked Coward. He admitted that their way of playing it, so that the audience laughed at and not with the play, was remarkably effective. But he wasn't ready to be laughed at. Coward was not mad about the girl: he was mad at her. And when the play came to Broadway he wrote a letter to the press agreeing with their criticism of Tallulah as Amanda. When he had first played in *Private Lives* opposite Gertrude Lawrence in 1931 he'd called it quits after six months, despite full houses, because he was bored. Tallulah's fight against boredom included her satirizing the part and paying off her creditors from a salary of $4,500 a week.

"Tallulah would often say: 'I'm not only a great actress, I'm a great personality,'" recalls Buff Cobb. "She'd frequently quote herself and then laugh like crazy. You either were pro Tallulah or you hated her. She was an element, she wasn't a human being. She was a wind or a storm. But with it, she had Southern manners. We had to call her 'Ma'am' and knock on her dressing-room door before going in. I had a play I thought she'd like, so I told her about it. She said: 'Buff, is the woman common?' And I said: 'Yes, Tallulah, I think she is. Funny and common and. . . .' She said: 'No point in reading it. I couldn't POSSIBLY play it. My dear, I can play a whore, I can play a lady, but I cannot play anybody common.' Yet I've seen her do some things that I thought were rather common, but she had a kind of elegance and elan—it worked for her. With anybody else you'd just say: 'Oh my God, lock them up.' I was amused once when she called out: 'Wait, I'm not dressed! Now you can come in.' And what she called dressed was lipstick and a bra."

Though Coward wasn't pleased with Tallulah, her director Martin Manulis was. "It was an enormously successful revival with audiences," he says. "It ran almost three years in New York and on the road, which is incredible. Tallulah gave a very strong performance, really a personality appearance. It had a kind of circus color to it and was very wild. At the beginning Coward didn't feel she was right for the role and we started it as a short-term production, perhaps just to run in the summer in New York. We went to Chicago to play what was to be a few weeks of break-in engagement, but it played there over a year. For all her high jinks and everything Tallulah was very reliable in the theatre.

"I really was enormously fond of her. She was very demanding and demanding of your time, she lived such an odd life. To the outer world it might have sounded marvelous and glamorous, but night after night it wasn't."

"I don't think you've seen *Private Lives* unless you've seen Tallulah in it," says Cleveland Amory.

On October 21, 1948, just before *Private Lives* opened in New York, Tallulah broadcast a speech to introduce Harry Truman. Part of it was her family history: "There were Alabama Bankheads in one or another of the Houses of Congress for sixty consecutive years. My father was Speaker of the House for four years, served with the body for twenty-five. My grandfather, John, sat in the Senate for thirteen years. My uncle John spent twelve years of his life in the Upper House. They all died in harness. I would be outraging their memories, I would be faithless to Alabama, did I not vote for Harry Truman. Yes, I'm for Harry Truman, the human being. By the same token I'm against Thomas E. Dewey, the mechanical man. . . . Mr. Dewey is trim and neat and tidy, but is he human? I have my doubts. I have no doubts about Harry

Truman. He'd been through the wringer. And by the wringer I mean the Eightieth Congress. That Eightieth Congress which ignored his passionate pleas for veterans' housing, for curbs on inflation, for legislation to aid and comfort the great mass of our population. . . ."

Ten days later Truman spoke to a crowd of twenty thousand at Madison Square Garden. Tallulah spoke too, and next day a photograph of her kissing Truman's hand was on the front page of the *Daily News*.

Before the year ended *Time* magazine zeroed in on Tallulah.* "Even when it was new, seventeen years ago, Noel Coward's *Private Lives* was no great shakes as a play. When it was revived this fall on Broadway, it had plainly not improved with the years. But last week, as it has for the past six weeks, *Private Lives* was packing the Plymouth Theater with as many standees as the New York Fire Department will allow. What the customers were crowding to see was not so much a play as a remarkable personality with a remarkable name: Tallulah Bankhead.

"On stage, as well as off, Tallulah Bankhead mugs, flings, shouts and croaks her boisterous way through an outrageously amusing imitation of Tallulah Bankhead. Many a mediocre play has been dragged beyond its deserved life span by Tallulah's gaudy brilliance, but this time she has turned one into a smash hit singlehandedly.

"Tallulah is not the first lady of the theater. She is the theater's first personality. The theater's current first lady is a composite of Helen Hayes, Katharine Cornell, Judith Anderson, Lynn Fontanne—and Tallulah. But Tallulah does not fit neatly into a category, and other ladies of the stage, whatever their virtues as actresses, pale beside her as stars pale when a bonfire is lighted. . . ."

At home, glancing through the papers, Tallulah saw that Kirsten Flagstad was in New York. She'd heard her sing in *Tristan und Isolde* while *Private Lives* was in Chicago. She

* November 22, 1948.

wrote a far letter to the opera star, enclosing a letter from the Honorable Nathan D. Perlman, chairman of the fund-raising committee for the Foster Parents Division of the Labor Zionist Committee. The letter was an appeal to Flagstad for a contribution. Flagstad replied, enclosing a contribution, and the exchange of letters led to a meeting.

When Tallulah learned that Flagstad intended to see her in *Private Lives* she begged her to ignore the singing. In the play Tallulah had to sing "Some Day I'll Find You." And she had a problem. She couldn't always hit the right note to start with.

The opera star ignored the singing, loved the play, and invited Tallulah and friends back to her apartment where they talked themselves hoarse until six-thirty the next morning.

XX

Tallulah Makes
the Greatest Film Test Ever but
Loses *The Glass Menagerie*

1949 Tallulah went backstage to congratulate Laurette Taylor for coming out of years of retirement and an alcoholic haze to play the mother in Tennessee Williams' *The Glass Menagerie*. It was a performance that left the audience in no doubt that they were seeing the greatest actress of the age. Laurette clutched Tallulah's hand: "You," she said, "must play the part on the screen."

Four years later, in 1949, Hollywood was ready to bring it to the screen. And Tallulah got the news from her agent that she was to be tested for the part. Not just an ordinary test. It was planned to take three days and include six scenes. Irving Rapper, the director, was to fly from Hollywood to New York to direct this unusually extensive test.

Tallulah was thrilled and scared. Rapper was thrilled and scared too. He had seen Tallulah in *The Little Foxes*. He and actor John Garfield made it first on their agenda during a trip to New York. Both thought her overwhelming. But it was what he had heard about Tallulah that frightened Rapper to death. Bette Davis was known as an iron-willed woman who was as flexible as a ball bearing. Rapper had worked with Miss Davis more often than any other director and he found her less than the legend—tough but not traumatic. Tallulah, he understood, was worse than her reputation and could be even tougher and more tormenting than Bette

Rapper was, in fact, both frightened and fascinated, because he sensed that Tallulah was one of the brightest women in the theatre and that if he could tame her, the effect would be extraordinary.

When he reached New York, he telephoned her at "Windows." She invited him to spend the day with her and their mutual friends Glenn Anders and Mildred Dunnock. There, to his surprise and relief, he found Tallulah to be the very opposite of her legend. She was kind, sensitive, and considerate. "I never in my life found anyone so cooperative and intelligent,' he says.

Next day Tallulah was in a New York costumier, trying on a hat for the test. She called Rapper to look at it—and the hat was all she had on "She was so serious and I took my work so seriously," says Rapper. "There she was standing in the nude and I was looking her in the eyes and saying: 'Darling, any hat you like. It's only an impression of you for a second in close-up.' I don't know if she intended to shock me but I was a little shocked—and amused."

The night before the test, Tallulah stayed at the Algonquin Hotel. She phoned Rapper from there to say she was worried and afraid and asked him to come over. But he'd promised to go to Leonard Bernstein's birthday party that night and, having to get up at six next morning for the test, he tried to calm her over the phone.

The test took place in a low-ceilinged room in a studio in the West Fifties, during three sweltering summer days; days that Rapper and the camera crew will never forget.

Rapper went into her dressing room to wish her well and

noticed an unopened bottle of whisky on the table. She said to him: "Whatever you suggest, darling, I'll build on. And whatever I say, you build on."

She walked with him toward the camera and the waiting crew and began the first of six scenes.

"I was absolutely floored by her performance," says Rapper. "It's the greatest test I've ever seen in my life. I couldn't believe I was seeing such reality. She totally submerged her own personality and became the woman she was playing. I'll go so far as to say she was giving as brilliant if not a greater performance than Laurette Taylor. Miss Taylor had many mannerisms and stuttered as if she'd lost her reasoning. Tallulah was absolutely natural, so moving, so touching without even trying.

"The crew were stunned, too.

"After the test was completed—the most elaborate test I've ever done—I went to Tallulah's dressing room to hug her and thank her and I noticed then that some of the drink had gone. But she hadn't touched a drop during the three days she'd worked. Now, she was taking a drink as a release."

Next day, a well-known leading lady was tested and Karl Freund, the cameraman of great experience, said: "How can I work today, after working with Tallulah?"

Rapper and the crew thought there was no doubt that Tallulah would get the part and give the greatest performance of her life, and one of the greatest ever seen.

Others who saw the test were equally affected. Bill Orr, Jack Warner's son-in-law and head of Warner's television department, took his wife to see Tallulah's test. They both came out with tears streaming down their faces.

Some weeks later Tallulah's agent called her with the news. The part had gone to Gertrude Lawrence.

Tallulah didn't say a word.

But Errol Flynn cost Tallulah the part. Jack Warner had suffered because of Flynn's bouts with the bottle and dreaded the same problems would occur if they employed Tallulah.

So the studio decided not to take the risk. And for some mysterious reason, the film of Tallulah's astonishing, brilliant performance was ordered burned.

XXI

Radio Star:
Tallulah Sings

1950 Goodman Ace was in the office of an eye, ear, nose, and throat specialist, awaiting treatment for an allergy. The door burst open and a woman came in, lifted her skirt, and turned her back. The doctor reached over and gave her a shot. And the woman walked out.

"Who was that?" Ace asked.

"Tallulah Bankhead."

Probably the only silent appearance Tallulah ever made.

But Ace, a comedy writer, had been enchanted with the little he saw of Tallulah. When he heard she was to star in a new radio series he took a big cut in salary to work with her.

NBC radio had called on Tallulah in a last-ditch attempt to recapture power and glory. Bleeding from raiding parties made by rival CBS who had snared some of their top attractions, weakened by creeping television, NBC radio saw Tallulah as the shot in the arm needed to bring about a massive recovery.

But a month before the radio show opened she agreed to do a lecture tour. If the radio show failed she'd have something to fall back on—as well as something to talk about. Her first lecture was in the auditorium of the Southern Methodist University in Dallas. Every one of the 2,800 seats was sold.

She came on stage, calling out "Hello, darlings" to the crowd, then gave them a preview of her autobiography. A *Life* photographer took a photograph of her standing on one leg, a tiny, very upright figure on the stage, before a microphone and a table with a glass on it. "I bet you think this is gin," she said as she took a swig. "I wish it was." If Tallulah, as she claimed, hated a liar more than a murderer, she must have hated herself at that moment. She shook with nerves as if she had malaria, sang without anything being thrown, and did impressions. The audience shook, too—she had them convulsed.

"Miss Bankhead showed the lecture world a new trick," wrote John Rosenfield in the *Dallas Morning News*. "There are two types of attractions, one with a message, and the other to stalk personality. Here is an ideal formula for projecting celebrity. She gave the paying customers what the lecture committee ordinarily reserves for itself in a postperformance cocktail party."

And another anonymous critic was reported by Richard Maney to say: "There is no doubt that Mr. Charles Laughton, tonight's lecturer, has what vaudevillians call 'a tough act to follow.' " Come to think of it, that critic was probably Maney himself. But she had been great entertainment. And she flew on to Chicago and Wilmington, within the week, to repeat with some variations her solo performance of words, music, mimicry, and memorabilia, all by Tallulah.

Between flights and lectures she rehearsed for the upcoming radio show. She recalled grimly: "I walked through the rehearsal like a woman under water, numb with humiliation."

Why? Because the writers seemed to have relegated her to a back seat. That she would endure only in a cab.

But she had to quit the lecture tour as too exhausting. And, after all, she'd already seen America in *Private Lives*.

The program, called "The Big Show," was to run ninety minutes every Sunday night. Tallulah was to be mistress of ceremonies and hostess to the world's most wanted people.

Now, whenever she dropped a name, its owner would sing with her, act with her, trade quips, cut up, comment, answer questions, ask questions. All that activity couldn't be left to the ingenuity of the stars. So writers, Ace among them, crowded into a little room with ham-on-rye sandwiches and black coffee, and imagined what they'd say if they were Tallulah and her guests. "Darling . . ." three writers wrote, got stuck, and sent down for more coffee.

Up with the fresh coffee came news that brought a spurt to the typing. Ethel Merman was opening on Broadway in *Call Me Madam* on Saturday, the day before the debut of "The Big Show." She had agreed to appear on that first broadcast and to sing chunks from the entire score of the musical.

"Ethel sings," wrote one writer and then, unblocked, he continued as follows:

"Tallulah: Thank you Ethel, that was wonderful.

"Ethel: Thank you Tallulah. It was such a pleasure being on your show.

"Tallulah: It was our pleasure Ethel. Thank you again.

"Ethel: Thank you, Tallulah, for having me.

"Tallulah: Thank you and goodnight."

The writer whipped this dialogue from his typewriter and took it to the producer, Dee Engelbach. Engelbach glanced at it and nodded approval.

The writer showed Goodman Ace a carbon copy and said: "Engelbach likes it."

Ace flipped and flew to Engelbach.

"Are you going to use that?" he asked.

"I think so."

"But this is the first chance Tallulah gets to talk on the show and all she's doing is thanking Ethel."

Engelbach looked puzzled: "That's what you're supposed to do."

"In that case we ought to do it Tallulah style," suggested Ace.

"What's that?"

"I'll show you." Ace went to his typewriter and wrote: "Ethel Merman sings for eight minutes. (Audience can be expected to give ovation.) Tallulah says: 'Thank you Ethel Merman, and better luck next time.' "

Ace took it to the producer, who weighed the paper in his hand without looking at it: "It seems kinda long," he said.

But Ace persuaded him to look—and he looked and liked. And that style set the entire mood of the show.

"For chrissakes!" said Tallulah after seeing the finished script for the first broadcast. "Ethel Merman's got all the fucking jokes! Why not call it 'The Ethel Merman Show' and have done with it?"

The dialogue was transposed. Ethel played straight woman—Tallulah got the laughs.

When Ethel saw the revised script on Sunday morning only hours before show time, she wanted to transpose the producer—and telling him so, hit a high note that split four ways. She objected because Tallulah had now lassoed all the laugh lines.

Tallulah countered that Ethel had all the songs. Did she want all the laughs as well? Apparently she did.

So Tallulah demanded at least one song—and got it. "Give My Regards to Broadway" was within her range but each time she started on a different note. Composer and orchestra conductor Meredith Willson was called upon to work a musical miracle. How could he get Tallulah to strike the right note every time?

He approached her cautiously. "Miss Bankhead," he said, "you have perfect pitch." She purred. "But you haven't got relative pitch." He took her into a corner and suggested a remedy.

They came out of the corner beaming. Willson started the orchestra for "Give My Regards to Broadway," and just before she was to sing, he hummed the starting note in her ear. It worked every time.

Ethel wasn't too happy about Tallulah having all the laugh lines AND someone to hum in her ear.

Tallulah fought for every line and every laugh because she was afraid that she was going to be overshadowed by guest stars who were celebrated for their work in revues, musical comedies, or vaudeville or who, like Ethel Merman, had outstanding singing voices. As a dramatic actress Tallulah felt that trading a few quips with comedians and introducing each act was going to diminish her. Her depression showed. The producer was unnerved. He couldn't imagine anything but failure with Tallulah going through her lines with the vivacity of a patient etherized upon a table.

Goodman Ace, shut in his writer's room (writers weren't allowed in the same room as performers), heard Tallulah's depression coming over the microphone, her voice like a foghorn going down for the third time. That evening he joined an invited audience in the theatre to watch the first broadcast performance, hoping the people there would give Tallulah enough lift to please the radio listeners.

The live audience did it.

Critic John Crosby, a man who thought radio was dying, wrote with enthusiasm: "One of the fastest and funniest ninety minutes in my memory. It was housed in NBC's newly acquired Center Theatre (three thousand seats); it had a forty-four piece orchestra and a sixteen-voice choir presided over by Meredith Willson: it cost about a trillion dollars—and, well, it was big. . . . Tallulah even sang 'Give My Regards to Broadway' in a voice that almost had more timbre than Yellowstone National Park."

In one night Tallulah acquired thirty million fans.

And what must have stilled her deepest fears, was critic John Crosby's line: "She succeeded somehow in outshining even the most glittering names on that glittering roster."

The Metropolitan Opera's leading baritone was a nervous guest on "The Big Show" even though he had only two words to say—his name. But he had never spoken on radio before and was afraid he would lapse into a childhood stutter. According to the script, Tallulah would announce: "For the next hour and thirty minutes, this program will present, in person, such bright stars as . . ." And when it came to his turn he was supposed to jump in with his name. Tallulah sensed he was not at ease, dropped her script, and said spontaneously. "I heard this beautiful boy sing today. He has a great voice and I love him."

A relaxed young man stepped up to the mike and said: "Robert Merrill." Word perfect—and no stutter.

In his autobiography* Merrill says he was trusted with a few lines in the next show and even invited to take part in the script conference. "She had the best team, headed by Goodman Ace, but she lashed them like sled dogs. Her long legs in floppy slacks propped up on the desk, puffing a cigarette—she screamed and groaned and exploded in raucous sarcasm. 'If I can't get any writers with balls, I'll have to write it myself!'

"She took a phone call from Ethel Barrymore: 'Ethel, I want you for a simply lovely sketch. About the old days in the theatah. And here's the blackout line. I say, "I just loved your brother's performance," and your line is "What did you see John in?" and I say, "Bed!" . . . But, daahling! He really *was* the best I ever had . . . Well, let's have lunch . . .'

"Since she dreaded to be alone, she invited me often to parties in her house off Sutton Place. I suppose I was the straight man, relief for all the comedy of the exotic flora that surrounded her. I'd sing a few numbers and go home by midnight. Tallulah was on till five or six. I never saw her in daylight."

"She was a great actress," says Goodman Ace. "I saw both Jeanne Eagels and Tallulah in *Rain* (Tallulah played in a

* Robert Merrill with Robert Saffron, *Between Acts: An Irreverent Look at Opera and Other Madness* (New York: McGraw-Hill, 1976.)

revival on Broadway for forty-seven performances in 1935). Jeanne Eagels was superb, one of our greatest actresses, but Tallulah was great, did it beautifully. She could have done a lot of things if she'd been more disciplined. She listened when somebody else was on, she didn't just stand there waiting for her cue. She was a real pro.

"During 'The Big Show' she'd suddenly burst into laughter right after she'd spoken a funny line and say: 'I just got that one darlings.'

· "We wrote a number of sketches for her that came under the heading of 'Tallulah Against Conformity.' One was her learning to drive. And another was her going on the subway for the first time.

"My wife has a little joke she thinks is funny. I don't. Once Tallulah called the house and asked for me when I wasn't there. And she said to my wife: 'Darling, I've got to get in touch with him because he writes so wonderfully well for me. How he's captured my character! Everybody thinks we're sleeping together.'

"We writers adored the character of Tallulah. We didn't have to invent a character. We just elaborated on what we heard about her."

It was decided they needed a theme song for the show and, inspired by a deadline, Meredith Willson remembered the farewell his mother sang to her class as a Sunday school teacher and wrote: "May the Good Lord Bless and Keep You." Tallulah took to it as though she'd been waiting all her life for this kind of farewell to audiences. Meredith hummed the first note in Tallulah's ear and the guest stars all did a phrase.

Next week the show was broadcast from Hollywood, and everyone flew out there. Tallulah stayed on a few days to say hello to Ethel Barrymore and other friends. Meredith Willson was just about to board the midnight plane back to New York when he saw Tallulah hurrying across the field toward him, her tawny hair streaming and her white ermine coat floating behind her, and fans at her heels. She was crying

out: "Darling! Darling! Wait, darling!" When she reached
him and got her breath, she said: "Oh, darling, that song.
We must never, never leave the air without that song. I don't
care if we lose the commercial message, let the sponsor go,
but never, ever cut that song." And she threw back her head,
quite conscious of the little circle around her now, and sang
in her inimitable way:

> · May the good Lord bless and keep you,
> . . . er . . . er . . .
> In all the old familiar places.

XXII

Tallulah on Trial

1951–1952 "The Big Show" traveled to England for two weeks in September, 1951 and Tallulah held a press conference in the Ritz Hotel, where she stayed when she first went to England in 1923. She climbed on a chair, removed her shoe, poured champagne into it, said, "To Britain, God bless her," and drank.

British radio audiences heard the show too but weren't ready for insult comedy. The British critics generally blasted the blend of sentimental and sour.

But back in the United States Tallulah was an attraction to almost everyone with a radio set. It was the ideal life for her: after rehearsal and performance, she was free for the rest of the week.

And then a court action involving Evyleen Cronin, a former secretary-maid, threatened to ruin her as "America's darling."

Tallulah spent several days before and after Christmas, 1951 in a New York court as witness for the prosecution of Mrs. Cronin. The trial took place before an all-male jury in a stuffy, overheated courtroom while a snowstorm either threatened or raged outside.

Tallulah went into court on that first day with a pocketbook crammed with telegrams. Vincent Price and Estelle were playing in *The Cocktail Party* on the West Coast. They and all the other members of the cast had sent her a good-luck telegram. Scores of other such telegrams arrived from almost every company then touring America.

"She was absolutely deluged with wires," says Vincent Price. "Actors particularly liked her because she wasn't a phoney. She was an improbable character to begin with but she was not a phoney."

Evyleen Cronin had been charged with altering Tallulah's checks and pocketing the difference. Mrs. Cronin's attorney, State Senator Fred Morritt, tried to take the spotlight off his client and put Tallulah on trial as a cruel and immoral woman and a drug addict. He charged: "Mrs. Cronin's jobs included paying for marijuana, cigarettes, cocaine, booze, and sex. Mrs. Cronin will testify that Miss Bankhead taught her to roll marijuana cigarettes. She became adept and in five hours could roll ninety-eight of them. When my client went to Miss Bankhead for money she was beaten at least fifty times. She beat her unmercifully. She also took care of Miss Bankhead's gigolos. We are going to prove that as part of her duties Mrs. Cronin would be told to give money to her lovers."

Morritt then shouted to the judge: "Throughout my opening statement, Miss Bankhead is making remarks, facial expressions, or sounds which might be all right on a radio program but not in a court of law. I ask the court to direct her to keep her mouth shut and to censure her."

Judge Harold Stevens, presiding at his first major case, replied quietly: "I am not censuring Miss Bankhead. I advise all witnesses to act in accordance with the respect due to the court."

As Tallulah swept angrily out of the court, reported a *Daily Express* correspondent, she said: "I'm disgusted with the tactics of the defense attorney. I've a natural bronchial condition. My cough is an old addiction. As far as the defense counsel is concerned I can't even cough in court."

More than three hundred people, ninety-eight percent of

them men, and many of those bald and middle-aged, lined up for seats to see the trial. When a cameraman took a photo of the line one man hid his face with a newspaper, saying: "Do you think I want my wife to know where I spent the day?"

On the ninth day of the trial, attorney Morritt became very angry and was standing up, waving his arms and shouting. The judge ordered court attendants to push him into his seat. When he calmed down, Mrs. Cronin gave evidence. She admitted that she was a former striptease artist, "down to bra and panties—like they do on Broadway today," and testified: "I once said to Miss Bankhead: 'Baby you're spending too much money.' And Miss Bankhead got mad and hit me in the breast, saying: 'I don't want you ever to talk to me about money. This happens to be my business.'" Then Mrs. Cronin wrote out the language Miss Bankhead had used, which was apparently too hot for the jury to be shown.

Mrs. Cronin said she used to buy clothing and food for Tallulah, to bathe her and give her rubdowns, and: "I just did everything I could for her."

Why did she raise the amount on the checks? To pay for Tallulah's entertainment and charities, she claimed. "One night Miss Bankhead told me to give forty dollars to Bill Langford who was playing in *Private Lives* so that Miss Bankhead and he could go to a nightclub. Next night she told me to give him twenty dollars when they went out. Once she told me to give an extra ten dollars to a cab driver who had told her some story about his child.

"I also paid out money for ginger medicine for Miss Bankhead's laryngitis. There was a lot of alcohol in the medicine and it cost $7.50 a bottle. Miss Bankhead also had a small bottle of champagne every night at the theatre for which I paid."

As Tallulah left the court someone shouted: "You have all the Giant fans behind you!"

Tallulah beamed: "Oh good," she said.

Every time Tallulah was introduced to the audience before

"The Big Show" went on the air (it was broadcast from a theatre), she'd bring up the subject of the trial and the audience would cheer. "They were all on her side," believes Goodman Ace. "She was outspoken and candid about it."

Buff Cobb, who'd toured with Tallulah and Bill Langford in *Private Lives,* told Tallulah she'd be delighted to testify on her behalf, but it wasn't necessary. "The whole thing was Tallulah's fault," says Buff. "Because Tallulah was so cavalier about money. Dola Cavendish (who normally handled Tallulah's money) was sick and had gone up to Canada and this Cronin woman, who was really a mealy-mouthed thing—and Tallulah didn't realize this—was turning into the greatest 'yes' woman of all time. She was trying to push her way into Tallulah's inner circle and she finally made it. Not up to Tallulah's standards at all. Tallulah trusted her with everything. She'd bring all the checks to her and Tallulah wouldn't even look at them."

There was a break for Christmas, then the trial went into its eleventh day on December 28, 1951. Mrs. Cronin continued her evidence with a refreshed memory, listing among the things she'd bought for Tallulah "bobby pins, beer, birds, a birdcage, liquor and lobsters, port wine and pillowcases." Someone in court was heard to murmur, "and a partridge in a pear tree."

Mrs. Cronin said she paid fifty dollars for cocaine and about as much for Tallulah's marijuana.

The trial ended on the thirteenth day—Tallulah's lucky number—when Mrs. Cronin was found guilty of stealing. Because of her age—fifty-nine—Judge Stevens gave her a suspended sentence of one to two years' imprisonment on each of three charges. He praised Tallulah for her generous attitude and for not expressing "a vindictive desire that Mrs. Cronin should be punished by imprisonment."

Mrs. Cronin died in a New York hospital a year later.

Tallulah felt no guilt over the outcome of the trial. Mrs. Cronin had been caught stealing, had tried to wriggle out of the charge by resorting to blackmail, and had lost. In her autobiography Tallulah writes: "My sins have left no scars on my conscience. Long since I've repented and atoned for such escapades as may have wounded others." Tallulah had begun tape-recording the story of her life, "as much of the truth as I dare," in the late summer of 1951. The trial had interrupted the tale. Now she got back to it, pacing the living room floor of "Windows." She'd already reached 150,000 words and was only halfway through. At the time she thought to call it "Ah, my foes, and Oh, my friends," but that was changed by mutual agreement to just "Tallulah." After Tallulah's tapes were transcribed, Richard Maney ran the story through his typewriter, simplifying, clarifying, and trying to avoid libel actions. There was one which Victor Gollancz, Tallulah's publisher in England, lost. Tallulah said in her autobiography that when Olga Lindo replaced her in *Rain* the play was an immediate failure. In fact, it ran for six months.

Tallulah's book, published in 1952, was a best-seller for twenty-six weeks.

That Christmas Tallulah's American publisher, Cass Canfield of Harper & Row, and his wife went to Tallulah's home "Windows" expecting a riotous party. But because of the deep snow, they were the only guests to make it.

They had a marvelous, quiet time, just talking.

"The Big Show" went off the air in the spring of 1952. Tallulah made her TV debut in the fall of the same year, as a regular star on NBC's new "All Star Review." "From the moment of her entrance . . . it was a Tallulah joyously and overwhelmingly alive" raved Jack Gould in *The New York Times*. John Crosby, his rival on *The New York Herald Tribune* joined in the applause: ". . . it demonstrated beyond the shadow of an option that Tallulah was a great television personality . . . She is a magnificent comedienne and NBC, I think, has corralled a really great success."

XXIII

Sleepless Nights and
Dear Charles

1954 Almost everyone who worked with Tallulah started out scared and ended up either sorry or with a fascinating friend for life.

Arthur Penn, fresh out of directing on television, was offered a chance to cut his teeth on a stage play called *Dear Charles* in summer stock. He was young and resilient, so—though anticipating trouble from the star, Tallulah—thought he could handle it.

Penn accepted an invitation to dinner at "Windows" to discuss the play. Tallulah was now fifty-two. Penn realized that she had once been a stunning beauty, the belle of the ball, a great sort of maverick, but that now she was living out the vestiges of that role—for which she was thirty years too old.

From midnight on she reverted to being a three-year-old who pleaded with him to stay and sit by her until she went to sleep.

Penn went with her and sat beside her bed. She took his hand and closed her eyes and battled to go to sleep. At one point she was almost off, then woke with a start. "I haven't been to sleep for three days," she complained. Finally, hours later, she freed his hand. And he tiptoed out.

At rehearsal next day the kitten was a lion. She wanted to play the part as herself. Penn wanted her to play the character.

"Tallulah," he said. "This isn't a serious play and we're not trying to penetrate the role all that deeply, but I want you to put yourself inside the play."

"You sound just like Kazan!" she yelled.

"Look," he pointed out, "there are only two ways to go, yours or mine. And since I'm directing the play I think you'd better go mine. Afterward you can do what you please."

As he watched her Penn felt that acting was an enormous strain for Tallulah. And he suspected the camp version of Tallulah that she wanted to present was partly an attempt to avoid the strain of building a character.

She struggled and objected and made counter-suggestions and raised her eyebrows and her voice. Then it became clear to Penn that he was asking her to do something she feared to do: forget Tallulah.

She invited him to dinner once more, once again begged him to stay with her until she slept. He did.

Next day Tallulah continued rehearsing the way Penn wanted—to the best of her ability. But it was obviously with reluctance.

The play began its pre-Broadway tour and Penn said goodbye to Tallulah. He had expected trouble and she had lived up to his expectations. "She was really, I think, profoundly a kind of Cinderella character," says Penn. "She would like to go to a ball every night, but the idea of maintaining her relationship with the prince was absolutely impossible."

But Tallaluh had been right about her performance. The audience wanted to see Tallulah in a play and not a play with Tallulah disguised as one of the characters. At Hyannisport it was such a success that a Broadway opening was arranged and Tallulah made a surprise phone call to dress designer Gene Coffin in New York City.

It was a Sunday when Coffin lifted the receiver to hear a

string of directions from Tallulah: "Darling, I need an evening gown, a cocktail dress, a morning dress, and then I need a dress for when I'm out cutting flowers. Come up on the plane. We'll meet you in Hyannisport with a car. And I want sketches of those dresses. Now catch the afternoon plane and we'll get together tomorrow night." And the phone went dead. Tallulah had hung up.

Coffin was frantic. He didn't have any drawing paper or a drawing board. The stores were closed. He finally used brown wrapping paper for the sketches. He caught the plane and took the sketches to Tallulah at her hotel.

She roared with laughter when he showed her one sketch of each dress—the Hollywood way, to which he was accustomed. On Broadway, an actress has a choice of several designs. But she said "They're beautiful" and gave him the go-ahead to start stitching.

Coffin arrived with a little Italian woman at four in the afternoon to fit Tallulah, now back in her New York home.

She had just got up and was suffering from near-to-opening-night nerves.

"I'm in a foul mood," she greeted them. "Haven't even had coffee. Let's get this thing over!"

The first dress was a good fit.

The second dress, fine, except for a minor alteration.

But she let the third dress fall off her and ran around the room in just her panties shouting and screaming: "Coming up here in the middle of the day to fit! The goddamned dress is so heavy, it's more like a battleship! And it's got too many beads on it!" And on and on and on.

Coffin sat and waited for the storm to die down.

But the dressmaker stood like a woman in shock. She had never witnessed anything in her life like this. It was as if she was watching someone go mad before her eyes—and she was the cause. She was so upset that she became ill in the cab on the way back to the costume house.

Next time Coffin saw Tallulah he said: "You know you did

something terrible to this woman. You shouldn't have performed like that."

"Darling, I wasn't performing."

"Maybe it was for real. But she'd never seen anything like this. She lives out on the Island in a little bungalow probably, but she's a terrific seamstress."

A few days before opening night in September, 1954, Tallulah sent the woman four tickets to the opening night and a tremendous bouquet of American Beauty roses. And the card read: "The flowers are for you darling." It was Tallulah's way of saying she was wrong—and she had made another friend for life.

Coffin was in for more surprises from Tallulah. The next one came after the Broadway opening, when his telephone rang at two-thirty in the morning. Coffin jumped like crazy and heard: "Tallulah, darling."

"What's the matter?" he asked.

"Nothing, darling. But I know you, you poverty-stricken son of a bitch, you probably don't take the *Wall Street Journal*. Neither do I, but I've got a copy here with a review. I want to read the first line: 'Tallulah made her comeback to Broadway after six years.' Now of course, anybody else would say I look like a million dollars. But the *Wall Street Journal* says: 'Looking like several million dollars . . . in gowns by Gene Coffin.' I want to tell you one thing. Now you're in the second paragraph. Next time, if you're in the first paragraph, your head goes. Goodnight." And she hung up.

Back on Broadway, Tallulah tried to revive her triumphant days. At Christmas she gave a big party and ex-husband John Emery was one of the first to arrive and one of the last to leave. They behaved like good friends. It was obvious that he still found her a delight in small doses.

William Roerick starred opposite Tallulah in *Dear Charles* and was incensed when friends would say, after a performance, such things as "Now you can't tell me she wasn't drunk tonight, the way she fell over the sofa."

Roerick would indignantly reply: "It was all worked over and rehearsed. Every bit of what seemed like fabulous clowning was very precisely figured out. Tallulah never throws anybody onstage by doing anything unexpected. No, she was not drunk."

Roerick enjoyed Tallulah when she wasn't maintaining the Tallulah legend for public consumption. He was one of the few who saw the other, radically different side of her. "Alone I found her mystical, attentive, and eager to learn," recalls Roerick. "Then she was a quiet, strange woman and I liked her very much. She used to pump me to get information. I once mentioned Ikhnaton, husband of Nefretete. As far as anyone knows he was the first monotheist, a very interesting and curious man. Tallulah finally got out of me everything I'd ever read about ancient Egypt."

When the play reached Los Angeles, Tallulah asked Roerick to escort her to lunch with Bing Crosby in the Paramount Studios commissary. She had just been seeing playwright George Kelly and he'd given her books by Madame Blavatsky, the Russian mystic. Tallulah was talking about this, racing along like a well-oiled machine gun, and garbling her words. Then she took a breath and said to Crosby: "Bing darling, do you know what I'm talking about?"

"No, Tallulah, I don't think I do."

"Neither do I, and I like to know what I'm talking about." And she changed the subject.

After the last performance of *Dear Charles*, Roerick went into Tallulah's dressing room and said: "I won't be seeing you anymore."

"I know, darling, you have your place in the country and I have mine. But we'll be seeing each other."

"You don't understand what I'm saying, Madam. I won't be seeing you again. You know I'm deeply devoted to you, but I can't stand your public personality."

She stared at him for a moment, then said: "Darling, isn't it awful? I make vows that I'm going to stop all this nonsense, but people come around and it takes over, it takes over." And as she spoke, the public personality took over. While she was talking, it was as though she were being possessed by another creature: Tallulah Bankhead. And she went on, quickening her pace. "After all, darling, we can't go around showing people what we're really like. I mean pearls before swine, dear. Pearls before swine."

XXIV

No Sex—Just a Matter
of Geography

Philip Hall wandered into Tallulah's life one Saturday afternoon and stayed five years. A friend had invited him to spend a few hours in the pool at "Windows." One thing led to another. He went back to stay longer each time, and hazy weeks merged into years. He became her secretary and friend. He learned to move at a snap of her fingers, and he found that to try to live at her pace was an almost deadly occupation. The thirty-six-hour days could only be endured by a superman or a yogi. Sometimes he and Tallulah were so exhausted that they'd fall asleep in the same bed—and wake up with no memory of how they got there. "It was just a matter of geography," says Hall. "And Tallulah would ask: 'Did we byze last night?'" Hall survived the Tallulah treatment, though only after undergoing four major operations. He remembers Tallulah with delight, affection, and pain.

But Stanley Haggart needs more time for the smoke to clear. "We were quite close and perhaps intimate and we knew each other very, very well," he says. "We had lots of talks and shared lots of things but I don't remember her with delight—not yet.

"Philip Hall used to work for me when I was designing for television, and his hours became more and more peculiar, and I found out he had got caught in the world of Tallulah. He'd turn up later and later and later and finally he quit and worked with her full time. He was her cigarette lighter. That's the function of her secretaries. This was during 'The Big Show.' I spent about twelve to fourteen hours with her that first meeting at the Elysee Hotel. Hall and I had stopped by for a four o'clock drink and stayed until dawn. Even then she was hard to get away from. She decided that I was for her.

"One of her things that evening was to 'play' the hostess with me on 'The Big Show' by getting all the people she knew across the country, on the telephone, to meet me. She was in love with the idea of being the hostess, on 'The Big Show' and even in her own life. She introduced me and told them who I was and then I had to talk to them whether we had anything to say to each other or not—it didn't matter. One was a man who had a puppet show on TV every night. Another was Ethel Barrymore in California. It was terrible. I said to Ethel Barrymore: 'We were sitting here trying to think of where you would be at this particular time. And I figured you were at a double-feature movie at the Grauman's Egyptian with a bag of popcorn.' She roared her deep laugh. Then I explained what Tallulah had insisted that we do. And she said: 'How very like her.'

"At the Elysee Hotel when we were having dinner she said very grandly and elaborately that the dog had to eat off her plate. There was still some left over, so she said: 'No waste of food for me,' and she called the maid and butler and gave it to them.

"She told me her daddy had taught her to do recitations from the Bible and Shakespeare. 'Give me a theme and I will do it.' So I suggested something impassioned. She chose a scene from the Bible. Then I chose the theme 'love.' She used these as devices to make advances.

"She said: 'Will you byze with me?' Then I didn't know what in the world it meant. And then she said: 'It will be the most fabulous experience of your life. You've never had an experience until you've had it with me.' And she insisted upon the great, wonderful sex experience of my life that I could have with her if I wanted, it would be the great thing of all time.' Finally, at this point, Hall and I escaped together, because it really was not my dish of tea. She did a real Tallulah Bankhead thing then. He got the door open finally and there in the public hall was an artificial fireplace that she had had banished to make room for her radio set. She ran past Philip into the hall, threw herself against this artificial fireplace with her head high and cried: 'You can't leave now!' It was all stage scenery. She was quite serious but I felt it would be so theatricalized and so artificial and such a production. She used those devices as well, I believe, to cover her rejections.

"She shocked me tremendously. I'm a Puritan. I took a young man to meet her backstage and he went home to her apartment. She said: 'Put me to bed.' And he took off her clothes and tucked her in. What shocked me most was her ruthlessness and selfishness in conversation and her thoughtlessness of others. She was an expert at destroying the men around her, at putting them down.

"My affinity for Tallulah Bankhead and the affinity of many fellows I know . . . it's part of our own psyche to be attracted sometimes to monster women, to distortions of womankind. And we have that need sometimes for being involved and we use it one way or another. That was a phase I went through.

"I think 'The Big Show' was the beginning of the end for her. It was like a bizarre funeral, a bizarre national funeral in which she was the goddess and became the caricature of herself and whatever possibilities she had as an actress were buried and gone.'"

XXV

Tallulah in
Las Vegas

1954   Tallulah treated her body as though it belonged to someone else whom she wanted to hurt, and she was bombing her career by performing in lightweight plays that ran forever out in the sticks or flopped fast on Broadway. She excelled in *The Little Foxes* and *The Skin of Our Teeth*. But what else? As a girl she had made an effort to be in a great play by a living author—Shaw's *Heartbreak House*. She wanted that part so badly she'd gone into St. Patrick's Cathedral and prayed for it. For ten days she rehearsed the part, then the Theatre Guild told her Ellie Dunn was taking over. Ellie had recovered from an illness and they'd only been using Tallulah to keep the rest of the cast in rehearsal. The bitterness and disappointment remained forty years later. Tallulah had a brief liaison with greatness in Ibsen's *Hedda Gabler*, televised in 1954. "A lioness playing Puss in Boots," wrote a critic.

Now, with the chance to create Tennessee Williams characters conceived in her likeness, she put her foot in his face and grabbed for frothy comedies in which she could give vaudeville performances. "Tallulah gives her throaty laugh." "Tallulah does a triple take." "Tallulah imitates TALLULAH." While Tennessee Williams was turning out *A Streetcar Named Desire* (1947), *Summer and Smoke* (1948), *Rose Tat-*

too (1951). *Camino Real* (1953), *Cat on a Hot Tin Roof* (1955), Tallulah was tussling with the abortive *The Eagle Has Two Heads*, cavorting in almost three years of *Private Lives*, a few months of *Dear Charles*, stock revivals in summer theatres, and playing herself as mistress of ceremonies on the radio.

She held off Tennessee Williams as if she dreaded the inevitable encounter, feeling perhaps that she was so far gone into playing a superficial version of herself that she would not have the self-discipline needed to create the fresh, deeper, Tallulah-inspired characters he wrote.

His *Cat on a Hot Tin Roof* was being cast in 1954 when Tallulah took off for Las Vegas to star in *Ziegfeld Follies*.

Ted Hook, a chorus boy at The Sands Hotel in Las Vegas, was on tiptoe with expectancy. His idol, Tallulah Bankhead, was coming to head the show. He had done a paper on her in college, based on a *Time* magazine feature, and had gotten an A-plus on it. He'd never dreamed he'd ever work with her. Now he and three other chorus boys, beside themselves with anxiety, waited during rehearsal for this great lady to arrive. And down the aisle of the theatre she came with Dolores the Maltese and Gabrielle the Pekinese. And she was furious! The smile fled from Jack Entratter's face as she screamed at him: "How dare you, darling! I will not have this! My name always comes at the top of the bill. It should be 'Tallulah Bankhead starring in the Jack Entratter Production of Ziegfeld Follies!' In minutes the boys were on the ladders to give Tallulah top billing.

"She didn't let us down on that first meeting," says Ted Hook. "She threw a marvelous tantrum. But she was amusing throughout and she was only sticking up for her rights because she didn't have an agent in those days. She walked up the aisle and she saw the four of us and the choreographer introduced us and she said: 'Come along darling, we're going to be burning the candle at both ends for the next four weeks.'

"And she wasn't kidding. Because every night after the show the four of us sat at the foot of her bed and listened to her fabulous stories. And we'd finally take turns because we got so we couldn't take it. She had perpetual insomnia and she'd keep us there until noon and one o'clock the next afternoon. The room was pitch black and she had the air conditioning going full blast. Whenever she got hungry she'd pick up the phone and all sorts of hors d'oeuvres were brought immediately.

"One time they told her that the cook had gone off duty so she found out what his room number was. He was living at the hotel. She called him up and told him she'd give him fifty dollars if he'd whip up some little goodies because she and her friends were hungry. So of course he ran down and got them, and when he came by she gave him a hundred dollars."

The surprise was mutual when opera singer Robert Merrill spotted Tallulah in the bar of The Sands hotel, in Las Vegas.

"Daaahling! What the blazing hell are you doing *here?*" she asked as she kissed him energetically and crushed him against the bar. He explained that his solo singing act followed hers.

"You poor misguided bastard! The only act that can follow Tallu is King Kong with an erection!"

That shut him up for a moment. In fact, he didn't get a chance to open his mouth for almost an hour as she launched into total recall of her radio show highlights and complaints about the &%$!$%&+ desert sun and air that was ruining her hair and complexion. But she was overjoyed to tell him about her new shape.

"I've had the most blessed event in my young life—silicone injections—and my bazooms are absolutely virginal—oh, lawdy! I'm born again!"

Merrill records in his autobiography, *Between Acts: An Irreverent Look at Opera and Other Madness,* how Tallulah showed him "her beautifully formed bosom, fuller than a Bali maiden's but obviously virginal.

" 'They fill it with glop, but you can't tell the difference. Have a bite.'

" 'Delicious,' I said.

"I first saw Tallulah Bankhead in 1939, from a second balcony seat in her American triumph, *The Little Foxes*. Another hit, *The Skin of Our Teeth*, then a disaster, and the stage abandoned her. She stormed into network radio, drawing the biggest audience in the country, and here she was at The Sands, caricaturing the grotesque gossip-column image of herself—booze, boys, girls, men, all in a swirl of ferocious energy. A force of nature, like Mount Vesuvius, that could not be denied. Only the blue eyes and voluptuous mouth remained of the honey-haired beauty of *The Little Foxes*. She was utterly honest with herself, and the separation from the legitimate stage must have hurt—but 'Whattahell honey, I've got it where it counts.' "

XXVI

Tallulah and Tennessee

1955–1956   "Don't touch me! I can't stand to be touched!" Tallulah screamed, and Tennessee Williams flinched. Christ Almighty! He was only going to put his hand on hers because he felt great tenderness for her and sensed a tremendous vulnerability in the woman.

And what happens? She acts like a . . . like a Tennessee Williams character. Ironic his first play should be called *You Touched Me!*

They were in an elevator together going up to a party when the outcry occurred. Later at the party he was brooding in a corner of the room when someone asked what was the matter.

"Oh, I feel depressed. Tallulah hates me."

And she called fast and loud across the room: "I do NOT. I love you!"

Why Tallulah hated to be touched is a mystery, but both Ted Hook and James Herlihy had explanations that could have stopped Williams' depression—if they'd only told him.

"I was there when Talllulah shouted 'Don't touch me!' to Tennessee Williams," says Ted Hook. "She'd broken her hand not long before."

"It wasn't only that," explains Herlihy. "Tallulah couldn't bear to be touched and Tennessee didn't realize that. I've seen her reacting to being touched on a hundred different occasions and it was always difficult for her, especially in an unexpected situation.

"She was warm in her compassion and in her spirit but she was not a warm giver of great hugs and so forth. She was no cuddlebunny. I can't imagine her sitting around necking with anybody. She just wasn't physically warm: I'm sure of that."

But because nobody told Tennessee, he was hurt by her reaction. In fact they were always hurting each other and probably unintentionally.

These are the facts. Tallulah had insulted Williams each time he brought his plays to her, plays written for her and almost, though not quite, about her. "Take your dirty play! Take your miserable play and when you've written something that's clean, I'll read it!" Or words to that effect. Worse, probably. At such moments the words people remember saying and others remember hearing are always somewhat different.

And pride was involved. When Williams became a great Broadway success, Tallulah was sliding. But she did the equivalent of swallowing her pride, and phoned him at Key West to ask if she could play in his *Milk Train*.

"Tennessee, darling, I've read your new play and I'd like to do it."

"Tallulah, I wrote the play for you but it wasn't ready for you, so I tried it out in Spoleto with an English actress, Hermione Baddeley. She was so terrific that I staggered into her dressing room after the Spoleto opening and said: 'Hermione, this play will be yours if you want it next season on Broadway.' I'm terribly sorry, but . . ."

Tallulah hurts Tennessee. Tennessee hurts Tallulah.

Next time they met, they quarreled.

Then they met again:

TENNESSEE: Tallulah, I'd like you to meet a very close friend of mine.

TALLULAH: Oh, how nice of you to like such a homely person.

(Later she came to like him, says Williams.)

"There was a rather up and down relationship between us," says Williams with a slightly worn laugh. "I always loved Tallulah but got awfully angry at her at times. I think maybe she sensed in me a person as lonely as she was. She was fragile as they come, physically: she just lived on her nerves. Unfortunately I only knew her after she had become addicted to pills, sleeping pills, or whatever they were. I only saw her take sleeping pills. Whether she took cocaine or not, I don't know. But whatever they were, they ravaged her."

They quarreled, then refused to speak to each other. It seemed that Tallulah would never appear in a Tennessee Williams play.

Then their friends conspired to unite them.

James Herlihy and Stanley Haggart told Tennessee that Tallulah was so important to his psyche that every woman he wrote about had the echo of her and that they must therefore get together. They told him how much Tallulah loved him and reminded him of his words: "When I wrote *Streetcar* I could hear Tallulah deliver the lines."

They told Tallulah that they knew she was dying to play in a Tennessee Williams play. How could that come about unless they met and talked?

A party was arranged at Tennessee's apartment. At first they stood across the room from each other, hostile, but their hostility gradually dissolved. It was arranged that Tallulah should play Blanche Dubois in *Streetcar*.

At last Tallulah was to play Tennessee. But already it sounded like a contest.

"She had never seen *Streetcar*," says Gene Coffin. "She had a mental block about seeing it because she'd turned it down. So when she was going to play it, we went to Warner Brothers over on the West Side, to the viewing room. They were going to run the film for her (with Vivien Leigh and Marlon Brando starring). Tennessee Williams was there, and Bankhead and Jean Dalrymple. And Tallulah said: 'Now everybody must be quiet.' And there were only four or five of us. 'Everybody must sit far apart, sit in a corner and have a lot of space,' because she wanted to hear it and watch it very closely. Williams didn't say much of anything. I think he was a little upset at her not having done it in the first place and then turning down *Sweet Bird of Youth*. So the picture started and the credits were interminable. They ran on and on and on. And at the end of the credits when the picture really started Tallulah just went: 'SHHHHH!' There was nobody talking anyway. And Williams got up and stomped out of the viewing room and just before he slammed the door he said: 'Fuck you all.' "

The play was to open at the Coconut Grove, Miami, and to tour before opening in New York's City Center.

"I brought a young lady to her apartment in New York when we were casting *Streetcar*," says Tennessee. "The young lady was of rather aristocratic Russian descent, and I wanted her to play Stella opposite Tallulah. Tallulah took a very dim view of her but received her with great cordiality. And immediately afterward she called me on the phone and she said: 'How DARE you bring that Cruikshank cartoon to my apartment and tell me that she looks like my sister.' (He chuckles.)

"I'll never forget Tallulah in Coconut Grove. When we arrived she didn't like the set and she suddenly bellowed out: 'Hey, where is the IMPOSTOR?' meaning the manager. And she rushed up the theatre aisle, saying 'IMPOSTER! Where are you?' "

The play went into rehearsal.

"In the evenings during rehearsals she was surrounded by young men," says Williams, "minions for her who took care of her, and she would dispatch one of them upstairs for her sleeping pills, and she would tell him which ones she wanted and he would come down with the pills and she'd take them and say: 'In about twenty minutes I will become slightly incoherent and then in about half an hour I will become unsteady on my feet and start to fall. You must pay no attention. Peter [Pell] here will see I don't hurt myself.' And it would be exactly as she described."

Streetcar opened at Coconut Grove.

"There were all these faggots in the house," says Williams. "Tallulah began to play to them. There was hardly anything else she could do. They insisted on it. And I got very drunk and at the conclusion of the evening I was sulking around and somebody said: 'Come over and speak to Tallulah.' And I said: 'I don't want to. She pissed on my play.' It was repeated to her. I suppose that hurt her. Later, the next morning, after the notices came out, Herbert Machiz, the director, and I went to her house to consult her about the future course of the rehearsals, and she was lying in bed looking like a little girl. She said with a sort of wounded bravado: 'Well, wasn't I the best Blanche you've ever seen?' And I said: 'No, the worst,' which was an awful thing to say but it happened to be the truth.

"And Tallulah said: 'Over that way is the bay. Why don't you take a swim in it, straight out?'

"The revival of *Streetcar* approached New York with several stops on the way," recalls Williams. "Despite my savage love for Tallulah, I didn't attend them, but the director told me that Tallulah worked with the strictest dedication to the inner truth of the part."

"She did," agrees the stage manager, Peter Pell. "After Tennessee and Herbert laid it on the line, she fussed and fumed but she buckled down and really went to work to attempt as best she could to do it."

Then came the time to get costumes for the New York opening. Says Gene Coffin, "I stayed at her place on Christmas Eve arguing and fighting until four in the morning—our first and only battle—over the price of the costumes. Of course my family was furious when I finally got home. Just before I walked out she said: 'The price is impossible, prohibitive. You know it's City Center. You have to have civic pride, darling.' Well, this is the thing that threw me, when she kept throwing 'civic pride' around. 'The price must be lowered.' But it couldn't be: I was giving her rock-bottom price then. This was not my salary. It was for the making of the clothes. So she said: 'The trouble with you darling is you have no civic pride whatsoever.' She was getting very angry at this point. She was not drinking, by the way. 'You know they get the biggest stars in the world there for eighty-five dollars a week. They could get Helen Hayes for this.' And I said: 'I know this. I want to ask you something. Are they getting you for eighty-five dollars a week?' And she just drew herself up very haughtily and said: 'Darling I'm the only woman in the history of the theatre that has received one third of the box office.' And I put on my overcoat and hat, picked up my sketches, and left. I didn't go to see the play but I did send her a wire opening night."

Tallulah's secretary and friend Philip Hall was at the first night of *Streetcar*—and was horrified by the audience, "Directly she entered the stage they took it as a comedy. Because she had a a deep voice they thought she was a lesbian, which of course she wasn't. I was always so nervous on opening nights that I had to see everything twice anyway—but that first night was horrible."

Actor James Kirkwood was in that audience. "It was a dreadful audience. They were all of her fans I suppose, but they wanted to see her do tricks. I thought that she wasn't going to make it. It seemed as if the whole homosexual community was up in the balcony and they wouldn't give her a chance. Whenever she had a line that could be construed as camp, like the one that refers to a constellation of stars and she says, 'The girls are out tonight,' it got a huge laugh and a hand. Well, Jesus Christ, that was so rude of the audience. And I could tell she was shocked and stopped by it. It was supposed to be a very touching moment when she said that. I was hoping that she would say something to the audience like: 'Would you please give me a chance? This is not a joke.' "

Tallulah, thrown by her reception, was thinking of saying something like that. But she didn't say it. She kept at it.

"Of course if she had stopped, it would have blown her performance," admits Kirkwood. "But she did her very best to fight the audience and gave a remarkable performance."

She saw Philip Hall after the show. She was shaken and disappointed: "What can I do?" she asked. "I can't stand in the box office and sell tickets."

Tennessee Williams saw that performance: "She was quite fabulous: she had a great struggle because she had acquired a following among a certain type of audience and they were awfully hard to play to because they wanted her to camp it up. She mastered her following. She didn't give an inch and she brought out the tigerish side of Blanche more than anyone had. Tallulah had a sort of bravura in the role that no one else had. A lot of actresses would have quit after the Coconut Grove experience. But Tallulah went on and mastered the part and the audience. She had great gallantry and courage."

Williams admits he shed tears almost all the way through and that when the play was finished, "I rushed up to her and fell to my knees at her feet. The human drama, the play of a woman's great valor and an artist's truth, her own, far superseded, and even eclipsed, to my eye, the performance of my own play. Such an experience in the life of a playwright demands some tribute from him, and this late, awkward confession is my effort to give it." That was part of a letter dated March 4, 1956, and published in *The New York Times*. It resulted in a letter from Tallulah with the guiding hand of her press agent Richard Maney, implying that Tennessee Williams was moved more by booze than by Blanche.

Not true. Seven years later in *The New York Times*, December 29, 1963, Tennessee Williams revealed he was still moved by Tallulah's courage and talent. He wrote: "The Tiger-Moth called Blanche was superbly played by such stars as Jessica Tandy and Uta Hagen before that part and Tallulah got together, under circumstances that probably only Tallulah Bankhead would have the quixotic valor to confront without fear, or any evidence of it.

"Tallulah played Blanche with that Tiger-Moth quality of the lady and star who had haunted the skylit workroom in which I had caught Blanche Dubois in the paper facsimile of a jungle trap.

"Some people who saw Tallulah's interpretation of Blanche have mistakenly said that she was too strong for the part of this neurasthenic creature, but I feel she gave a magnificent portrayal of the role. Blanche is a delicate tigress with her back to the wall. The part must be played opposite an actor of towering presence, a Brando or a Tony Quinn, to create a plausible balance, but circumstances necessitated her playing it opposite an actor who would appear to best advantage as the male lead of a gently poetic play such as, say, something by Chekhov, Synge, or Yeats. And he made Tallulah's incandescent Blanche seem a bit too incandescent."

XXVII

Welcome, Darlings

1956   James Kirkwood had been part of a real-life murder mystery, was a soap-opera actor, and a novelist: an altogether sophisticated young man of the world. But the thought of meeting Tallulah Bankhead gave him the shakes.

Kirkwood had met her briefly before at a "Windows" party. "James Kirkwood?" she had greeted him then. "The son of James Kirkwood, the actor?"

"Yes."

Tallulah stood up and made a very slow definite cross to him from one side of the room to the other, while the roomful of guests stopped talking and watched. She took Kirkwood's hand and said: "I knew your father . . . very well." And the room broke up.

Kirkwood knew that Tallulah and his father had been lovers in London in the 1920s, and he joined in the laughter.

That one encounter (which she'd apparently forgotten) made him, if anything, more nervous of meeting her again. He believed some of the legends about her must be true. He had watched her fight the mob in the *Streetcar* revival and show her steel. Friends assured him that she was a terror and rode over everyone on twelve camels. But despite his qualms he couldn't turn down the opportunity to play opposite her.

It was arranged that he would audition for her in her New

York apartment directly after he finished his daily stint on the TV soap opera "Valiant Lady."

When the time arrived he was shaking so much that he swallowed a Miltown to at least appear calm, and rang the bell. The butler told him, "Miss Bankhead is just getting up." It was one in the afternoon. Kirkwood went upstairs to the living room and waited.

Then he heard her wild voice and thought: "Oh my God, now I'm going to meet my Maker."

Down she came wiping her eyes: "Oh this crap!" she complained. "My eyes are packed with it every morning. Do you have it too?"

"I do, I do," he said nervously. "I believe it's called dried-up sleep."

Tallulah stood on the stairs for a while trying to focus on him. "James Kirkwood," she said, "I see you every day on 'Valiant Lady' and I think you're a very fine young actor. Do sit, darling. I'm really hooked on soapies. I watch 'Valiant Lady,' 'Love of Life,' and 'As the World Turns.' Now I understand you have some comedy material you want to show me. What sort of stuff do you do?"

"Well," said Kirkwood, 'well, . . ."—stalling for time to give the Miltown a few more moments to work and dreading doing a comedy audition of nightclub satire material to Tallulah Bankhead in her living room in the afternoon. But he couldn't "well" forever. "Well, I have this take-off of the *Reader's Digest*. . . ."

"Darling," Tallulah interrupted, "I did this number in *Ziegfeld Follies* and I came down the staircase and my first line was. . . ."

It ended up that Kirkwood spent the entire afternoon with Tallulah auditioning for him.

Then she said: "I think you'll be just perfect."

"But how d'you know? I haven't done any material for you."

"You obviously have good breeding, darling. I think you're very handsome and clean-cut. I don't want any of these dirty comics working with me. I think you have class, and you're going to be just fine."

After praising Kirkwood until he blushed, Tallulah had to get back to herself. She suddenly pulled up her robe and put her legs across the coffee table and said: "Don't I have the most beautiful ankles?"

So Kirkwood was cast to play opposite Tallulah in the musical revue *Welcome, Darlings,* which was to tour the summer circuit. Everyone in the show, except Tallulah, was young. Her previous review, *Ziegfeld Follies,* had been next thing to a disaster and now she rehearsed as if her entire career depended on how she did in *Welcome, Darlings.*

Kirkwood's dressing room was next to Tallulah's and on the first night, just before his entrance, he met her in the hall.

"I was nervous," says Kirkwood, "and I thought that Tallulah Bankhead never had a nervous feeling in her life. When she took my hand and said: 'Jimmy, walk me up to the stage,' her hand was shaking, it was like a cold claw, and she was bent over. She looked like an old woman. I thought: 'God almighty, I've never seen anyone gripped by such fear.' Now my first number was right after the opening in which she did a song number with boy singers and dancers. Then I came and did a monologue about how I was terrified of working with her and how my insurance was canceled and my mother said, 'My poor baby,' when I'd said: 'Guess what? I'm going to play opposite Tallulah Bankhead.'

"Opening night I was standing in the wings and I could see the boy dancers and singers were doing their opening number before she came down the staircase and joined them.

"I'll never forget her climbing the back part of those kind of fake stairs, and standing there, and she was hunched over, holding her shoulders, trembling.

"I kept watching her: I knew the cue was coming up. I thought: 'My God, I'm going to be in the theatre the one night Tallulah can't go on or is so gripped by nerves that it hampers her performance.'

"About thirty seconds before her entrance, she suddenly stood up terribly straight and spread her arms out and pulled herself together and tugged at her dress, and a smile came on her face. I want to tell you, it was like . . . it was like a miracle. The curtains opened and she came down with all the aplomb in the world and just killed them."

On opening night, at another theatre in Westport, Kirkwood hurried offstage for a very quick change but the girl who should have been there to help him had gone to the other side by mistake. In his frantic rush he came on zipping up his fly and his shirt was caught and it got a huge laugh. The audience, and the cast dancing the Charleston, broke up. And Kirkwood chortled his way through his singing introduction to Tallulah.

"Tallulah came out with flames. You could almost see the smoke coming out of her nostrils," says Kirkwood.

When the first-act curtain fell, Tallulah turned to him and said: "You little BASTARD! Who do you think you are? The most unprofessional behavior, for chrissakes! Coming on like that and laughing all the way through my introduction!"

Embarrassed in front of the cast, Kirkwood said: "Oh go and fuck yourself!"

Tallulah screamed, rushed to her dressing room, and slammed the door. And then nothing could be heard but breakage. Tallulah smashed glass, threw hairbrushes, smashed a vase, then she grabbed a large pair of shears and went for her wardrobe. Rose, her maid, locked in the dressing room with Tallulah, screamed: "Miss Bankhead, no! No, Miss Bankhead! Your gowns! Your beautiful gowns!"

But Tallulah, livid, lunged and ripped.

Kirkwood stood next to the stage manager, frozen. "God," whispered the stage manager. "Don't say any more to her. Play it cool and stay away from her."

But that was impossible. Tallulah and Kirkwood had

several more sketches to do together as well as a couple of musical numbers.

She came out for the second act and she went onstage but she never once looked Kirkwood in the eye.

At the end of *Welcome, Darlings* she always introduced the entire cast, one by one, to the audience. Kirkwood came last and she would say: "And my own, my own very special darling, my own Jimmy." Kirkwood would come downstage, take Tallulah's hand, and everyone would sing 'May the good Lord bless and keep you,' and the final curtain would come down.

Kirkwood wondered how she'd handle it now she was in a rage. She managed it by introducing everyone but Kirkwood and then closing ranks and starting to sing, "May the good Lord bless and keep you." Kirkwood was left isolated upstage all by himself, and it got a laugh from the audience. He thought the only thing to do was to disappear. So he turned and began to tiptoe off. And that got an even bigger laugh.

Tallulah stopped the singing, whipped around and said: "Oh yes, and I almost forgot this little bastard!" And that was the curtain line.

Still smoldering, Tallulah said the show was sloppy, gave hell to everyone, and called a rehearsal for next day for all the cast except Kirkwood.

Next morning he went to pick up his mail backstage but they were painting the set and he had to go through the auditorium. As he entered, Tallulah was onstage with her back to him, giving hell to everyone. As he walked up the steps she almost backed into him and he thought, "Oh what the hell!" and put his arms around her waist, kissed her on the neck, and said: "Good morning, Madam."

She turned around. "Thank Christ," she said. "I thought you'd never apologize!"

"I didn't apologize. I only said good morning!"

"You little bastard!" she roared. Then she broke up, and they were friends again.

That night she tried to break him up onstage by lowering her upstage eyelid very slowly during one of his lines.

When they reached Rhode Island with the show, Adlai Stevenson was making a television speech as a presidential candidate and, being a great fan of his, Tallulah wanted to hear it.

But the speech was scheduled to start before the show normally ended. Tallulah persuaded the cast to hurry so that they sounded like chipmunks. Then, after the first curtain call, she said to the audience: "My darlings, I know we've been in a rush. I know you all want to hurry home to see Adlai, that dear, sweet man. So we're not going to take any more curtain calls—sothankyouandgodblessyou." And the curtain came down and Tallulah was out.

After several weeks of the tour Kirkwood began to notice how insatiably curious Tallulah was about other people. When he came into the theatre in the early evening to collect his mail, she'd invariably be in his dressing room and greet him with: "You've a letter from your mother. Where is she? How is she?" And then she'd say: "What did you do today?" She wanted all the details from the moment he got up.

"She loved mystery and intrigue, ghost stories and gossip," says Kirkwood. "She used to say of two kids in the show: 'D'you think he's byzing with her?' And of two boys: 'D'you think they byze together?'

"I'd say: 'Why d'you think that?'

" 'I saw them in a convertible together and they went to the races together when we were playing near Saratoga.'

"I'd say: 'Maybe they just went to the races.'

" 'I think they're byzing together,' she'd say. 'You find out.' "

XXVIII

Eleanor Roosevelt
and Governor Ribicoff Get
the Tallulah Treatment

1956   What more could Tallulah do to hold her audience when she was at home? She desperately needed an answer. If she didn't entertain them, they'd get bored and leave her alone. Tallulah had now become terrified of solitude.

There was her body. She was still very proud of it. She'd strip and say: "It's not like an old woman's, is it?" And it wasn't. She'd show where she had her breasts lifted. There was nothing lascivious about it, no hint of trying to entice. It was simply: "Well, what do you think of that?"

There were her stories that seemed to have been threaded on a circular needle. Scheherazade had to tell one blockbuster a night to survive; Tallulah told a hundred.

But perhaps her brightest invention was her "Who are the people you'd most like to meet in the world?" game. James Kirkwood was in Tallulah's hotel room with others still on tour with *Welcome, Darlings* when she asked. They all had a turn and then Kirkwood said: "Laurence Olivier and Mrs. Eleanor Roosevelt."

Tallulah said: "I'll fix Mrs. Roosevelt. She lives across the street."

Sure enough Tallulah fixed Mrs. Roosevelt. When they got back to Manhattan, she invited Mrs. Roosevelt to tea. Kirkwood was told his wish had been granted and he went to Tallulah's home to wait expectantly for the great lady.

She arrived while Tallulah was watching a soap opera called "Edge of Night." Tallulah greeted her.

"Shhh!" she said.

Kirkwood says: "Mrs. Roosevelt looked at her with that dear face of hers and Tallulah snapped: 'Wait till it's over. Can't you be quiet for ten minutes?' "

Mrs. Roosevelt nodded.

Kirkwood felt as if a taboo had been broken.

He pretended interest in the soap opera, while his pulse protested.

Tallulah pointed at one of the soap-opera performers: "That's the bitch that told that one's father that he was living with another woman. She's a bitch. You've got to watch her."

"Oh, I see," said Mrs. Roosevelt.

"Shhh," ordered Tallulah.

Mrs. Roosevelt sat silently beside Kirkwood on the sofa.

When the soap opera ended, Tallulah allowed Mrs. Roosevelt and Kirkwood to talk and after ten minutes they were all in the middle of a friendly argument.

Tallulah suddenly stood up and said: "I've got to go to the john, but I don't want you to say another word until I get back, do you hear me?" She backed out of the room, backed down the hall, talking as she went: ". . . because if you do I'll never forgive you. I wouldn't miss this for the world." She started to undo the waist of her slacks and when she got to the bathroom she let the slacks drop. The bathroom door was wide open and the john in full view. She sat and peed, still talking, got through a piece of toilet paper, flushed, pulled up her pants and returned to the guests, still talking.

On the sofa, Mrs. Roosevelt and Kirkwood had the best seats in the house and they almost upset the tea service. Kirkwood was determined not to acknowledge what had happened and Mrs. Roosevelt avoided his eyes.

As soon as Mrs. Roosevelt left, Kirkwood exploded:

"Oh, God, Tallulah, why would you ever do that? Now really! That was so embarrassing."

"What do you mean?"

"Getting up and going to the bathroom in the middle of the conversation and taking your pants down and sitting there with the door open."

Tallulah gave him her queenly look: "Mrs. Roosevelt knows we all have bodily functions. That was no news to her."

"I know she knows but that's no reason not to shut the door."

"Oh, well," she said. "I don't know what's the matter with you."

Couldn't he understand that she just didn't want to be bypassed in the conversation when Mrs. Roosevelt was there? was Tallulah's unspoken question, and very few of her questions were unspoken.

Kirkwood never met Laurence Olivier, but he did have supper with Governor Ribicoff.

The governor of Connecticut and his wife came to see *Welcome, Darlings* and asked Tallulah out to supper afterward. She invited Kirkwood to be her escort. They went to a lovely old inn in Connecticut where Tallulah downed five very quick bourbon and ginger ales.

Normally Tallulah went on chemical reactions, but her reaction to Governor Ribicoff was magnetic. If she'd had her way, she would have sworn him in as president that night. She kept saying: "He's a Jew, the only Jew. . . . They've never had a Jewish governor in this rotten state until now."

When some of the cast came by she was getting quite drunk and she said: "This is Governor Ribocrop, Robercoff, Roober . . . well you know, he's the governor for godsakes and he's a Jew. Isn't that marvelous?"

She leaned over to Kirkwood and whispered: "You know he's really a very attractive man."

Mrs. Ribicoff was getting a little nervous, and the governor showed signs of strain.

It got to be about one a.m. and there was a little pause and Mrs. Ribicoff said to her husband: "Darling, I think it's about time that we . . ."

And Tallulah snapped her head around and said: "WHY DON'T YOU GO HOME!"

The place cleared almost before the glasses stopped shaking. And shortly after, Tallulah and Kirkwood found themselves trapped by a group of bores.

Kirkwood went to the men's room for respite but to his astonishment, Tallulah followed him inside and slammed the door.

"What the . . . ?"

"How can we get away from those awful people?" Tallulah asked.

"Let's get out of here, first," Kirkwood suggested, already having trouble trying to open the door that had automatically locked.

They called the manager. He couldn't open it. The manager called the state police. They couldn't open it. Eventually Tallulah and Kirkwood climbed out through a window.

Kirkwood recalls: "I thought: 'Oh God, here's one of those Tallulah Bankhead stories.' Someone said that it was going to hit the paper that the state police had to get us out of this men's room. Actually it was just a mistake."

It never did get in the papers.

XXIX

"Don't Go Right
to the Body"

1956   Tallulah's idea of heaven would be a roomful of handsome men, all with a fund of fabulous tales in reserve for when she got laryngitis. But she only met a few who were up to her standards. James Kirkwood was one of them. He had been involved in a real-life murder mystery. He had in fact found the body of a murdered man, and his mother, a Hollywood actress, was a suspect. Kirkwood wrote a novel based on the murder called *There Must Be a Pony.* It fascinated Tallulah so much that at almost every party, while and after they were touring in *Welcome, Darlings,* she asked him to repeat it.

"Darling, tell them about *There Must Be a Pony.*"

"But they've heard it before."

"Not all of them. Tell them, darling."

"Well, when I was fourteen I found this body. . . ."

"No, no, no, darling. Start with. . . . Where were you born?"

"But, Tallulah, they don't want to hear that."

"Yes, they do. His mother was Lila Lee and his father was James Kirkwood. He was born in Los Angeles, California. . . . And how many schools did you go to?"

"Fourteen."

"Fourteen. Well tell 'em that! Don't go right to the body!"

Some critics have called Tallulah an undisciplined amateur,

but in her own way she strove for perfection and demanded it from others. Kirkwood must tell the story from beginning to end. Everything must be just right . . . even the stage curtains. And the night they weren't is not easily forgotten.

Welcome, Darlings had arrived at a new town. They weren't playing that night because the set was being put up. Tallulah had been drinking and, Kirkwood recalls: "She came into the theatre and, dear God, I've never seen a woman do anything like it in my life. She had it in her contract that there was not to be a white curtain. And there was a white curtain. She stormed up the aisle and she got up on that set and she clawed it down. She screamed all the while and when the curtain came down, she fell in it. She struggled out . . . and then she didn't know what to do. The theatre had filled with technical people and the cast by that time. And then she went after the set and broke chairs and knocked tables over and smashed dishes and poked her fist through flats and kicked and scratched and I thought: 'My God, she's going to have a heart attack!' I want to tell you, she demolished the stage. She was tiny, small-boned. I don't know how the hell she did it. We had no rehearsal that night. We were all sent home while they reconstructed the set and new curtains were found. They were working until eight the next night putting everything back together.

"Next day when we continued rehearsals, she wanted me to cut one of my lines and I said I wouldn't take it out. We had a little argument over that. The line was 'There is sex after death.' The number was a satire on *Reader's Digest*. It went: 'America's Number One Killer: Zippers. Do the Duke and Duchess? Are American Tennis Balls Underfuzzed? I Bailed Out of an Eagle.' All crazy alarmist titles that they have. And at the end of the number I said: 'And finally, a condensation of America's number one best-selling novel that's causing people all over the world to shoot themselves (fanfare): There Is Sex After Death.' She didn't think it was funny. Said it was in bad taste."

She'd had the same reaction to Tennessee Williams' *Battle of the Angels* where the mixture of sex and religion had offended her.

The mean, destructive side of Tallulah was aroused when she felt threatened by incompetence. And she really cared about the audience, so much in fact that she had injured her career and talent by using gimmicks—her characteristic hoot, for example—to keep them amused when she thought the material was lousy. She handled so much lousy material that she couldn't get out of the gimmicks even when the play was good.

"But even then," says Kirkwood who played with her and watched her from the audience, "Tallulah had some magic, God-given quality that asserted itself the moment she stepped on the stage. You knew damn well that there was somebody rather extraordinary there.

"She could, God only knows, bore you and sometimes she could be quite rude to someone she took an instant dislike to. She could be very overbearing. Those were the times you really wanted to spank her.

"She asked me to come to dinner one night, and she was very serious. 'Jimmy,' she said, 'what do you think's going to happen with my career?' I said: 'I think you're going to go on picking these dreadful plays and giving kind of freakish performances until you're so down and out that you'll finally turn yourself over to a good director and just be an actress and do what they tell you to do. It'll probably come to the time when you'll do a Laurette Taylor and you'll get a play that may not be as good as *The Glass Menagerie* but a play with some substance and you'll be so frantic at what you've been doing that you'll just give in and then you'll probably have a fantastic comeback and I hope you do.'

"At that point she swore at me and threw a wine glass. And she said: 'What a terrible thing to say to anyone!' I said: 'I said it with all the love in the world.' And I said: 'I think that's what probably will happen.'

"Then she cried and left the dining room and went upstairs to the living room. And I sat and picked at my food for a while. I finally went up and then we talked a little more. I really adored her.

"The thing that used to break my heart was that she had a terror of being alone and I'll never forget the evening after the performance when she would invariably try to trap you into staying up with her until she fell asleep. And invariably she'd get you to sit on the edge of the bed, and sometimes she would put her hand gently on your arm. She'd taken a sleeping pill that would knock out a horse, but she would sometimes, somehow talk through it, it would be just like a record. Maybe two or three of us would be there and we'd be looking at one another as if to say: 'Thank God we can go home and get to bed soon.' And she would get to a story and her voice would get like a record running down and then sometimes she would start picking up and we'd look at one another with panic and then she'd be up and we'd be in the kitchen cooking. A couple of times I thought she'd really gone to sleep and she had her hand on my arm and as I attempted to move my arm to leave, it was like a reflex, the hand just clutched my arm. There was something very touching about it."

Morton Da Costa, who had lived at "Windows" for a year when he was working with Tallulah in *The Skin of Our Teeth* as the broadcast announcer and Montgomery Clift's understudy, had since become a director. He hadn't seen her for years. Then Gus Schirmer asked him to see Tallulah in *Welcome, Darlings,* which had reached a summer theatre run by Harold Kennedy. He recalls: "When I went backstage she was quite rude. Gus said, 'Harold wants us to have a drink with Tallulah,' and I said, 'Screw, I'm not going up. She was fucking rude.' Anyway they persuaded me to go up and we sat around and Tallulah avoided me the entire time and then she got onto *Skin of Our Teeth* and she turned to me and said: 'And I saved your job in that for you.' And I said: 'Yes,

Tallulah, and I've dined out on it ever since.' And she said: 'Oh, have you darling?' And then she just dissolved. The thing was that in that period I had become rather successful as a director. She was playing the summer circuit and what she was presuming was that my attitude would be patronizing toward her now, which was something she couldn't take, which was a nonsense presumption. But I could see the insecurity in it and that's why I said I'd never forgotten it and had been dining out on it.

"And indeed, I hadn't forgotten it and still thought she was great. And then we embraced.

"Next day she phoned. I wasn't in as a matter of fact. It was hard to do, but I didn't return the call because I saw another year of captivity."

XXX

"Around the World
in a Mackintosh"

or

Another Turn of the Screw
for Henry James

1956–1957 Everyone was whooping it up at the opening night party for *Street-car*—except Tallulah. Tamara Geva found the star of the show alone in the bedroom, quietly sobbing. Had the humiliation of an audience that laughed at her instead of empathizing with her broken her spirit at last? Would she call it quits, settle down in the country with her pets and press cuttings?

Not on your life!

When Herbert Machiz offered her the chance to create the starring role in *Eugenia* she grasped at it like a girl just out of drama school.

She'd shown him she had the guts and discipline to play *Streetcar* straight, while the audience camped itself silly. Let them throw her to the lions again—this time she'd really tame them. And in a part that would be her own. For nearly twelve years she had followed other actresses in shopworn roles, and she was inevitably compared with them, the originators. She could put her stamp on *Eugenia.* Tallulah put her stamp on *Eugenia*—with a vengeance. It remains a Tallulah original.

The play was based on Henry James' novel *The Europeans,** adapted for the stage by Randolph Carter.

Carter had first met Tallulah seventeen years before in 1939 and had not forgotten her. He had made a play out of *Wuthering Heights,* and John Emery, halfway through his four-year marriage to Tallulah, was rehearsing as Heathcliff. Tallulah was in town and at her height in *The Little Foxes.* She described her role as "soulless and sadistic, an unmitigated murderess. For profit she would have slit her mother's throat, but not before so staging the crime that the guilt would be pinned on another." She seemed to have carried the role with her offstage. Carter recalled with apprehension that Tallulah watched the dress rehearsal of *Wuthering Heights* and then ripped into Emery. She savaged his performance and so demoralized the poor man that he slept the night in the theater rather than go home to her.

Carter knew that Tallulah could still draw a crowd—but would she wreck his play in the attempt?

Nothing prepared him for what did happen.

Tallulah had dictatorial power over the cast and script and she quickly used it, firing one actor she claimed she couldn't hear and attacking the play as if it were the enemy. There were new scenes to learn every day because she couldn't stand or understand the old ones. And Tallulah was having trouble learning anything.

When Carter brought back his rewrites of rewrites she tore them to confetti as he watched, thinking this was more like a wake than a wedding.

"She fought with Machiz all the time," says someone who was on the tour. "He was a monster. An extremely intelligent man, a marvelous talker and extremely witty. But a vicious and malicious man. He more than met his match in Tallulah.

* A 1979 movie version of *The Europeans* starred Lee Remick as Eugenia.

She was more than a match for anyone in the world at that period. NOBODY could handle her."

"One day she would destroy everything you did," recalls Carter. "The next day she would have completely forgotten and be the most adorable, affectionate, and charming person."

Some nights she would make Carter stay with her until five in the morning and then put her to bed. "She was frightened to death and totally insecure in the play and the part," he says.

If ever a pre-Broadway tryout seemed headed for disaster, this was it. But Tallulah wouldn't give up or give in. She slammed her hand against a door—not in anger, but to give dramatic punch to a scene that dragged—and broke her little finger. Too vain to wear glasses, though she needed them, she smashed into something and cracked several ribs. Taped and tormented, Tallulah kept on playing. But it was a different play every night.

She always found it hard to sleep. Now, the pain and tension made it impossible. She demanded painkillers, and when Tallulah demanded, people delivered. The doctor gave her Tuinal. She tripled the dose he advised, added Benzedrine, Dexedrine, Dexamyl, and morphine, and washed them down with a daily quart of bourbon in a dangerous attempt to kill pain, steady her nerves, and get the sleep she now desperately needed.

Machiz saw her gulp nine pills and asked, "How many would be fatal?"

"Thirty five," she said. They were not the best of friends by now.

She was creating a vicious circle for herself. The more lines she killed the more new ones she had to handle. The drugs she took to smother pain had made a mush of her memory.

Carter was dazed and bewildered by her unending cries of "I can't do that! Change that!" Her criticism was totally arbitrary. One evening she would look at the new material, seem to approve, even apologize for making so many changes.

Next day she would look at the script and bellow, "Who the fuck wrote that?"

"She really didn't know what was happening in the play," Carter recalls wryly. "The only thing that interested her was when she came on. She'd stand impatiently in the wings and say, 'Cut the lines! I'm coming on! Fuck it! They're waiting for ME. They don't care what you're saying!' And that awful Herbert Machiz tried to point out that possibly the lines of the other actors were a build-up for her entrance. But she said, 'I don't need any build-up, shit-head! I'm coming on!' And she did."

It's a wonder that the play got on at all and even more that an audience stayed to watch. But there were times when Tallulah was magnificent.

"It opened at New Haven on Thursday," says Carter. "For the first Saturday matinee Tallulah gave the most beautiful performance I've ever seen in my life. She was very tired and she didn't yell and scream, and the play had not yet been torn to pieces. If it had come into town then, it would have been quite a different story. But six weeks on the road and it was in shreds. It wasn't the play I wrote at all. It wasn't Henry James or anything—it was in tatters."

No, Carter wasn't punch-drunk from the battering—and misjudging her performance. Boston critic Elliott Norton confirmed that Tallulah was in top form.

In Baltimore one night, actor Tom Ellis sensed that Tallulah was slightly drunk onstage. She fluffed a few times, but covered it with mumbles and an air of bravado that suited the character. Once, when Ellis tried to feed her a forgotten line, Tallulah muttered, "Don't be so right!" and made up some words of her own until she stumbled back on the track.

But now she was in trouble. She didn't know where she was or who she was. She just stood and stared. There was a growing panic in the wings as her silence stretched out so that the audience began to suspect the worst.

And still she just stood there.

Would this be the inglorious end of Tallulah's career—at a loss for words? That in itself might rate a headline, as well as her stage obituary.

Now Ellis felt the tension on both sides of the lights—but was going to let her save or sink herself. With Tallulah anything could happen.

And it did.

Suddenly, to his astonishment, Tallulah spoke—and with a new vibrant authority. "Get the bonds!" or something like that. He remembered that line—but it wasn't from *Eugenia*. He knew it because he'd played in *The Little Foxes* at school.

Tallulah had regressed to her biggest triumph.

Ellis fed her a few lines from *Foxes*. She played hers back, gathering confidence and authority. It was an incredible, wonderful performance. The audience—with probably rare exceptions—had no idea they were listening to the wrong play. They were at what was now a special event, Tallulah showing what a spellbinding actress she could be.

When the curtain came down, the audience went wild.

What a *New Yorker* writer later saw as a snarling, gurgling Tallulah, manipulating her parasols like pool cues, her fans like discuses, and laundering the stage with the skirts of her spectacular gowns, was a desperate, drug-diminished woman trying to duplicate her triumphant performance as Regina Giddens. Too many critics had convinced her that the play was not the thing—Tallulah and only Tallulah was. Didn't she resurrect and bedazzle *Private Lives* as a one-woman show? Hadn't Arnold Bennett, who knew everything about everything, said that the world came to watch Tallulah, period?

And what Randolph Carter saw as a selfish superstar savagely rejecting his work and demanding unending rewrites that were never good enough was a terrified Tallulah looking for a different play. Even Henry James, whose novel inspired *Eugenia*, had admitted his work was lightweight.

But Tallulah could glimpse the similarities between

Eugenia and Regina. They were both ruthless, scheming fortune hunters. Her Regina had been called "an almost Satanic figure" by one critic, and "cold, calculatingly and calmly cruel and yet absolutely true and fascinating."

In her attempts to re-create moments of terrible truth onstage as Eugenia, her fellow actors saw her approach the Satanic—offstage.

Yet Tallulah still had marvelous moments. "I saw her work in a way I've never seen anybody else work," says Ellis. "When she was unsure, when she had to be intuitive and instinctive and try to find the material she was as wonderful and moving as Kim Stanley. The moment she knew what she was doing, she became as bored as a child who understood its new toy and could do nothing with it. And she began camping it up and kicking it around. But as long as the material was out of reach and we were struggling for it and it wasn't working yet, it was thrilling."

Maybe there was method in her madness. Could she have been trying to keep the part alive by demanding new material almost daily?

Toward the end of one act Tallulah had the stage to herself—and nothing to say. But even so, some of the cast waited in the wings to see what atrocity she'd commit next. All Tallulah had to do was walk up a flight of stairs and stand silently at the top, as the curtain slowly closed. But nothing was that simple with Tallulah.

The walk was according to the script. But then she did the unexpected. Instead of standing silently at the top of the staircase, as she had done at every performance till now, Tallulah said:

"I shall go around the world in a mackintosh."

Had she finally freaked out? Forgotten where she was? None of the above. Tallulah had demanded a curtain line. Standing mute was asking her to do the near impossible—especially with a captive audience and an imminent curtain.

Carter provided the line at the last moment, when there was no time to tell the rest of the cast.

He was even ready to respond had she greeted the line with: "Who wrote this crap?"

"Henry James," he would have replied. It was taken verbatim from the novel.

But Tallulah had accepted the line almost gratefully. And ironically, it was the play's most memorable line.

The Broadway opening felt like something akin to walking the plank in shark-infested waters. Tallulah's performance caused critics to clash: one griped that she was totally incoherent, another said she flirted with greatness. They must have seen her on different nights.

After about five or six Broadway performances, Carter took Tallulah out to supper. She was in a mellow mood. "I really think this is a lovely play," she told him. And then, "I don't think we changed it much, do you?"

"It was an indirect apology," says Carter. "It was her way of saying she was sorry she'd destroyed it."

Despite conflicting but mostly cool reviews, the Saturday matinee was sold out. Minutes before curtain time Tallulah was missing. Her phone rang but nobody answered it. The stage manager took a frantic cab ride to her home. She had no understudy. The audience had come to see Tallulah—and no substitute would do.

The stage manager found her hopelessly drunk or drugged or concussed. She said she had fallen in the bathtub—and look, look, here's where I hurt myself.

There was no Saturday matinee.

Tallulah crippled *Eugenia* and the critics polished it off. It lurched through eleven performances. But no mere critics could kill Tallulah's spirit.

"Miscast?" she roared at *New York Post* reporter Jim Cook, a few days after *Eugenia* folded, "Of course I'm ALWAYS miscast. I'm Tallulah Bankhead and I'm the only one."

"What do you want to do next?" Tom Ellis' agent asked him.

"I don't care," Ellis said. "Send me onstage with Olivier, Anderson, and an orangutan."

After Tallulah you can face anything, he said. "The illness that you go through with Tallulah, the fear is so great . . . You have to be willing to die when you go out there with her. Because she will throw everything up at any minute and say: 'Aw, this is a lot of shit!' and walk off. So you learn not to have any fourth wall with her, and that's wonderful."

Twenty-two years later he says, "I learned probably everything I know about acting from Tallulah."

And Randolph Carter made the most of his trauma by writing a play about Tallulah called *The Late, Late Show*, in which a star watches her old movies with a couple of people and reminisces and carries on the way Tallulah did—like crazy.

Even though she dismembered his play, he says: "Underneath all this was a great talent. When she was onstage you couldn't take your eyes off her. She was an absolutely fascinating creature."

XXXI

Crazy October

1958 Novelist James Leo Herlihy had seen Tallulah in *Streetcar* and thought her "brilliant and the greatest actress alive." Now he had her in mind for the lead when he turned his short story into a play, *Crazy October*. He took the manuscript to Tallulah's home on East Sixty-second and read it to her. She liked it. And Herlihy loved her. "The most interesting person—male or female—that I've ever met in my life." But she was close to physical and mental collapse, was perpetually drugged to stay awake or to sleep. She drank to such an extent that she couldn't remember how many pills she'd taken.

Herlihy wanted her in his play, but he suggested that before rehearsals started she should go to a hospital, to get off drugs, and then relax and recharge herself at his home on Johnson Street, Key West. Tallulah agreed.

She arrived in Key West loaded with presents for everyone she met. A woman reporter who had lost her hearing interviewed Tallulah for a Key West newspaper. Tallulah bought her a dog trained to let her know when the phone or the doorbell rang. Tallulah saw children who wanted bicycles, she'd buy bikes for them. "She tried to give people whatever they needed to make their life better," says Herlihy.

"Everything she did was funny or original. She was an exceptional person—one of the original mind blowers. We'd gone to see *The Fugitive Kind* in Key West, a movie made from Tennessee Williams' play *Orpheus Descending*. After it was over she said: 'Tennessee they're ruined a perfectly terrible play.' She liked that so well she called up **Walter Winchell** when she got back to New York to make sure that everybody knew about it.

"She also used to commit spoonerisms that worked and then she'd simply take a bow when people laughed.

"Tallulah was a mixture of almost everything: the little girl, the sophisticate, the warm human being, and the brilliant actress.

"I didn't know people could speak so interestingly and at such fantastic lengths until I had met and known Tallulah. Before that, the rule in the theatre as in life, was that everybody had to take turns, and they had to be short speeches. I didn't know that somebody could monologue fascinatingly and hold people, and that has affected my theater writing.

"Tennessee had a big yard but he hadn't done much with it when Tallulah was there and she said of him: 'Tennessee Williams is a poet. All the flowers are in his mind. He doesn't really need a garden.'

"Another evening, when she was there, she asked the producer of *Crazy October,* Walter Starcke, 'Do you believe in God?' and he started to answer, but before he did she said: 'Because I don't. If there is a God he's deaf, dumb, and color-blind, so fuck him in the first place. But of course he is there, you know, darling. He's there.'

"She was deeply religious but she couldn't bear to hear anything commonplace or fatuous said about a religious question," says Herlihy.

Stanley Haggart, the man who had resisted her advances, was in the group at Key West and Tallulah didn't recognize him, to his relief. But he saw a different Tallulah from Herlihy's.

"Tennessee Williams, Herlihy, Tallulah and myself went to a theatre one night to see an amateur group. In the middle of the first act she let out a bellow and got up and stormed out. She was bored and hated the amateurishness of it. She humiliated everybody but couldn't have cared less. When we went to a nightclub she took over the microphone. She drank less than people thought. Her behavior was due to a combination of things she took, pills and drink. She lost her sense of judgment and became a bit of a ham doing 'The Big Show' over again.

"When *Crazy October* was being rehearsed Herlihy and Tallulah had a terrible fight, their one fight, over her being unprofessional. He came to grips with her temperament and he gave her notice to leave. He was going to replace her. She really loved him and she did what he wanted. He was the only one who could prevent her from garbling her words when she was on stage.

"She, Estelle Winwood, and Joan Blondell got along beautifully. When they were traveling by train from Washington all three were supposed to have a drawing room each. Tallulah held up the train for twenty minutes with all the congressional people on it because she found out that there were only two drawing rooms on it. She had a fake fainting fit in her hotel. Finally they had to go on separate trains to have their drawing rooms.

"Yes, there was a shocking, terrible temper, a rude-to-people-unnecessarily side to her," admits Herlihy. "I've seen all that. She used to say herself that everything ever said about her was true. For example, she was never self-conscious about nudity. She enjoyed it. It seems to me after all it is our natural condition. . . . She might have enjoyed the reactions of other people to nudity, but as a child who finds it very puzzling. She never quite understood why people disliked their genitals and their 'boobies' so much that they had to keep them so carefully hidden. '

Stanley Haggart was called in to help design the sets and costumes. Then Tallulah took over. "She said: 'You know I can't wear orange if someone else is wearing yellow.' And I answered: 'You can because you're the hottest part of the fire.

Orange is the color of fire.' She just loved that and accepted orange. I was still feeling embarrassed in case she recognized me from our earlier encounter, but she didn't."

As rehearsals progressed, Tallulah gave Herlihy exactly what he asked for. "She was a perfect instrument, entirely adaptable and flexible," he says. "Naturally there was no question in anyone's mind that it was Tallulah. To disguise herself she'd have had to put dark glasses on her voice."

XXXII

Kennedy, Capote, Parker, and Sandburg

1958–1960

It was midnight, October 17, 1958, and Ted Hook was asleep in his Los Angeles apartment. The phone woke him. A friend said: "Tallulah's on the Jack Paar Show and she's blasting *Time* magazine because they claim she sat on Harry Truman's lap at a luncheon for ex-presidents' wives, to which she was asked. She said she did not sit on his lap: she knows better than that, her father being Speaker of the House and all that, she knows the protocol." Before Hook's friend had finished, Hook's TV had warmed up and there was Tallulah telling them off.

"So I watched the show," says Hook, "and I thought, 'goodness she's in town.' Because I knew she was opening the next day in James Leo Herlihy's *Crazy October*. So I called every single hotel in Los Angeles never dreaming that she would be at a hotel like the Huntington, which is right around the corner from the theatre. So I finally telephoned there and in each case I would call and say: 'Tallulah Bankhead, please,' as if I were her long lost brother—and I was just a chorus boy who hadn't seen her in years and wanted to rekindle an old acquaintanceship. So, finally, they put me through. And she answered the phone herself. I thought she was at the studio. I hadn't realized the Jack Paar Show had been taped that afternoon. And this voice came on and said: 'Hullo.' I said: 'Miss B?' I always called her that. She answered: 'Yes.' 'This is Ted Hook from The Sands; and she said, 'Oh, my God, come around, darling, come around.' So I did and I asked, 'Why did you answer the phone?' She said: 'It's the first time I've answered the telephone since 1934, Rose is becoming impossible.' That was her maid. They'd had a fight that day. I really think it was the first time she'd answered a telephone since 1934. So I came over.

"She was having a big party in her suite and Joan Blondell was there and Estelle Winwood and James Leo Herlihy and Walter Starcke the producer and Gert Macy and Jack Western, who played her son in that play. And they were all sitting around and having drinks and everything and finally when they all left, she'd had quite a few drinks herself and I could see the sleeping pills were taking effect, and she said: 'How would you like to come to work for me? I would love to have you be with me and just sort of take over my life. I need somebody to take charge and to handle my tours and my press and to be an escort and to be there in the darkest hours, which are late at night, and when I'm loneliest.' And she said: 'I will give you a fabulous salary. . . . You'll never have to pay for your rent, or your food, or your liquor, or your laundry or cleaning, but I insist you buy your own goddam cigarettes.' And I thought she was kidding, I thought it was just the liquor talking, so I said: 'Well, Tallulah, that's very sweet and you know I'd love to do it.' She said: 'You have till twelve noon tomorrow to make up your mind.' Then I got to thinking: maybe she does mean it. Because I'd been with her in those moments and I knew she *knew* what she was saying no matter how many drinks she'd had, or how many pills. Until the moment the whole body collapsed into a lethal sleep, she did remember. So I went home and I stayed awake all night and I thought: she can't mean it, really she can't mean it.

"So the next day I called about eleven o'clock and Rose was

on the phone and said: 'Well, have you made up your mind?'
Rose was very hostile. I told her: 'Yes, I have, I've decided I
will.' And Tallulah got on the phone: 'Come round, darling.
Move out of your place.' So I said: 'I can't just move out of
an apartment.' So she said to tell the landlady she'd give her
six months' rent in advance. I said: 'You don't have to do
that. I'm on a month-to-month basis. Nobody's used to that
type of thing. I'm just staying in this filthy $65-a-month apart-
ment.' So she called the landlady, who's dead now, and she
said: 'Cleo darling, this is Tallulah Bankhead.' And of course
the woman thought it was her daughter making a joke. She
said: 'I'm going to pay you six-months' rent in advance
darling.' Well, the whole thing sounded more preposterous
every minute. So sure enough she had me write a check
and give it to my landlady. I think that's what killed her. So
I went to work for her. I'm a kid who's been a chorus boy,
who came from a middle-class family in Oakland, California,
who had worked in motion pictures as an extra. And that
very day she said: 'Do you have a dinner jacket?' And I said,
'No.' I didn't know it was synonymous for tuxedo to begin
with. So she had me go out and rent one and that night I'm
standing at a stage door at the Huntington Hartford Theatre,
saying: 'I'm sorry, Miss Crawford, Miss Ball is in there right
now. And Mr. Preminger is right after you.' I'm lining up
movie stars and celebrities that I'd read about all my life.
And her husband John Emery was there—Tallulah adored
him—and Polly Adler: it was just a wild, wonderful night.
And that's how it all started. Then we went from Los Angeles
to San Francisco that Christmastime and Rose got in a huff—
they'd been together for twenty-five years—and Rose left,
never to go back. Tallulah kept her on the payroll, I think,
until the day Tallulah died.

"She always got up at ten of four. On the button. The
soapies. 'My soapies. I've got to watch my soapies.' 'Brighter
Day,' 'Secret Storm,' and 'Edge of Night.' Ten of four she
was gotten up, went right into the tub, the water was all

ready and the two bowls of ice cubes. She always put ice cubes on her face and other areas to firm things. And then into the dressing gown and then planted in front of the TV until Jack Paar was over and then right back to the bed. The days never varied for years on end.

"Once in Chicago she lost her temper with me and then she cried for two days because she felt so bad about it afterward. Sometimes she tested me. She told me she was testing me. Two days after I was hired she'd come out of the stage door of the Huntington Hartford Theatre and my job was to have a taxi waiting for her. Well I'd gotten the cab and always was told to have him push down the thing, no matter how much it cost, no matter how long she was detained, she wanted her cab waiting there—and her hotel was exactly one block away. So I had the cab waiting and all of a sudden some woman came out of the stage door in a mink coat: the taxi driver probably didn't know who Tallulah Bankhead was. And this woman saw the cab and popped into it and he probably thought that was Tallulah and he went off. It was the funniest thing. Jamie Herlihy was with us that day. And she said: 'Ted for godsakes you're not doing your job! For *chrissakes*, what'd you think I hired you for? I've got to have a taxi waiting for me. Stars *always* have transportation, either in the form of a chauffeur or taxi!' And she was just furious. And I was shaking all over. She said: 'What are we going to do, for godsakes? I can't stand out in the street! I've never been left alone in the street in my life. Even as a little girl in Alabama I always had an escort, for chrissakes!' And I said: 'What do you want me to do Tallulah?' She said: 'Well, where's the hotel?' I said: 'It's around the corner.' She said: 'Well, why didn't you say so? Let's *walk* for godsakes!' And I couldn't believe that she was actually going to walk. When we got to the door, I said: 'Oh, Tallulah, I'm so sorry.' And Jamie was terrified and I was terrified. And when we got upstairs she said calmly: 'Perfectly all right, darling. I *loved* the way you handled yourself. I was just testing you to see if you could live through this *storm* of Tallulah Bankhead.' She said: 'You've passed the test.' She said: 'For chrissakes, why didn't you tell me it was so close? We could save money on taxis. We'll walk all the time.' "

Something was tormenting Tallulah so much as Christmas approached that she decided to play the real-life part of Scrooge. When Joan Blondell asked her to pay her share for a cast party, Tallulah refused. She angrily called Ted Hook into her dressing room and gave her orders: "There will be no fucking presents, no fucking parties, and no fucking good cheer this Christmas." A few days before the twenty-fifth she saw a little Christmas tree in Joan Blondell's dressing room and greeted it with a Bronx cheer.

But two days before Christmas a miracle happened. "I know I said no Christmas this year," she told Hook. "But I'm a star, darling, and a star is entitled to change her mind." She sent him out to buy for the boys in cast and crew a silk dressing gown and bottle of liquor apiece and, for the women, two cashmere sweaters each.

After the Christmas Eve performance, she made a pitch to the audience for the Actor's Fund, danced a frenzied Charleston, and almost sang her way through "May the Good Lord Bless and Keep You," before breaking down in tears.

Now she just couldn't wait for Christmas and ordered everyone to try on dressing gowns and sweaters there and then. One stocky stagehand found his dressing gown was too large. Tallulah was incensed. "I told you medium fat, not FAT!" she shrieked at Hook.

Joan Blondell laughed with surprise when Tallulah handed her a bottle of perfume. "For chrissakes, Tallulah, you're the one who wasn't going to have Christmas this year."

Tallulah commanded silence, then called out: "Merry Christmas, darlings. And I hope it will be my last."

But she had several to go yet.

"She reminded me of John Barrymore," says Joan Blondell. "She had the beauty of a Barrymore. And she was a lovely, lively person."

Ted Hook recalls: "Dola Cavendish sort of took over as her secretary for a while, not really, because Dola was terribly wealthy. She just did it for a lark. That was a case of complete adulation. Dola was not a lesbian. Dola was a lonely, old, ugly, hideous alcoholic and I say that with compassion, because Dola was a warm, wonderful person, extremely well-educated. But she came from a family of thirteen girls, eleven of whom died by their own hand in a sense, either through suicide or alcoholism. She took a shine to Tallulah because she'd always had a crush on stars and she was going to will Tallulah the world; and whenever Tallulah came to Canada, of course, Victoria, British Columbia, was hers. And Tallulah loved to go up there, because Dola had a beautiful, beautiful house, and lovely trees and good bridge companions and servants that took care of Tallulah's every need and a fireplace in every bedroom and it was just kind of a haven of rest for Tallulah.

"She used to snap her fingers to have her cigarettes lighted and I used to just roar. She and I were on such a channel that she could look at me and I knew whether she wanted her lipstick or her frownies. She wore these marvelous little V-shaped things you buy in the store that are called frownies and you pull your frown apart, you lick it and you put it on. Estelle Winwood wears frownies and wingies. Wingies go on crowsfeet. When Estelle goes to bed her face is a sea of stickum tape. And Tallulah would put them on her forehead and we'd get in a taxi and she'd say: 'Don't forget to tell me to take my frownies off, darling, before we get out of the taxicab.' And taxi drivers used to turn around and say: 'Oh, Miss Bankhead, what did you do to your forehead?' She'd explain: 'They're frownies, darling.' I could look at her and know when she wanted her frownies, when she wanted a frownies that was on removed, when she wanted her lipstick; when she wanted a pill; when she wanted a drink. We got so after the first year, she used to tell people that we didn't even communicate. I just *knew*.

"There was a rumor that she and a big TV star might do a show together. Then Tallulah read in a gossip column that the TV star would not appear on the stage with a woman who had to have the curtain rung down because of excessive drinking—and mentioned Tallulah Bankhead. Well she went into a state of melancholia for thirteen days. Robert (her butler) and I used to have to pick her up bodily and lay her on the floor while we made the bed. Because she stayed in that dark room and she wouldn't speak to anybody and she wouldn't eat. She did nothing but. . . . Oh, it was just frightening. She was going to sue and everything and Donald Seawell, her attorney, said don't bother, you never win anything in these suits, and it just makes it sound worse. She said: 'I was not like Jeanne Eagels. I have never had a curtain rung down on me because of my drinking. When I drink I drink and when I work I work.' And she was right.

"She was in bed one night, and she got up, she'd had too many sleeping pills and too much alcohol—this was during the melancholy period—and she apparently went to go to the bathroom and she fell. And about three in the morning I heard her screaming my name: 'Ted! Ted!' Well I was used to that, because lots of times, if she'd had drinks or had too many sleeping pills or something she would call out to me or she would want me to come down and just talk to her, tell her she was loved, and things of that nature. So it was almost like crying wolf at that point because she'd done it several times that night And finally when I went down I heard this terrible wheezing coming from her rib cage and I realized that something serious had happened. So I called the doctor and they came and got her out on a stretcher and carried her down those stairs and took her to Flower Fifth Avenue Hospital and she was in there for some time. She had really broken her ribs and it was very bad. She had had no food and was in a terrible state of melancholy and that's what happened.

"Tallulah was first and foremost a Southern lady. She had the most exquisite manners of any male or female I've ever met in my life. The only thing she cared about, she told me in her later life, when she said: 'Darling, the only thing I care about are good manners. If the waiter serves the soup with a surly attitude,' she said, 'I'd just as soon pay the check and leave.' 'Slit my throat but smile when you do it!' She was that all the way.

"She did the so-called shocking things purely for effect. It got the exact effect that she desired. It was her little attention-getter. But it was never done in a vulgar fashion. She would go in and whistle on the john. She would always say 'I've got to go looloos now' and things like that. She always did it with great charm and she was fey—an old-fashioned word I know but that's just what she was.

"She was disappoined that in the early days she didn't marry somebody. She always said that it wasn't right for stars to be married, that was the main reason she didn't. And because of that, she had so many things to keep her from having babies. I think her biggest frustration in life was not being a mother, more than anything else. She would have been a magnificent mother. Because she was a mother to animals and to everybody else. She picked up people on the street—and I don't mean that in a crude way—we'd walk down the street, people would talk to her and she'd invite them back to the house for drinks, total strangers, because she was so starved for companionship. And she couldn't just call up the world and invite them over."

Ted Hook flew down to Washington with Tallulah on April 13, 1959, when she appeared with actress Peggy Cass, representing Actors' Equity before the House Ways and Means Committee in support of federal unemployment compensation for actors.

"I got there the night before," says Peggy Cass, "and in the morning I went to meet her at the airport, and my dear, she'd had a lot of sleeping pills, she was the last one off the plane and she was really quite sleepy, like drugged. And she was with this fellow, Hook, who was her secretary. She looked absolutely marvelous, she had a brown and white dress, very pretty, and she said: 'I want a little Jack Daniels, darling, to warm me up.' She said she was terribly cold. It was April, a spring day. We went to the Jefferson and she didn't have a drink, instead she had coffee, and my dear, by the time we got to the Senate hearing, she, my dear, was in absolutely sensational shape and she was marvelous, absolutely marvelous, lucid, witty, brilliant, the whole thing."

An AP report said: "Surrounded by mink, cups of ice water and cigarettes, Miss Bankhead opened with a frank admission to the committee: 'I haven't heard a bloody word you've said, so I don't know whether you're for us or agin us.'"

Leaning heavily on Ted Hook, because she'd twisted her ankle, Tallulah told committee members she had never collected unemployment compensation but actors needed it because they're out of work so much. "Maybe they shouldn't be actors but maybe you shouldn't be elected to Congress, who knows?"

The bill didn't pass.

"Then I left to go to the airport to see her off," says Peggy Cass. "I wasn't going home with her. I took the train. She was in the airport restaurant and asked for bourbon and branch water. And they said, 'We sell only wine here.' And she said, 'You mean to tell me a Bankhead can't get bourbon in Virginia?' And then the plane was called."

Tallulah had moved from "Windows"—the cost of snowplowing the road to it could have financed an off-Broadway show—and was now living in a house at 230 East Sixty-second Street, Manhattan

It was here she surprised Ted Hook one day by saying: "If you could have anybody to dinner tonight, who would you like?"

Thinking it was just another party game, Hook said out of the hat: "Truman Capote and Dorothy Parker."

Tallulah went to her phone book, got their phone numbers, and called them. They were both free.

"I went and picked up Dorothy Parker, who lived nearby, and Capote arrived a few minutes later.

"I remember Capote asking Dorothy Parker if she'd seen the recent Guggenheim exhibit. And she said: 'No. If I go above Seventy-second Street I get a nosebleed.'

"That was the most fantastic night. That and the night Carl Sandburg came over were the two most exciting evenings I've ever spent with anybody. Tallulah had sent Sandburg a wire once and he always carried it in the pocket next to his heart. He called it, with affection, 'My wire from Miss B.' Sandburg said he had never stayed up beyond one o'clock in his life and this time he stayed until five.

"She also introduced me to Kennedy, which was one of the most exciting things ever: we had gone to his hotel. She had never met the man herself. Janet Leigh introduced us. Janet Leigh said—he wasn't President at the time, he was running—"Tallulah I'd like to present John Kennedy. John Kennedy, Tallulah Bankhead." And then Tallulah said the same thing she said every time she introduced me to anybody, she said: 'Mr. Kennedy, I would like you to meet my very dear friend Ted Hook, who happens also to be my secretary.' Now I said: 'You do *not have* to say I'm your good friend. I'm working for you, I'm in your employ, I'm paid well and I love my job, every bit of it. You do not have to preface every introduction to Carl Sandburg, and Joan Crawford, and Truman Capote with 'my very dear friend.' She said: 'But I feel that way.' And I said: 'That's very sweet of you and very gracious and I do appreciate it.' And that's the way she was."

A good preparation for working for Tallulah would be a refresher course in *Alice in Wonderland*. She treated her staff as buddies one moment, then raged at them for being too casual; offered them drinks and called them dipsos for saying "thanks." A cook was fired for answering the door with nothing on but high-heeled shoes; a maid for smoking pot during working hours.

One of Ted Hook's final, frantic duties for Tallulah was to hire a replacement cook. After days of screening unlikely candidates he found a marvel who could cook, clean, and even do secretarial work Ted introduced the tiny, very old black woman to Tallulah. "She can cook, clean, type. . . ." "Yes, yes," Tallulah interrupted, "but does she play bridge?"

She didn't play bridge. but Emma Anthony got the job. And in time Tallulah treated her like a well-loved old relative who had to be guarded from harsh realities. She made a superhuman effort not to shock Emma, almost imitating the painful stuttering of Somerset Maugham in an effort to stop herself in mid "shit, fuck, or bastard." In time, Tallulah, began to spell out these words, when Emma was around, though it was clear to Ted that Emma could outspell Tallulah.

XXXIII

Campaigning for Adlai and Jack

1960 Actor Tony Randall loved Tallulah on sight—and out of sight. On their first brief encounter during rehearsals of *Skin of Our Teeth* he was captivated, and though World War II kept them apart, he cherished that meeting. After the war Randall studied great acting close up—playing in *Inherit the Wind* with Paul Muni. And he studied the glamor queens, acting opposite almost every one of them on stage, screen, and television.

A man of startling views—believing that tenor opera stars have a mating season and a season of abstention to protect their voices—a man with an eye for the comic and outrageous, Randall never ceased to be entertained by Tallulah. He was one of the many she couldn't quite place when they met again, and they often saw each other after the war.

Says Randall: "When you ran into Tallulah you'd think she didn't remember you and then suddenly she'd say: 'Oh, yes, you were in such-and-such a show.' She did recognize you but she talked compulsively and even if you were in her vision she couldn't stop talking about what she'd started on.

"Practically anywhere you met her, unless on the street, she'd have a glass in her hand. She'd say: 'Just so you won't be disillusioned, darling, it's bourbon.' I remember meeting her at a costume fitting and she came over and spat down my neck for luck.

"She knew everything about the theatre, her instincts about the theatre were always right. At the time John Gielgud made his gigantic success over here in *Hamlet* in 1937, they were having a problem. The director Guthrie McClintic told me this. And someone said: 'I know who can help us, let's go talk to Tallulah.' So they went over to Tallulah's house to ask her advice about whatever this problem was. And she was in bed. She got very interested in the problem and sat up and the covers fell down. She was naked to the waist, which never in her life bothered her. But Gielgud was so embarrassed that though they stayed there for over an hour talking he never once looked back her way.

"I've never known anyone anywhere like her. She was so funny and so fast. Guthrie McClintic worshipped her and he told me one time they were in Paris and one of these terrible women performed who could pick up a coin from a corner of a table using—to use a euphemism—her thing. And immediately Tallulah wanted to try it! She was unstoppable. She would do anything that came into her head.

"She was a little girl show-off, a little girl being bad all the time to get attention, being naughty and being darling.

"We campaigned together for Stevenson and then for Jack Kennedy in 1960. We did a performance for Jack Kennedy in Teaneck, New Jersey. There were some ten thousand people in this armory and some seven thousand outside, a bitter cold, rainy November day. And he was five hours late. He was making many appearances that day and the weather held him up. And all those people stayed and the performers who were supposed to entertain them didn't stay. Three or four of us stayed the whole five hours and tried to keep the audience amused so they wouldn't go away. Tallulah was one. She had this habit of blinking her eyes in a very annoying way, but when she was 'on' she didn't do it. You know the old joke 'Squeeze me with your eyes. . . . Not so tight!' Her whole face would close up with it. It would happen very quickly and often but when she was in front of a camera or an audience she could absolutely control that thing and didn't do it. Here for five hours she held herself before the audience looking young and smart and in good spirits and full of fun and it must have been a terrible effort for her. We hadn't prepared a show. All any of us had prepared was to get up and say: 'God Bless You.' In those shows the singers are the lucky ones, they can get up and sing a song or two or three or four. But us actors have to ad lib. I ended up leading the audience in community singing and I led them in the same song 'George Washington Bridge' over one hundred times. And it became hilariously funny. Tallulah sang along. We'd say, 'We have another request.' And we'd do it again and again and again. They all stayed. Nobody left. And nobody was angry when Jack Kennedy arrived five hours late.

"She tried to shock you by saying 'Shall we make love?' and things like that but I'm unshockable. She loved to shock the rubes.

"Tallulah was a glamorous actress. That's a rare thing for me to say because I don't think they're glamorous, because I know them all and they don't have any theatrical glamor or air about them. She also came at the tail end of a period that expected its actors and actresses to be colorful vagabonds and gypsies. They wanted them to be like John Barrymore, to be eccentric.

"She was often surrounded by homosexual men and it's psychoanalytically interesting why she chose her companions this way. I think they chose her. She's exactly the kind of woman that they make cults about. Judy Garland and Maria Callas. If you've ever been to a Maria Callas performance you can't believe the atmosphere in the opera house. And Callas can't sing at all. She never had a good voice. She had an extraordinary personality on that stage, but for the last ten years her voice has been gone. But they carry on with an hysteria that is manic. And of course there's never been a homosexual cult around a man. These homosexuals don't fantasy about men. I mean about themselves as men. They all want to be women. And they want to be women like that: they want to be roguish, world-beating women. Maybe they all had mothers like that. These women are a bit like homosexuals in drag themselves."

XXXIV

Traumatic —
Midgie Purvis

1961–1962 Tallulah was lying in bed when theatre producer Robert Whitehead came in with Burgess Meredith. They wanted her to play in *Midgie Purvis*, by Mary Chase. It was a wild, tempestuous meeting. Tallulah acted as if they'd come to turn off the electricity. She was still pretty blotto from last night's bourbon.

As they went out, Meredith, whose early passionate encounters with Tallulah had brightened his Broadway days, said to Whitehead: "If we use her we're only asking for trouble."

"She's the name we want," Whitehead replied. "I'm sure she'll shape up."

At first it appeared he was right.

Tallulah arrived for the first rehearsal, steady and clear-eyed. She took directions well and learned her lines quickly. She was sweet to the children in the play—which was about the generation gap, how parents through lack of imagination fail to share their children's world.

And it was becoming evident that in this role Tallulah could show all her critics that she did not reduce all parts into a caricature of herself.

Then some changes were made in the script. Tallulah

went home to learn them. Came back next day, word perfect. But the scene didn't quite go as Whitehead and Meredith expected. That scene was rewritten on the spot by Mary Chase, who was as quick and imaginative as the children she wrote about. Now every day brought new changes in the script, and Tallulah began to snap at the kids and scream that they were moving on her lines.

The hysteria spread. Everyone was terrified, anxiously awaiting Tallulah's next attack.

Meredith tried to stop it: "Unless this play is frozen soon, we'll never open with anything, good, bad, or indifferent."

Meredith asked Tallulah to meet him in the theatre alone one time. When she saw no one else was there she asked why.

"Because I have no notes for the rest of the cast, only for you."

Her screams and curses shook him and left him stunned. She walked off refusing to listen to his criticisms.

It was only a few days before the first night. Meredith and Whitehead discussed the possibility of writing Tallulah out of the show. They had driven her to distraction by the constant changes in the script and now they couldn't handle her. "Perhaps she'll leave," Meredith said.

But Tallulah wouldn't leave.

The play went on.

"What we did achieve was a kind of a miracle," says Burgess Meredith. "The play sort of staggered in and came to life. And Tallulah captivated the critics pretty much. Walter Kerr said she was quite amazing, but thought the play had not been brought together."

One of the audience, Christopher Hewitt, thought she was marvelous in *Midgie Purvis.* "As the old lady she was quite incredible. She got away from herself and was playing the character, not Tallulah. But the play bombed."

"Her sense of the comic is unerring, her timing is as right as rain, and she plays upon that remarkable voice of hers the way Rubinstein plays his piano. It warms the heart to see her slide down the bannister in the big house where everybody has insisted on her being a lady," wrote critic John Chapman in the Sunday *New York Daily News.*

Meredith was so upset by the experience that he vowed never to direct Tallulah again, but recognized a large part of the blame was his for allowing too many changes to be made in the script.

Tallulah was nominated for the Antoinette Perry Award for her performance, and Ted Hook agreed to be her escort. A week before they went he told her he'd been offered a job as a choreographer. What should he do?

"Ted," she said, "I would keep you for the rest of my life, but you're very young, and it's a chance for you not to be sheltered under the identity of a star. I could die tomorrow and then you'd have built the better part of your life around me. And that's no good. I think you should do it."

So he took the job.

When he was on the road she would do telephone taped interviews with him and tell people how much she enjoyed him, and hoped Ted's show would be a success. The tape was played on local radio stations to give Ted's show publicity.

Tallulah wasn't without a secretary-friend for long.

XXXV

Here Today

1962 Tallulah's poor memory for names could be covered up by calling everybody "Darling."

But what could she do about her poor memory for faces? She accepted an introduction to playwright George Oppenheimer four times until, hurt, he said: "Tallulah, this is damned insulting. Maybe I'm not the kind of man women recall, but this is at least the fourth time we've been introduced."

She cried.

"She was without a doubt one of the most kindly people to other actors I've ever known," says Oppenheimer. "When we were auditioning for *Here Today* in which she starred, she attended the auditions and whenever anybody came out she'd jump on the stage and say: 'I'm Tallulah Bankhead,' as if they had to know. And 'Good luck.' And this is terribly kind and put them greatly at ease.

"God knows she was wonderful in my play (which broke an eighteen-year-old box office record at La Jolla Playhouse), but once Tallulah had been in a play for a long time, she became pretty undisciplined. Oh, God, she was so campy when I saw her six months after she'd started!

"She was a thoroughgoing actress ham. I shared a radio interview with her once and all I got to say was 'hello.' Every time they handed me the microphone she'd say: 'He's too modest'—and grab it."

Tallulah's wardrobe mistress for *Here Today* was Harriet Beal, a one-time dancer in the theatre. The past year and a half she'd been with Marilyn Monroe, had taken care of her personal mail, often helped her learn her lines, and autographed all her pictures.

Tallulah's butler, Robert, hurried over to Harriet one August morning in 1962 and said: "Harriet, see if you can get Miss Bankhead out of that bed, because we have to leave by limousine for the next town."

Harriet went into Tallulah's bedroom and called gently: "Good morning, darling! Get up. Get up! We've got to go."

Tallulah tried to open her eyes, rubbed them, then opened one cautiously. "Oh, Harriet," she said. "I've got to tell you something. Marilyn Monroe committed suicide."

Harriet fainted and fell on the floor. Tallulah apologized for days afterward. It had just slipped out. She and Robert had agreed to keep the news from Harriet until they reached the next town. But it was almost impossible for Tallulah to keep news to herself, even the tragic.

Robert and Tallulah had their fights on tour as they did at home. But one morning, at two o'clock, in Falmouth, Massachusetts, she insulted Robert and he quit on the spot.

Tallulah sent an SOS to Harriet's cottage and Harriet woke in a hurry, got dressed, and went to see her.

It was obvious to Harriet that Tallulah had been drinking. She still had a glass in her hand, and when she tried to brush hair out of her eyes, she missed.

Harriet tried the tough approach: "What on earth is going on at this hour of the morning?"

"Oh, Harriet, Robert has quit and I don't know what we're going to do."

The two women talked until dawn. Then Harriet went out to look for Robert. Someone found him in a motel and he agreed to see Harriet.

Tears running down her cheeks, Harriet pleaded with him: "You can't leave her like this. She needs you so badly."

Robert, who did everything for Tallulah, paid all the bills, bought all the food, usually controlled her drinking, practically ran her life, now wanted out.

"I'm not going back," he said. "She called me a black son of a bitch."

Nevertheless Harriet persuaded him to go back and talk to Tallulah. And Harriet said: "Now Miss Bankhead, will you please tell why you called Robert a black son of a bitch?"

And Tallulah replied: "I didn't call him a black son of a bitch. I called him a son of a bitch. I know he's black."

"It was so funny the way she said it," recalls Harriet Beal, "and in the course of this meeting they got back together."

Tallulah told Harriet: "If I ever ask for a drink when I come off the stage, don't give it to me."

Tallulah came off the stage a few nights later and asked Harriet: "Have you got a drink for me honey?"

"Oh, no."

"You haven't? You mean to tell me I can't have a drink?"

"Now, what did you tell me? Didn't you tell me not to give you any drink?"

"Yes, but I thought you'd surprise me."

"She was a marvelous woman," says Harriet. "I've only met one other person in my whole life that I could sit and listen to and never open my mouth other than to ask her questions. She was so well versed on everything, you were always learning something from her. The other was a young lady, a librarian in Chicago.

"I worked for Vivien Leigh, Eve Arden, Eartha Kitt, Marilyn Monroe. I loved them all so dearly. People say that Miss Arden was my favorite but there was something different about Miss Bankhead that I admired. There were ugly things told me about Miss Bankhead but I never saw that side of her. In my book she did stand out."

XXXVI

Tallulah Catches
the Milk Train

1963–1964 Tennessee Williams was in Mexico watching Elizabeth Taylor watch Richard Burton watch Ava Gardner watch John Huston watch Tennessee Williams' *Night of the Iguana* turning into film.

But when he wasn't watching, Williams worked on a new version of *The Milk Train Doesn't Stop Here Anymore*. An earlier version had died after two months on Broadway, during a newspaper strike.

Late one night Tennessee finished the new script and put a call through from Puerto Vallarta to New York City. The call reached Tallulah at midnight. It was early November, 1963.

They exchanged "darlings" and then he offered her a part: "*Milk Train* now says what I wanted it to say from the start, but couldn't get down on paper."

"When do we start rehearsals?" she asked.

"In three weeks."

"Who else is in it?"

"Ruth Ford, Tab Hunter, and Marian Seldes. And Tony Richardson will direct."

"I'll be there, darling."

It was par for the course for Tallulah to be burned, bruised, or bleeding. She prepared to rehearse for what was to be her last Broadway play with a painful injury. She had dropped a lighted cigarette which caught between her fingers and made a savage burn that turned into an ugly open wound. Let the air get at it, she was told, when it failed to heal. Now she jumped when anyone approached her right side suddenly. Onstage she would wear a chiffon square around her wrist to hide the wound.

A few days before the first rehearsal Marian Seldes got a phone call. It sounded like Tallulah inviting her over to discuss their scenes together. Tallulah was just a legend to Seldes—tough, glamorous, and daring—and for a few moments she suspected a friend was trying to fool her with a pretty good Tallulah imitation, until the actress convinced her she was the real thing.

Seldes went to the East Fifty-seventh Street apartment and took the elevator—room for two close friends—to the thirteenth floor for their first meeting. Tallulah greeted her wearing tight slacks and a loose silk blouse, chain-smoking and chain-talking, and doing everything she could to avoid going over their lines, like a child putting off homework.

Tallulah was anxious to destroy the self-perpetuating myths she had once gone along with in the spirit of "say anything about me, darling, as long as it isn't boring." Now, as she and Seldes dined together, Tallulah complained about the scandalous publicity.

She had certainly made herself a tempting target. When old father *Time* did a cover story on her as far back as November 22, 1948, the *Time* scribes told how she broke all attendance records in Boston during a blizzard that stopped traffic and closed the schools. Tallulah could fill the theater in a blizzard, not because it was the only warm place in town, but because she was her own mythmaker. And part of the myth was that there was NOTHING she wouldn't do or say.

Hence the *Time* contention that Tallulah "can quote readily, and at impressive length, from the Bible, Shakespeare, and a lavatory wall."

Truman laughed through Tallulah's autobiography and Roosevelt had roared when she appeared at the White House hard on the heels of a group of reformed female convicts and greeted him with, "We'll get along swell. You like delinquent girls."

It was her wit not her wantonness she wanted to impress on Seldes, as if rehearsing a new witness to be ready with answers to questions from the inevitable biographers.

She protested to Seldes: "I am a victim of bad publicity, darling. They say I'm a lesbian, a nymphomaniac, a dope fiend. . . ." She then told one of her favorite true stories of how she had had commiserated with Tennessee Williams after seeing the movie version of his play *The Battle of Angels,* saying, "I think it's a disgrace, darling. They've absolutely ruined a bad play." She laughed with delight. "Now that's the sort of thing they should write about me. Not that I go around naked. My figure's not good enough to go around naked."

Seldes was so taken with Tallulah that every day after rehearsals she recorded what the legend had said and done. It became a chapter in her book *The Bright Lights: A Theatre Life,* published by Houghton Mifflin in 1978.

Tony Richardson was to direct the play. Tallulah had not been his choice. He gave in to Williams and producer Merrick, who wanted her, only when they agreed quid pro quo to accept Tab Hunter as the young man. If Tallulah had known Richardson was after another actress for the part there might have been even more devastation than there was.

It was rarely less than an ordeal for a director to work with Tallulah in her last years. She searched for their soft spots and struck, circled for a blow to their self-esteem and—whack! Then she'd step back for a surprise attack from an unexpected angle. She had broken the spirit of more than one, and crippled several. She wanted people to be flawless.

Richardson was in no mood for difficult women. He was having trouble in his own life. His marriage to Vanessa Redgrave—as outspoken in her way as Tallulah and even more politically ablaze—was heading for the end.

When the cast assembled for the first reading in Tallulah's apartment, she let her little dog Dolores run interference—as if that was Richardson's first test. Could he take on Tallulah and Dolores and survive?

He had a lot going for him. He had shown the golden touch commercially and artistically. His movie *Tom Jones* from Fielding's classic earned raves from critics and box-office cashiers. He had just directed *Luther* and *Arturo Ui* on Broadway and the praise still rang in his ears.

Now he was gamely trying to make himself heard above Dolores' incessant yapping. Tallulah looked stunning as she sat, the equivalent of stage center, on a white couch with her matching white pooch beside her. "The play is about . . ." Yap! Yap! ". . . Death . . ." Yap! Yap!

Tennessee Williams arrived late and tried to sneak in undetected until Dolores' yapping gave him away. Disappointed that there were no drinks, Williams gradually covered himself with gray cigarette ash which was wafted about when he laughed at his own actor-read jokes.

Richardson was in no laughing mood. In fact, he found it so trying to speak above Dolores' yaps that he lost control and muttered "Fuck you!" at her.

At the height of Dolores' frenzy, Richardson tried to explain the meaning of the play and Tallulah scored one to the chin as she leaned forward disingenuously and said, "I can hardly hear you, darling. What are you saying?"

Had Richard Maney masterminded Tallulah's last Broadway appearance, he couldn't have surpassed this scenario: she was to portray herself, or, as she put it, looking fiercely at

Williams: "Everything in this goddamned play he copied from me!"

In Tallulah's own words, Flora Goforth, the character she was to recreate, was "a promiscuous, pill-ravaged rip, undernourished and overwrought. Born in a Georgia swamp, Flora has become a legend in her lifetime, thanks to her seductive design, her bedroom triumphs, her ability to outrage or exhilarate the peasants by her off-key conduct." Tallulah to a T—though she would never call herself promiscuous, and was born one state state west of Georgia.

Tennessee Williams hoped that Flora's character would evoke pity as well as laughter as she fiercely fought off swiftly approaching death. In real life Tallulah had rarely been without a young man at her side and beck and call. As Flora, she had a handsome gigolo, nicknamed the Angel of Death because of his penchant for comforting rich old women in their last days.

What happened was not fair to Richardson, nor to Tallulah. She was fighting for breath, with only five years of pain-wracked life left. But she heard Richardson was a genius and hoped he could work a miracle.

Rehearsals began in earnest on November 20, 1963, at the Lunt-Fontanne Theatre. In her book Marian Seldes tells how "we were rehearsing the first scene of the second act. From the stage Tab's voice was saying, 'We don't all live in the same world, you know, Mrs. Goforth. Oh, we all see the same things—sea, sun, sky, human faces and inhuman faces, but . . . one person's sense of reality can be another person's sense of—well, of madness! Chaos! And . . .' Tallulah didn't answer him. She cried out. Tony had interrupted to tell her that President Kennedy had been shot.

"She was weeping. Tennessee came holding his Boston bull terrier and some brandy which he shared with Tallulah. We stopped rehearsals for ten minutes. Then Tab began again: 'Madness! Chaos . . .'

"I took Tallulah home after the rehearsal. We talked about

her father Congressman Bankhead, whom she adored, and
Adlai Stevenson, whose voice comforted us on the taxi radio.
She was shaken but surprisingly controlled. The following
week was the most disciplined rehearsing for her. She had a
vitamin B shot every day and although she was tired, she knew
her words pretty well.

"One stunning, unforgettable rehearsal of the final scene
in the first act made us think that the project would be magi-
cally transformed and that Tallulah was going to give a performance that would be remembered with her work in *The
Little Foxes* and *The Skin of Our Teeth*. She took Tony's
direction and used it with thrilling intensity and power.

"She knew she was good that day, yet she went to Tony and
told him she could not do it his way. 'It would kill me. I'm
going to play it my own way.' "

Why couldn't she repeat that extraordinary performance
that Marian Seldes recalls as "terrifying and beautiful"?

"Because it was too personal, too devastating," Seldes explains. "You've got to remember she was really fighting for her
life all through that production, and so was the character. And
the secretary, the part I played, is trying to help her, trying
to keep her alive. And so was I in my life, trying anything to
make life a little easier for her. Somehow, in that one day, in
that one rehearsal it was Tallulah and it was Mrs. Goforth.
It was the actress and it was the woman—it was everything
that great acting is supposed to be. It was sublime.

"But I can understand why she often said she hated acting.
It didn't satisfy her as it does some actors. It didn't seem like
a craft to her. It was as if she was born with that talent—almost
a curse, and with her beauty. And when people are talented
and beautiful, other people tell them to go on the stage. And
that's really not the way to choose a life."

Despite Tallulah's denial to Marian Seldes at that first
meeting, that she went around naked, the younger actress often
saw her "with no clothes on. We were in the same hotel in
Baltimore and she would call me at two and three and four

in the morning, needing help, or reassurance, or just to talk. My guess is that she was proud of that beautiful body and had no shame about it. Nudity didn't seem unnatural to her."

In fact, writes Seldes, "my eight-year-old daughter's first glimpse of the fabled, wonderful Tallulah Bankhead [on Christmas Eve] was of a naked woman half covered with a sheet sitting in a hotel bedroom smoking, coughing, laughing, and talking.

" 'Do you believe in Santa Claus, darling?'

"Katharine looked at me and then at Tallulah.

" 'No.'

"Tallulah gave me a reproving look. 'Oh, my *God!* I did! I did, all through my childhood, and when I found out there was *no* Santa Claus'—her eyes filled with tears and she pushed her uncombed tawny hair back from her face—'it was the most terrible moment in my whole life, until I heard that Kennedy was shot.' She wept. Katharine said nothing. Then Tallulah gave her a red dress and white sweater. Katharine thanked her gravely and went out to play in the snow."

Whether news of Tallulah's erratic out-of-town performances or the pall of the Kennedy assassination was to blame, advance bookings for *Milk Train* at the Brooks Atkinson Theatre were very light.

And Richardson was not around to help. He had flown home in a fruitless attempt to save his marriage. Producer David Merrick asked Williams if he wanted to close the play before it opened on Broadway. "No!" he said. "It would break Tallulah's heart." "I didn't want to close, either," says Merrick. "When you work that long on a thing, you love it."

Williams had seen Tallulah at her best, or through the eyes of a playwright in love with his creation. He was so excited with her performance that he phoned Estelle Winwood, who couldn't make the first night.

"I didn't know Tennessee Williams," says Estelle Winwood. "He phoned me the night before they opened and said Tallulah was simply perfect and that she was so wonderful in the part. And I thought, 'Oh, hooray, Tallulah's got another big hit now.' And then you know she got dreadful notices and the play came off after a week."

One reviewer wrote only: "Miss Bankhead was hoarse and unhappy."

She would never appear on Broadway again.

The Hermit

1964–1965 Tallulah told her new secretary, Jesse Levy, "Darling, for the next few years, till the day I die, NO NEW PEOPLE, NO NEW PEOPLE."

Says Ted Hook, her former secretary: "She felt she'd met the world, for chrissakes, she didn't want to have to cope with meeting or explaining herself, or listening to the problems of anybody new."

She called herself the hermit of Fifty-seventh Street and hated to go out for any reason.

Tallulah used a portable oxygen tank to gasp air between cigarettes. "I've got emphysema, darling," she confided to friends and acquaintances, "but for God's sake don't tell anyone."

Drugs and drink and pneumonia after double pneumonia, broken ribs, burned fingers, and emphysema had changed Tallulah so that at times the woman who had started life as an astonishingly lovely girl looked, in the words of her friend Orson Welles, "like an old quilt. She was the most sensational case of the aging process being unkind. I'll never forget how awful she looked at the end and how beautiful she looked at the beginning."

But the player conquered the hermit when Tallulah was offered a role in an English film, at first called *Fanatic* and eventually *Die! Die! My Darling!* a thriller in which she was to play a homicidal maniac. Friends persuaded her to take it for $50,000 and ten percent of the profits.

Those who expected Tallulah to make a sentimental journey to the English sites of her triumphs in the twenties were surprised. On a previous visit, she said: "I've come to visit the scene of my former conquests—though most of them are married now."

But this time, in August, 1964, when she was sixty-two, Tallulah said: "I don't want to see a goddam thing in London. Even the Thames looks different. I want to remember London as I knew it. But English people, thank God, are the same. I've been asked to look at skyscrapers and meet the Beatles, but darling, we have all that at home."

A Rolls-Royce, by her demand, was waiting for Tallulah at London Airport and it took her to the Ritz. "I don't stay anywhere in London except the Ritz. In the Ritz they've held on to something that there was more of thirty years ago—dignity and peace." In her suite on the fourth floor, flowers and a bucket of champagne were awaiting her.

Photographers and reporters were also in wait for Tallulah and when she turned on the stairs to wave goodbye, she slipped and fell. The papers had their Tallulah-type headline once more: "TALLULAH SLIPS INTO THE RITZ." She brushed aside assistance and got up alone.

Later, she tried to trace her old friends in the telephone book and finally said: "They're all dead and didn't leave any forwarding addresses."

Tallulah's passion for telling the truth most of the time nearly cost her the role in *Die! Die! My Darling!* She confessed to so many illnesses to the insurance company representative that the poor man must have felt inclined to call for the undertaker. He vetoed Tallulah as an impossible risk, and Columbia told her she would be replaced. Tallulah tried pleading but dropped that quickly when she saw it wouldn't work on an insurance company. Instead she offered to gamble her fifty-thousand-dollar salary if she didn't make it to the final "Cut! And print!" They accepted.

An American actress, Stefanie Powers, was in the movie with Tallulah. She says: "Tallulah had laryngitis and all the psychosomatic ailments at the start of the picture. She was obviously very apprehensive. And we realized that to make her 'turn on' during a scene we'd have to set up a tremendously competitive atmosphere. We did it the first day of shooting and she had only one shot to do that day. So we did everybody's scene and her one scene. The next day we scheduled her close-ups to be shown last at the rushes, so she would have to see everybody else's scenes first. In that way we established a competition, and she had to come on strong. Toward the end of the picture she refused to have a stunt man double for her. This weak little lady, she really is tiny and I'm quite big, carried me, dragged my body down the stairs and in through the door because she didn't like the looks of the stunt man. And she lifted me with a tremendous amount of strength."

At the end of the movie Tallulah gave director Silvio Narizzano a medal inscribed with a devil. Wearing a mink coat over an orange sweater and black slacks, she drove off for the airport in a Rolls-Royce with registration plates HEL 777.

Said Narizzano: "No words can express my relief that the picture is over. She is magnificent but impossible."

When Stefanie Powers got back to America she always called on Tallulah when she was in New York. "Nothing in her life-style was mundane," she says. "It was always absurd, extreme, bigger than life. She never liked to go to the toilet alone. She loved to have an audience. 'Just keep talking! Keep talking!' And she'd say: 'I'm a natural blonde and I'm ready to prove it.' And that's why she never wore any underwear.

"She used to call me Patricia, which was the name of the character in the film, and thought it was very bad of me not to wear lipstick. I just adored her. She was my severest critic and my best and very well-respected friend."

The hermit wouldn't stick to her cave. She flew to Hollywood to appear on a Red Skelton TV show. Vincent Price was on a nearby set and: "I went for a minute to see her but I left because I saw her sitting there and she was so strapped up, everything was sort of pulled up, it was not the woman, it was like the makeup for a corpse. And she was suffering from emphysema terribly."

When *Die! Die! My Darling!* was seen in New York, Tallulah took James Herlihy and James Kirkwood with her to see it. "She held my hand very tightly as we watched," said Kirkwood, "and once said, 'God, do I look awful! Ugh!' It was obviously very painful for her."

At her first closeup she called out: "I want to apologize for looking older than God's wet nurse," as years earlier she said: "They used to shoot Shirley Temple through gauze. They should shoot me through linoleum."

The movie got mostly murderous reviews. One exception was by Dora Jane Hamblin in *Life*. Tallulah "is the saving grace of the film, and she may well be launched—at 60 or 65— on a new career." Save for that lethal basso profundo, "half-British, half-pickaninny," Dora Hamblin said she wouldn't have recognized Tallulah. But when she did, she wanted to stand up and shout: "Hey, everybody, Tallulah's back!"

In that film Tallulah gave her last sustained screen performance, and achieved what she had avoided most of her life: she subdued her personality.

The *Life* critic spotted her. But if you hadn't read the titles there were few clues that you were watching Tallulah Bankhead.

XXXVIII

Four Hours of
Tallulah's Talk

1966   "The burden of fame is being alive," said Tallulah to this writer on May 12, 1966.

"When I was twenty-one I dreamed of being a star, and then marrying a rich man I was in love with, and having three sons, and racehorses, and gambling all night, and being a good wife and mother. But none of that happened. I just came to realize that happiness is only something that lasts a day or two.

"Lately I've been jealous only of people who can sing, not Flagstad, or Caruso, whom I heard when I was a child, but of people who can come on and sing a good blues song. And I'm jealous of people who can play the piano without practicing."

Tallulah spoke for more than four hours—until one in the morning. She laughed, cried, sang, smoked, drank, as she sat in her thirteenth-floor apartment on East Fifty-seventh Street in a black chiffon gown, looking as though life had thrown her against a wall and she'd just covered up the scars with rouge and lipstick.

Her secretary, friend, companion Jesse Levy was with her, an ex-Navy lieutenant from Pittsburgh. Tallulah spent the early part of the night trying to persuade him to cook himself a steak and threatening to drink too much if he didn't.

The tape-recorded interview turned into a contest when Tallulah eagerly accepted my eight-cent bet—she upped it from five—that I would ask her questions she hadn't been asked before.

Four hours of Tallulah would make another book. Here are extracts:

"I'm called the Kleenex girl because I cry so easily. I think my tear ducts are too near my eyes. I was so embarrassed when I started rehearsing *The Lady of the Camellias*, I couldn't see the script I cried so.

"Everything I do is controversial but I think most people who dislike me don't know me. I think if they know me they don't mind me too much.

"I hate a liar more than a murderer. I can understand murder—unless it's premeditated, for gain. Blackmail, anonymous letter-writing, kidnapping—they're the only things I hate more than a liar.

"I never open my mail. I don't even open my wires.

"Katharine Hepburn has got great personality and beautiful bones and she's divine. I call her 'The New England Spinster.' Lord knows what she calls me.

"I'm the Malaprop, the Queen Non-sequitur, everything. You know what I mean? Get words all mixed up. I say capitulated for catapulted. I mean, I can't be bothered.

"I've never spat on a man whose wife's having a baby, that I didn't give him a boy. You'd better telephone your wife first to see what she wants.

"I've NEVER been psychoanalyzed. Why should I? I tell everybody everything anyway. Why should I pay to do it? I remember one psychiatrist saying (she chuckles), 'If everyone was like you, we wouldn't need psychiatrists.' But that isn't true. I probably NEED one more than anybody. I've got all the phobias in the world.

"I'm a naturalistic actress. Can't stand anything that isn't natural. And good or bad, people say: 'I don't know whether Tallulah's acting off-stage or on. She's exactly the same in her dressing room as she is on the stage.' I can't change my voice. Can't change my bone structure. I think it was Somerset Maugham—bastard—who said (she chuckles): 'You're never old if your bones are good.'

"I'm a person who blinks their eyes if somebody else does. Maugham said my *Fallen Angels* performance was the most brilliant performance he'd ever seen. And I'd just met someone else who stammered equally badly. It wasn't a stammer. That can be terribly attractive, I think. But this was ugh, ugh, ugh, ugh, ugh. It was apparent, when he wrote his great book *Of Human Bondage,* although, apparently, he denied it, the clubfoot was his stutter. It was always humiliating to him and it made him very bitter. Syrie Maugham (his wife) did my house. She's the greatest decorator in the world, you know. She started all the off-whites and the white flowers and all white things. He was apparently so evil about her. I only read the first installment in *Esquire* I think it was. And Beverly Nichols wrote this book in defense of Syrie. I don't think he defended her as much as he should. He said she was a great beauty. She was not that. But she had great taste and a marvelous skin, like magnolias, which mine used to be before I took suntans. She was a wonderful person who gave marvelous parties and was never a snob. He couldn't have had a beautiful home if it hadn't been for Syrie. . . . I wouldn't know how to supervise a thing. I don't think anyone liked him. Now this is a DRASTIC statement. I shouldn't say that. But there was nothing touching or lovable in him. Now usually someone who you know is struggling every moment . . . I started to say something and I didn't finish it. But it's so long ago. There was no warmth, nothing that you felt. . . . I don't think people liked Maugham. You admired him tremendously. I loved his book, *The Summing Up.* I think it's an amazing book. And I've read every book he's ever written, I think, and the only one I disliked was *Theatre,* which the Theatre Guild wanted me to do on the stage with Shumlin."

What shocks you?

"Bad manners is the ONLY THING I cannot stand. I really mean it. I say 'Cut my throat, but smile.' I'd rather they'd shoot me in the heart, because it would be quicker, except I can't stand blood."

How about cruelty?

"Oh, well of course, I loathe cruelty to animals. I've had two dogs stolen. I worry about them but they would have been dead for years if I still had them. Anything to do with children being murdered or raped—that's a deep sickness. They should be put away for life. Anyone who steals a dog I'd like to be killed and I'd kill him myself. . . . But cruelty has so many facets. The really deepest, most vicious cruelty in the world was Hitler's to the Jews and even other people, Catholics. . . . Of course the thing in Isabelle's time wasn't so good. But I do think Hitler's was the cruelest thing I know in history. I read an amazing book about Julius Caesar. I didn't realize how cruel he was, also so brilliant in every way, and brave and all that. I read it when I visited a great friend of mine, Cavendish. She'd die if I mentioned her name, but she's dead now. She's from British Columbia. She was the thirteenth child. They're all dead now. She was the youngest. And she had two enormous, long halls full of nothing but books, mostly biographies.

"I'm trying to give up smoking. I had to give them up all during the war. I've given up drink for Dunkirk. I either suffer from malnutrition or else I'm fat as a pig. I'd rather go without a drink—I don't mean water—I mean, you die of thirst in three days when you can live for fifty days without food. I'd rather give both food and drink up than cigarettes. I've given them up time and time again. It's just habit, like biting your nails.

"You can ask me anything you want, and if it shocks me, I'll say: 'How DARE you!' "

"Cleveland Amory says of you: 'She has an entourage of

priests, judges, jockeys, parakeets, authors, and outfielders.' "

"Absolutely true. He's left out dogs and a lion and monkeys, ministers, and rabbis."

"Was it tongue-in-cheek when you said: 'Cocaine is most certainly not habit-forming. I've been using it for fifteen years.'?"

"It wasn't a bit tongue-in-cheek, my dear. I've had laryngitis all my life and I had the King's doctor's assistant, Dr. Carterson—Sir something—the King's nose and throat specialist. And someone told me to go there. Like I had the Prince of Wales' dentist who couldn't get over that I'd never had a filling in my life, and apparently the Prince of Wales had only had one. And Sir Gerald (du Maurier) used to show me off like a horse. He started the naturalistic acting from the romantic type. He's the type who'd make love (onstage) by saying, 'Oh, you fool,' like that, instead of 'I love you, darling. Kiss me' and all that. Well, you see, Dr. Carter was his name. Sir Milton Reese was the doctor and his assistant would often be in my dressing room and pumping the stuff in my throat. And the doctors here would spray my throat with cocaine. It was supposed to stimulate your larynx. It had NO effect upon your brain or mind. And I got these menthol cocaine lozenges from Boots chemist, like we call a drugstore here. And I'd say: 'Darling, care for some cocaine?' And I'd go to sleep with them. That's the only reason, apparently, I ever had to have a filling in my life. And once in London I got this menthol snuff. . . . I've taken cocaine. I wanted so much to be an *actress*, so at parties I'd say: 'I don't drink, but have you got any cocaine?' just to try and make myself sophisticated. And suddenly, one day, somebody said: 'Yes, I have.' Well, I'd never been so frightened in my life. I'd had an acute gangrenous appendix and nearly died, I'd had my tonsils out— woke up in the middle of the tonsilitis operation when I was about six. And I thought, wow, it's going to be like ether. And I said, 'Y.e.e.e.s,' I didn't know how to take it. I thought I'd take off like a ROCKET. So he brought it out. It looked exactly like snow. And he put it on his thumb and inhaled. I said: 'I don't think I could do that.' And he said: 'Here, take this nail file.' Well, I blew it off, you know.

"And that was the pure stuff. It melted right in the palm of your hand if you had the slightest perspiration. And I was nothing but. So I wasted most of it. So I finally took a couple of puffs and I thought, 'Now they'll take me out, I'll disgrace my father and my grandfather, everyone I love. I'll disgrace myself. I'd rather be dead than find myself in some awful scandal of some kind, or any scandal.' And, my dear, it had the most divine effect. I felt wide awake and had a marvelous time. I didn't sleep for quite a while. But I used to say as a joke, 'Oh, yes, it's menthol snuff.'

"This great friend of mine, Napier, I won't give his last name [Alington]. We went to this offbeat nightclub. And so we take out this menthol snuff and put it up my nose. It didn't have any effect—we knew what it was. And policemen would come in and we were hoping they'd say: 'Come with us!' and 'What have you got?' It cost sixpence (ten cents). But they never did arrest us.

"And I had this great friend who was the brother of Audry Carten, who played the other leading part with Sir Gerald du Maurier in the first play I did in England. Kenneth was about ten. Audrey was two years older than I was. I was nineteen. And he just adored me. You know how children are. And he was going to be operated on for appendicitis and the nurse said; 'Well, now, think of something quaite naice,' in a rather refained cockney.

"And he said: 'I'm going to think of crossing the Atlantic with Tallulah Bankhead.'

"Well, she practically dropped her implements and said: 'Oh, dear, is that quaite naice?!' "

When Kenneth was twenty-one he asked Tallulah to get him some cocaine.

"I said: 'Why certainly, Kenneth, it would be the easiest thing in the world.' Of course, I'd never give something like that to anybody. So his sister and I got some menthol snuff. Do you know, he didn't have a drink, he took his up his nose and he went absolutely mad for three hours. And his sister and I were just dying. He thought he'd had cocaine. He had ten cents worth of menthol snuff.

"Herman Shumlin was a great director. He directed me in *Little Foxes*. He made me slow up [in speaking]. I didn't have much to say in the play. But you'd be surprised: people couldn't believe how short the part was because they always thought I was listening in or coming in, you know. And of course it was marvelous for me because I hadn't had much luck here in America. . . .

"I hate the words hip or hep or in or out, because you've got to be way out to be in. It doesn't make sense to me. And I've heard the word 'camp' ever since I first was in England. Remember Beatrice Lillie saying, 'I'm a Campfire girl!' you know? And she was a great artist. She was a female Chaplin and that's the greatest compliment I can pay anyone. I love her. I mean, for example, camp is like black humor. People have different senses of humor, different senses of the ridiculous. . . .

"I suppose no one is a real bore, but they might bore me or you. . . . I never thought I'd take to golf, but I'm watching it on TV. The putting I adore. The long shots, I don't follow them. I don't know where they're going or what. I mean, I'm a Giant fan. I'm an emotionalist when it comes to that. I'm not an expert on anything, you know. I became a great tennis fan in England with Bill Tilden, and things like that, and Joe Louis, but I don't know (laughing). . . . First of all I don't know what you asked me.

"There was a great jockey in England called Steve Donahue. They used to say 'Come on, Steve! Come on, Steve!' He was a great friend of mine. He was divine. I adored him. He's dead now, so I can tell something—because he can't be arrested. But he used to always hold his whip in his right hand in the paddock if he thought he could win, and his left if he didn't. And once he held it in his right. And I bet with Ladbrook's, which is legal there. I wish I could find a bookie here. I went to the Tote. He won fifteen to one. As a matter of fact, Prince George, who became Duke of Kent, told me that the only time he ever saw his mother—the Great Queen Mother with those strange hats—really lose her dignity, was when Brian Jack won a race six times in a row. And he said his mother just lost complete control and threw her arms around the King's shoulders and just behaved like any other person that was thrilled. And, how he got away with it—Steve, I don't know, because he had broken his wrist. But he did it (ignored his broken wrist) so he could ride Brian Jack.

"I read Madame Blavatsky and found it fascinating although I didn't understand half of it.

"I think the strongest thing in the world is habit. Not sex. Not 'in love,' because 'in love,' that's hard to keep, particularly if you're stuck together and then you're 'trapped like a trap in a trap,' as Dorothy Parker says.

"I'm a high Episcopalian agnostic. I'm not an atheist. I do not KNOW. Who am I to know? Unless you're a saint and have some ecstatic thing. Or unless you take LSD. And I'm not comparing the two, now don't get me in trouble with the saints. I'm in enough trouble as it is.

"My father never touched me, never spanked me. But I knew if I'd done something wrong because then he called me Tallulah. Otherwise it was honey, sugar, baby, or darling or something.

"I'm sorry Daddy went into politics because he would have made a great lawyer, like Clarence Darrow. I didn't see enough of him. I was in England eight years and I only saw him once. He was a saint in a way. I remember him saying when he was dying: 'Oh, Tallulah, this is going to be such an ungentlemanly election.' And I said: 'D'you love me Daddy?' And he said: 'Now why talk about circumferences?'

"I get nervous when I hear Billy Graham saying 'Jesus' when I think of all the Jews in the world and the other religions."

If you could live anywhere on earth where would it be?

"I wouldn't live on earth. If there's nothing better I'd rather be under the earth, if there's such a thing, because earth goes down pretty deep."

South of France, Greek island?

"Oh, NO. I've had a thousand years of suntan. I'd like to live where quite a few very good, amusing, understanding friends of mine are near at hand—at all times, like you, Jesse.

"Give me a drink. This is nothing but melted ice.

"Shakespeare hit the nail on the head about every situation in life. And some of the most beautiful poetry comes from his terrible comedies. They're like German comedies. If there is such a thing as reincarnation, now don't say this because it'll sound sacrilegious, but Shakespeare was the reincarnation of Jesus.

"Alfred Hitchcock is the gentlest of men and a real genius. Now I'm not comparing him with Socrates or Plato, but for his day and profession, he's a genius. The only great English movie I've seen, *Murder*—he wrote the script, was the director, the cameraman, set designer, and cutter.

"Death of one's father, that would break anybody's heart even if they hadn't got a heart.

"I make Tennessee Williams laugh every time I open my mouth: whether he's laughing at me or with me, I'll never know."

Furiously angry because she'd just discovered her TV interview with Merv Griffin had been shown on TV while we were talking, and she wanted to see it, and had invited three friends for another evening when she was told it would be aired; she said:

"I'm in the mood to bugger everybody . . . if I had the wherewithal. How DARE they not tell me! And all I get out of it—$177. I have NEVER been so angry. I don't mean about big important things. I AM NOT IMPORTANT IN THE WORLD, like wars or children who are born with afflictions. (Crying) I've never been so angry."

A few moments later she was laughing and talking about when her father took her to see President Theodore Roosevelt. And she kept talking like a child after tears who is searching for other things to keep the unhappy event out of her mind.

"I think dolphins are the most divine people in the world, and I call them people because they've bigger brains. They say that if they had digits they'd rule the world. They came first before the dinosaurs, looked around and—'oh, no, this is too depressing!'—and went back to the sea again."

XXXIX

"Tallulah! Tallulah!
We Love You!"

1967 Tallulah lay in bed in her thirteenth-floor apartment, her feet toward the East River. The world was a fingertip away: there were five phones in the house. Outside, the smart, the rich, and the talented of East Fifty-seventh Street were in their limousines, bound for Broadway, Greenwich Village, Kennedy Airport. Tallulah's light was still on when they came back, had a nightcap; still on when they finally hit the hay, still on when they got up for an Alka Seltzer or warm milk and calcium tablets.

She rarely went out. It was too exhausting and she'd done it all before. She would have traded one night's deep sleep for all the parties and plays in the world.

But when Truman Capote invited her to his masked ball at the Plaza Hotel, she responded like an excited schoolgirl asked to her first prom.

It was called the party of the century and considered so newsworthy that the entire guest list was printed in *The New York Times*. Many people of note, it was rumored, had flown the country to make it appear that they would have been invited had they been available. Two days before the party, Tallulah got a frantic call from Dorothy Parker, distressed because she hadn't been invited.

Tallulah telephoned Truman and told him about Dorothy. "I just forgot her," Capote said.

"That's the whole thing," explained Tallulah. "The only reason she wanted to go was so people would know she's still alive."

"I'm sorry." Capote said. "But it would be too rude to invite her now. You know, I sit up at night, aghast at the people I forgot to invite."

An hour later she was still talking to Capote about the party. Who was sitting where? Who wasn't coming? Who was coming? Would it be all right if she wore this? Wore that? When were the masks to be taken off?

When it was too late to speak to New Yorkers, she called friends in California.

Tallulah went to the party and watched the dancing and said hello to everyone. She stood next to Norman Mailer and they smiled and nodded. Not a "fug" was said. Frank Sinatra danced by (he'd been on her "Big Show"); Alice Roosevelt Longworth exchanged grins with her.

She had made a promise to herself that she wouldn't approach anyone. But she was afraid that it might mean hours of isolation. Who is that woman? Tallulah something or other. But she spent almost no time alone. And she even had an emotional reconciliation with her old enemy Lillian Hellman, insisting that their vociferous battles of the past were merely misunderstandings. If Capote had done nothing else he healed that hurt. At least for a night.

A few days later she invited her friend and agent Milton Goldman and her friend Arnold Weissberger over to talk about it. She made a special effort to impress them in a beautiful white gown. She pricked her finger on a brooch and a drop of blood stained her dress near the knee. And she rose to the occasion. 'Oh, damn!' she said. "Wish it were a little bit higher. It would be much more flattering."

Goldman took the opportunity to tell her of the TV shows he'd lined up for her. Merv Griffin would like to interview her. They wanted her to guest on "Batman"—that would mean a trip to the Coast. And the Smothers Brothers were keen to feature her on their TV comedy show, also in California.

She allowed them to talk her into it. True to form, when they tried to leave, at two a.m., she protested, and as they walked out, screamed after them: "You cheapen yourselves!"

The palaver of getting ready for the TV shows exhausted and exasperated her. "By the time the hair dryer has my hair dry it's so hot my head starts to perspire! I hate the heat. I'm from the South of course, but it kills me," she told an interviewer.

She couldn't sleep for forty-eight hours before any appearance now. She dreaded making a fool of herself, and tried without success to steady her shaking hands. The frantic pace and brevity of TV rehearsals bewildered her.

But though times had changed, she hadn't and still insisted on the star treatment, the limousine, a suite of rooms, a secretary, wherever she went.

The Smothers Brothers had expected a raucous old dame and they found a sick old lady, desperate not to let the side down, scared as a kid on her first audition. They phoned her agent, Milton Goldman, for advice. "Give her less to do," he said. "Then she'll be all right. Don't make her do too much." Tallulah got through with less.

The "Batman" engagement required her to run all over the place. Because of emphysema, it was a painful effort for her to walk. But she ran.

For weeks afterward, Tallulah resumed the life of a recluse in her New York apartment, but even though exhausted, she kept in constant touch with friends by phone.

On October 9, 1967, Marlene Dietrich gave a one-woman show as her Broadway debut, and Milton Goldman called Tallulah to ask if she'd go to the opening with him. "Darling, you know how I loathe openings. I never go to the theater now. Still Marlene is such a good friend I can't say no."

Maureen O'Sullivan shared the car with them as they drove from the East Side toward Broadway. At the sight of so much cement she sighed for the home she'd had in the country:

"Oh, I do wish you'd visited me when I had 'Windows.' There were acres and acres of flowers."

"No vegetables?" Goldman asked.

"Of course, darling. I grew mint for my juleps and chives for my vichyssoise."

As they drove up Forty-sixth Street toward the Lunt-Fontanne Theatre, the crowds were lined up on both sides of the street. A mass of limousines blocked the street.

Then the crowds started moving east and looking into the car windows, celebrity hunting. Someone shouted: "There's Tallulah! There's Tallulah!" And the crowd began running toward her and the air was full of photographers' flashlights.

"Shoot from above, darlings. Shoot from above. It's much more flattering," Tallulah called out. She seemed slightly dazed by the excitement. It had been years since she'd had such attention.

The car slowly moved forward and as it stopped at the theater, fans broke through police cordons and shouted: "Tallulah, we love you! Tallulah! Tallulah, we love you!"

That night was a great occasion for Marlene Dietrich and at the after-theater party in the Rainbow Room she embraced Tallulah while Milton Goldman, Olivia de Havilland, Louis Nizer, Joan Fontaine, Burt Bacharach, Angie Dickinson, and a few hundred others looked on. But what made it memorable for her were the cries from the crowd outside, a nostalgic echo from her early career: "Tallulah! Tallulah, we love you!"

X L

Tallulah Lives

1967–1968 Tallulah never wanted to go out, so why stay in the city? She planned to semi-retire in a little cottage in Maryland, near her sister Eugenia. She went down to look it over and found that Tamara Geva would be her neighbor. The rivals, the widows of John Emery, who had once wanted the same man, now coveted the same territory.

Tamara Geva invited Tallulah to dinner while they were both in Maryland and was shocked to find her looking so sick. Tallulah came in plastered at six in the evening, proudly refused all food that was offered, and drank steadily through dinner and until midnight, when she left with the help of a man friend and Eugenia.

Back in her New York apartment she resumed her diet of drink and cigarettes, smoking one after another. "My darling," she'd say to anyone who was there. "I have emphysema. It's a terrible thing." Then she'd light another cigarette.

On New Year's Day, 1968, she talked very simply of death to her friends, without any sign of fear but with no great longing for it. The painfully gaunt, frail, little woman whose life seemed almost like one long suicide attempt could still find things to live for, still delighted in her friends.

In November, 1968, her one-time secretary Philip Hall went

to see her. And she said to him: "You know Philip, I think I'm going to die." He was shattered at the thought.

A few days later James Herlihy phoned Tallulah. He was on his way to California. They had a wonderful, lively conversation and agreed to meet as soon as possible.

There was an epidemic of influenza in December. Tallulah, susceptible to everything, caught it. The influenza developed into pneumonia. She'd beaten even double pneumonia before, but now she was a much weaker and older woman. The doctor confirmed Jesse Levy's fears, and Tallulah was taken to St. Luke's Hospital. Levy telephoned Tallulah's agent, Milton Goldman, with the news: there wasn't much hope of her pulling through.

Goldman put down the phone. When he last saw Tallulah she was in a kind of dressing gown that she wore all day. She'd almost become a recluse: hated to get dressed, hated to go out. Did she want to live? Would she put up much of a fight? He thought not.

Dr. A. L. Loomis, Jr. was waiting for Tallulah at the hospital. He had been taking care of her since 1965. Even her first visit to him at St. Luke's had been dramatic. She and Jesse Levy had gone to the wrong hospital—Presbyterian—and called him from there. Then raced to him in a cab.

"She had very bad emphysema," Dr. Loomis recalls, "and was quite resigned to the extent she wanted to do what she could to help—except to stop drinking or smoking. But she accommodated to it and never wore it for pity.

"Her visits were the highlights of my office hours. She was very effervescent and dramatic. She was always pleasant and a pleasure to be with. She had a flair about her.

"She hid her fears behind alcohol, sedatives, and cigarettes—and behind her dramatizations.

"Tallulah used to call me frequently to ask for medication and ask if anything further could be done. She was ready to try anything new, including a medication from England, which I gave her.

"One of the last parts she played was in 'Batman and Robin' on TV. She used to dread any part and have to decline it if it involved many costume changes. It was dreadfully difficult for her losing her breath for a moment: she had a desperate shortage of oxygen. And she'd say, 'If only I could get a little better,' and she'd talk of glorious parts she'd been offered but had to turn down because they were too strenuous.

"Emphysema is ninety percent reversible if people don't smoke. The incidence of it without smoking is very small. She wanted to do anything (except quit smoking and drinking) to get a little better, and if she'd stopped smoking she could have lived several more years."

On that last trip to St. Luke's, "I think she knew it was fatal. She had flu and then pneumonia. If she hadn't had emphysema, she might have recovered.

"Tallulah wanted to be sure that her sister knew about her—because I think she knew the end was coming and she accepted it, with some dramatization.

"She really wasn't the hellion as has been reported. Of course she expected nurses to be on hand all the time. She demanded a lot of sedation. I suspect she could have got several from different physicians. But she deported herself quite like a lady. You knew you were dealing with an extraordinary person with an extraordinary will."

It was during her delirium that Tallulah called out "codeine—bourbon"—her last coherent words.

Then her heart and breathing failed.

"Her heart had to be restarted, and a tube inserted in her trachea. She was put on a respirator which breathed for her. During her confusion she pulled out the intravenous tube," said Dr. Loomis.

She was in a coma for several hours.

Tallulah's friends began to hear of the news and go to the hospital to see her. Ted Hook was one of the first, but when he reached there Tallulah was already in a coma. He told Stanley Haggart that she couldn't last the night. They spent the evening together. Hook called Herlihy in California, who said he'd fly back to see her.

But Tallulah died that night, December 12, 1968, of pneumonia complicated by emphysema.

"She always told me she had absolutely no fear of death," says Tennessee Williams. "She even told me at times she would like to be out of it all."

But James Kirkwood believes that even at the end she had a strong will to live. "I think of her death as . . . they just slipped in and caught her when she was weak."

Tallulah's sister granted an autopsy. Seventy percent of her lungs was found to be involved with emphysema. "Her liver," says Dr. Loomis, "strangely enough, was not badly damaged. She must have had good bourbon."

How does he remember her?

"I was enriched by knowing her," he says. "Although she had many qualities one hardly admires or wants to emulate— she made a deep impression on me."

XLI

Tallulah's Will

She left her Baldwin grand piano and bench, a quarter of her estate, and $10,000 to Jesse W. Levy; to Philip Hall, a pair of white jade vases, "the painting by me with a red staircase called 'Room at the Top,' and two paintings by him which I possess," and $10,000; to Estelle Winwood, a diamond and sapphire pendant, and $10,000; to Edie Smith, "my gold necklace, my gold and moonstone brooch and my moonstone and sapphire bracelet," and $10,000; to Eugenia Bankhead, "mink coat" and $5,000—and Tallulah canceled all her debts and gave her an annuity of $250 a month; to Ted Hook, "the painting by Grandma Moses which I possess," and $1,000. Although Tallulah had lost contact with Robert Williams, she left him $500.

Eugenia Rawls Seawell was left "Renoir, mink cape, aquamarine and diamond ring, six-pointed aquamarine and diamond brooch, and, except for film print of *Lifeboat* all of my films and 16 mm. movie projector." Mrs. Seawell and her children also shared one half of Tallulah's estate.

The final quarter of her estate went to her sister's two grandchildren. And she left $5,000 to their father, her nephew, William Bankhead.

Tallulah also gave Mildred Dunnock, "my white porcelain tulips"; George Cukor, "the portrait of me by Ambrose McEvoy"; Edie Van Cleve, "my gold-weave cigarette case"; Ruth Mitchell, "my white jade statuette with teak base and film print cf *Lifeboat* which I own, if same can be found among my effects"; and to Elliott Reid, "the painting entitled 'Harbor of Dieppe,' by Max Bond."

She gave James Herlihy $2,500 and Rose Riley $2,000.

XLII

The Summing Up

1902–1968 Tallulah Bankhead brutalized her body, broke her bones, deprived herself of sleep, smoked marijuana, sniffed cocaine, took uppers and downers, boozed bourbon, gave the coat off her back, cherished her friends, infuriated her rivals, pained puritans, and was a joy to fellow nonconformists—and if she had worked at it, could have been the greatest actress of her time.

Tallulah was one of the greatest personalities, with a mystical, probing, sensitive side to her that only a very few ever knew about.

There was much more of the child than the woman in her, despite her justified reputation for indulging in almost everything that is frowned on by the righteous and condemned by the cautious. But she paid for all her excesses with a nervous system that was its own instrument of torture. Having led a life that some might call depraved, she still retained a childlike, innocent quality. And one of her greatest fears was that she would disgrace her beloved father, a man she loved uncritically and whom no other man replaced in her affection.

"People have a picture of Tallulah being sexual or vicious," says Tom Ellis, "and they decide to take any story you tell them and take those parts out and reprint them to support it. It doesn't matter that that story may have some of those qualities in it when you're trying to tell them something wonderful about Tallulah. And you get to the point—and people refuse to put in the point of the story, but only the tawdry bits leading up to it. People always say: 'Oh, she said "shit" did she? Oh!' And they put that down. It doesn't matter that she was giving two million dollars to a child at the time. That never gets put down.

"She was a prototype. Nobody's that frightened or that wonderful at the same time. A lot of things got picked up and blown up out of proportion and got to be what she was about.

"People are puzzled why she couldn't stand to be touched. Taking barbiturates makes you very sensitive and she was taking lots of them every day.

"As for her monologues—it all depended on your moods. She was like a wonderful hunting dog. She worked absolutely instinctively. If it bored you and she realized it, she might bore you some more just because she wanted to make you bored, or she'd say, 'Why don't you leave now?' or 'I'm going to bed,' or turn it on somebody else.

"And she always made everybody tell the truth. That was the greatest thing about her. She took the party game into reality, and that was what her life was about."

She was a weird mixture of the Southern lady, who would forgive a murderer if he took his hat off in an elevator and had clean fingernails—but who, herself, at times behaved like an unhousebroken cat and was as subtle as a sledgehammer. She couldn't stand cruelty, especially to animals, yet she sometimes got her dogs drunk. For a woman who lived a completely unrestricted sex life, she was amazingly prudish, becoming almost a Mrs. Grundy when sex and religion were mentioned in the same breath—although she was an agnostic. She was often generous with and sometimes careful of her money. Her temper tantrums were almost unbelievable, so sudden and so quickly over that she could change from scream to coo in midsentence. She was self-centered, her con-versations were meandering monologues; yet she was incredibly curious about others, often wanting to have a second-by-second account of their activities. She had superhuman energy and staying power in her youth but maltreated her body with drugs and drink so that when she craved sleep it played cat and mouse with her. From a ravishing beauty she became a pathetic mask of ruin. She was in fact selfish, spoiled, arrogant, rude, crude, but with such other qualities that hundreds found her fascinating and lovable.

As an old woman she still had a childlike enthusiasm for games, challenges, animals. Her easy tears, curiosity, quick laughter, and compassion for the unfortunate reflect the reactions of an unworldly girl. She never stopped falling in love. Her last romance was with Edward R. Murrow. She fell in love with him after he had interviewed her at "Windows" for his "Person-to-Person" TV show. By all accounts it was unrequited, but it made her happy as a girl over her first romance, and she never lost track of him until his death.

It was as a girl looking for new experiences that she ran into cocaine. To appear sophisticated whenever she was offered a cigarette, she'd refuse and ask for cocaine instead. When, to her surprise, it was first offered—on a nail file—she kept up her bravado by sniffing it. It cleared her brain and made her feel extra wide-awake. From then on such drugs were part of her life.

She took them for more than thirty years, not as often as her former secretary implied in court, nor as rarely as she claimed in her autobiography. "Don't believe a word Tallulah says about it," warns Estelle Winwood. "Whatever you've heard about Tallulah taking cocaine, you've only heard what Tallulah wishes to tell. She was taking cocaine like mad at one time."

And Joan Crawford agreed with Estelle Winwood. "Tallulah tortured her body. She never took care of herself. She was ravaged by pills and drink. And after so much drink she didn't know how many pills she'd taken."

Tallulah swallowed pills to wake up, to drop off, to kill

pain, and to kill time. Drugs were part of the reason why as a woman she would cry like a baby for pills to put her to sleep.

Her stripping naked was to shock and attract attention. Treating her toilet seat as just another spot to carry on a lively conversation startled, amused, and even endeared her to those exposed to it.

Tennessee Williams found this refreshing. "When I knew her later, Tallulah always impressed me by her honesty and gallantry and her lack of shame," he wrote in his autobiography.* "It is a quality I have discovered in Southern ladies of a certain kind. . . . I remember she never wanted to interrupt a conversation for bodily functions, and if she was carrying on an animated conversation with me and had to pay a call of nature, she would ask me to accompany her into the bathroom and sit on the edge of the tub while she completed her story and call of nature. This didn't shock me, in fact it delighted me by its forthrightness and lack of embarrassment."

Tom Ellis thought it was a test. "She'd take you by the wrist and drag you down the hall and say: 'Don't go! Stay here! Sit down!' It was a test. Are you going to stick around and play? Or can I make you crazy? We all have our standard routines and that was part of hers. If you were shocked it was too silly. And her strong language was to get rid of the assholes in her life."

Ellis doesn't think there was anything exhibitionistic or seductive about her stripping naked. "She took off her clothes because they told her not to put beans up her nose," he suggests.

Her love affairs with women for the early part of her adult life reinforce this view that she was sexually immature. Very few men were able to put up with tyranny from this child-woman. Although she kept her close friends all her life, no

* Tennessee Williams, *Memoirs* (New York: Doubleday, 1975.)

one man stayed with her more than a handful of years. Her closest friend, Estelle Winwood, was old enough to be her mother, and in fact did play that role. Her frantic need always to be in touch with people, to be with them until she struggled into sleep, was another aspect of her childlike nature. It could be that the death of her mother, when Tallulah was a few weeks old, was catalyst to this fear of being left alone. Psychiatrists will probably agree.* But, although her life was punctuated with pain, physical and emotional, she had an extraordinary interest in the world. Breathing with the help of a portable oxygen bottle because of her emphysema, the idea of going out to the theater became abhorrent to her, but she found "the best acting in the world" on TV soap operas and watched them as if she were part of that melo-dramatic world in which a bone breaks, a heart cracks, a sin is committed in every episode. Her political life was as unsophisticated as her TV viewing. Asked her opinions of Democrats, she would coo, reserving hisses for Republicans. She was a woman with guts, with a unique talent as an actress which she squandered in living, a woman who never stopped talking unless she met someone she wanted to hear from—and they were very few.

As a child she kicked out in all directions to find what would be forbidden to her. A stern parent would have kept her within bounds. But Tallulah had an indulgent father and a grandmother who couldn't always be around. So she had neither the discipline nor the feeling of safety and security that restrictions give to a child. As an adult she continued hitting out wildly, almost as if she were seeking someone who would restrain her. When she found such people, Robert, her butler, and Estelle Winwood, neither of whom

---

* The infantile or hysterical personalities thrive on attention and un-conditional approval and are hypersensitive to rejection. Their frantic pursuit of affection and applause often causes others to escape from their clutches. Then they fall into a deep depression in which they overeat, oversleep, and retreat from life. To avoid this depression, they arrange their lives to ensure a constant supply of loving approval and attention.

would take any of her nonsense and who treated her like a
wayward child, she clung to them.

But for them and almost everyone else she had to put on
her continuous performance. As a child she had a drive to
entertain but as she grew older it became compulsive, to the
extent that she would do or say almost anything to get a laugh,
or even a groan. She always denied that she was trying to
make up for the loss of her beautiful, spirited, daring mother,
the mother who had died three weeks after giving birth to
her. But some of her closest friends believe it has to be taken
into account in any study of Tallulah.

Ridiculous to compare Tallulah with Winston Churchill,
a man she worshipped, isn't it? But look at the parallels.

Both were weepers. A dead bird, someone in distress, a few
notes of music, could bring tears to the eyes of the actress
and the statesman.

Both were shockers, in reverting to innocent or provocative childish behavior. Churchill startled FDR, who went to
Winnie's room and found the British Prime Minister stark
naked. He began to retreat, but Churchill called him back.
"Come in. You can see I have nothing to hide," he said
with a wicked smile. Tallulah, in entertaining Eleanor
Roosevelt, hardly paused in her conversation as she walked
to the bathroom, left the door wide open, dropped her panties
and peed in full view of Mrs. Roosevelt, who continued to
chatter and sip her tea.

Churchill and Tallulah were steady and enduring drinkers.
Churchill once asked an Oxford professor of science, Fred-
erick Lindemann, later Lord Cherwell, to calculate the vol-
ume of the room they were in. "I've drunk about a quart of
wines and spirits a day since I was sixteen," said Churchill,
then sixty-two. "How much of this room would it fill?" Lindemann took out his slide rule and told the slightly disappointed
Churchill that it would not drown them—it would barely
cover their knees. Tallulah, without a glass in hand, seemed
somehow undressed.

What else did these two strippers-weepers-drinkers have in common? Each other. Tallulah boasted of only one meeting but he went to see her five times in *Fallen Angels*. He first appears on page two of her autobiography, *Tallulah*. Like Churchill, Tallulah was an amateur painter (she left some of her paintings to friends in her will). Both had the gift of gab, a love of words and literature. Both stayed in bed all morning, though Churchill was usually awake and working or holding court. Both were impatient and demanding. Churchill often broke into song, usually prompted by his wife; Tallulah did the same with the slightest encouragement. Both hated Hitler and were political animals. Both endured black moods of despair. Walter Graebner tells in his book *My Dear Mr. Churchill* how "he took as much delight in apocryphal anecdotes and epigrams attributed to him as in those that were true. 'Is that one of mine?' he would playfully ask, and would then carefully store it in his memory, to be used as his very own on a later occasion." Tallulah, too. Both had a passion for playing cards and played them with the absorption of children. They both indulged in sleeping pills, though Tallulah's were somewhat stronger and more plentiful. "My tastes are simple," said Churchill, "I like the best." It could have been Tallulah talking.

Both had unique voices that were instantly recognizable. Even their treatment of servants was strikingly similar. "Churchill talked to them, scolded them, gave them orders throughout the entire meal," reveals Graebner. "It was 'John, are you sure this bottle is properly chilled?' or 'John, where did we get these oysters? They aren't very good,' or 'Doris, *don't* take away the butter plates. We want to save them for our pâté.' Not for Churchill the upper-class English convention that table servants are invisible and can only be communicated with by surreptitious gestures and low mutterings."

Both idolized their fathers and adored their mothers, and were intensely proud of the family name and reputation.

Tallulah even went to court to protect hers. When Procter & Gamble used her name in a jingle to sell Prell shampoo, Tallulah sued and settled out of court for five thousand dollars.

They demanded to be the focus of attention at all times, were curt or worse with those who dared to interrupt them. And, when roused, Churchill could match Tallulah with expletives—though his biographers have skated over that aspect of the man.

They both married once only—but there they part company. Churchill's marriage was lifelong and comparatively serene; Tallulah's short and full of sound and fury.

The great romantic love of her life, Lord Napier Alington, was another wild, witty, unpredictable, charming child. As a lover he was fascinating and infuriating. Tallulah was rarely attracted to steady, reliable men who would have made good husbands. The rogues appealed to her. And she faced the consequences.

She was not deceived into thinking that the cheers and applause of her fans would sustain her: she cherished them, but knew it was her friends who would be there in time of trouble—not the audience in the gallery or the autograph hunters in the street.

Tallulah had a hell of a life, good and bad, and right until the end she kept her sense of humor and of the absurd. To those who knew her well she was part darling, part devil. But to the world who adored her she was always "Tallulah, darling."

INDEX